Mr & Mrs Smith

Boutique Hotel Collection

The Global Shortlist

www.mrandmrssmith.com

FOR TW

Mr & Mrs Smith – interesting name, isn't it? It all started with a real couple, as they drove back from a weekend break at a hotel that had promised far more romance than it had delivered. How could the guide they'd trusted have got it so wrong? Where were the people who understood what we really want from a trip for two – reviewers who could be relied on to report back with the honesty you'd expect from your best friend?

And so began Mr & Mrs Smith's journey: a quest to find and share the most romantic, stylish and special places to stay. The result was a hotel guide that took the British market by storm. Since 2000, that single volume has grown into a series of books, a collection of 500 great getaways across the globe and an award-winning website with a legion of loyal members. The secret of our success is simple: we're picky. A hotel in our collection not only has to have an unmatched ambience and hit the right style notes, it has to check our 'certain something' box: the welcome should be warm, without fuss or formality; rooms should be seductive and supplied with thoughtful extras; drinks must be perfectly mixed and dinners delicious; and, crucially, the stay must be memorable for all the right reasons.

Despite our sky-high standards, we have found plenty of wonderful hotels around the world that meet our criteria (all reviewed online at www.mrandmrssmith.com). For this book, we've selected 30 of our favourites, and sent a panel of trusted spies (including burlesque queen Dita Von Teese, Agent Provocateur supremo Serena Rees and fashion columnist Bee Shaffer, to name-drop a few) to try them out. And we've gone out of our way to bring you those in-the-know details and destination secrets you can't find anywhere else.

But Mr & Mrs Smith is about much more than nice-looking books: put us on your coffee table by all means, but don't forget to activate your free Smith card first (see page 4). As a member, you'll be entitled to free extras – from champagne to spa treatments – when you stay at any of the hotels featured in our collection, as well as exclusive room rates, travel discounts, shopping offers and much more. There's no charge for booking with us: you can reserve rooms online for free, or if you'd rather speak to a member of our expert travel team, you can call them on 1 800 464 2040.

We understand how precious your time is – you don't want to waste it on so-so stays. Rest assured: the vacation inspiration you'll find in *The Global Shortlist* is tried and tested, ensuring you get the address right first time – every time. That's a promise.

Best wishes and bon voyage,

Smith

Mr & Mrs Smith

(take)

advantage of us

This is your own personal Smith card, which entitles you to six months' free membership. The moment you register it (either online or by ringing 1 800 464 2040), you can access the members' area of our website, and find out about exclusive last-minute offers from our hotels. The card, which can easily be upgraded to SilverSmith or GoldSmith level (see right), also provides members-only privileges – such as spa treats, late check-out and more – when you book hotels through us. Look out for the *Smith* icon at the end of each hotel review.

A Mr & Mrs Smith membership card should be affixed here. If it has been removed, you can still buy the book – we'll send you a replacement card. Please send proof of purchase, with a return address, to your nearest regional Smith office:

LONDON
2nd Floor
334 Chiswick High Road
London W4 5TA
United Kingdom

NEW YORK
580 Broadway
Suite 1202
New York NY 10012
United States

MELBOURNE
Level 1
137 Flinders Lane
Melbourne VIC 3000
Australia

REGISTER NOW

To start receiving special hotel offers, shopping discounts and exclusive travel benefits, activate your card by registering online at www.mrandmrssmith.com/register-card or by ringing 1 800 464 2040 (it will only take a minute).

ROOM SERVICE

Activate your free BlackSmith membership today, and you will also receive our monthly newsletter *Room Service*. It's packed with news, travel tips, even more offers and fantastic competitions. We promise not to bombard you with communications or pass on your details to third parties. This is strictly between you and us.

AND THERE'S MORE?

If that isn't enough, you can even get access to VIP airport lounges, automatic hotel upgrades, flight and car-hire offers, and your own personal travel concierge, simply by upgrading your membership to either SilverSmith or GoldSmith. For more details, visit www.mrandmrssmith.com or ring our Travel Team on 1 800 464 2040.

Small print: all offers are according to availability and subject to change.

contents

[at a glance]

Rates may increase at weekends or in high season. All prices (based on current exchange rates) are correct at the time of going to press.

Belize

BELIZE

BELIZE
Blancaneaux Lodge

BELIZE

Mayans, Spanish conquistadors, colonising Brits and pirates of the Caribbean have all jostled for dominance of this petite swathe of Central America. And it's not hard to see its appeal: Belize is fêted for the astonishing beauty of its landscape, which shifts from white-sand tropical-island paradise to dense mountain jungle, and the unparalleled scuba scene at its Barrier Reef, the largest in the northern hemisphere. Belizean people are famously friendly, with a hybrid culture that reflects the country's diverse – and somewhat chequered – history. White-water rivers, lush rainforest, stalactite-hung caves and plunging waterfalls mark the inland Cayo region. Further south, manatee-filled mangrove swamps of the Placencia peninsula lie beyond vast prawn farms and a rapidly developing coastline, where the predominantly Creole/Caribbean population enjoys a slow-paced life of folk festivals, fishing, lively jump-ups and beach parties.

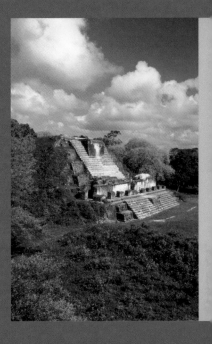

GETTING THERE

Planes Belize City is the main airport, serviced by American Airlines, Continental and TACA, among others. There is a departure tax of about $35 (a percentage of which goes towards conservation projects). Internally, you can catch frequent flights with Maya Air (www.mayaislandair.com) or Tropic Air (www.tropicair.com).
Trains Belize's surprisingly lumpy terrain makes rail travel an impossibility.
Automobiles If you plan to explore Belize in depth, a rental car can come in handy, but, thanks to some shoddy roads, a relatively short journey can become a lengthy test of patience – opt for a small 4x4 if you can. There's a branch of Hertz (www.hertz.co.uk) at the airport.
Boats Ferries and water taxis nip between the country's islands and link Belize City to San Pedro.

LOCAL KNOWLEDGE

Taxis Cabs are a cost-effective means of getting around – short trips within towns rarely cost more than a couple of dollars. Brace yourself for some bumpy rides, though.
Currency The Belizean dollar (BZ$) is currently pegged to the US dollar at a rate of 2:1. Check whether you're being charged in US or Belizean dollars before you pay.
Dialling codes Belize: 501.
Tipping culture Upmarket restaurants will automatically include a service charge, otherwise add 10–15 per cent. Drivers don't expect a tip, but you could add a dollar or so.
Siesta and fiesta Shops generally keep a long day, from 8am to 8pm, depending on the season. Banks usually close at 1pm, but you can also change money at an ATM.
Do go/don't go Belize has a moderate subtropical climate all year round, but outside of the dry months, it can be quite wet with brief but frequent showers. The first few months of the year are the best time to visit for full-on sunshine. Hurricane season is August to October.
Packing tips Insect repellent is essential for jungle trips and visiting mangroves; an umbrella is more convenient than a waterproof jacket for sudden showers. Take closed shoes for walking around the jungle, as flip-flopped feet can fall prey to nibble-happy red ants – especially at night.
Recommended reads Birds of Belize by H Lee Jones will help you identify the nation's vast array of exotic avians; for a flight of fiction, try Belizean author Zee Edgell's award-winning meditation on independence, Beka Lamb.

Cuisine Taking their culinary cues from an assortment of neighbouring cuisines, Belizean dishes exhibit influences from Mexico, Spain, the Caribbean and Mayan culture. Coastal delicacies such as conch fritters and grilled lobster vie for attention with mountain fare, including intensely flavoured mole chicken or light escabeche broth. Breakfast is often lavish and substantial; huevos rancheros (eggs served with refried beans, salsa and corn chips) is typical, as are deep-fried, doughnut-like jacks (fritters) in syrup.

WORTH GETTING OUT OF BED FOR

Viewpoint Buried deep in the Chiquibul Forest, Caracol is one of the most impressive Mayan sites in the country. Climb the Temple of Caana, Belize's tallest structure, and marvel at the rainforest canopy from the top. Look out for howler monkeys and toucans.

Arts and culture The Mayans left their mark on Belize, and there are some awe-inducing sites. Highlights include the sacrificial altars, capstones decorated with hieroglyphics and carved ball courts uncovered from the jungles of Caracol, as well as the pyramid temples and stucco friezes of Xunantunich. Gen up on the finer architectural points before your trip with the beautifully illustrated Taschen tome, *Maya: Palaces and Pyramids of the Rainforest* by Henri Stierlin.

Activities Belize has the second longest reef in the world, and the diving here is spectacular. Take the two-hour boat ride from San Pedro and dive the Great Blue Hole, a collapsed underwater limestone cave that forms a black circle in the turquoise water. Experienced divers can drop below the rim at 40 metres to explore the eerie stalactites and glimpse Caribbean reef sharks. Snorkel or scuba with Amigos del Mar (226 2706), one of the most respected dive schools in San Pedro, or try your hand at catching a tricksy bonefish or glimmering tarpon in the shallow waters of the reef. The Tides Dive Shop (523 3244) in Placencia can arrange for you to swim with whale sharks.

Perfect picnic Take a packed lunch and head off to wallow in the natural granite waterhole of Rio on Pools in the Mountain Pine Ridge Forest Reserve. On the way back, pop into the Green Hills Butterfly Ranch (820 4017) for an eyeful of natural colour.

Daytripper Tikal – one of the most astonishing sets of Mayan ruins in Central America – is a 90-minute drive into Guatemala from the western Belize border. The jungle trek to get there is as inspiring as the ruins themselves – the moment when you first see the temple-tops towering over the mist-hugged forest canopy is unforgettable. You can organise trips from Belize City or San Ignacio; visit www.tikalpark.com for details.

Walks Go on a subterranean journey through the Actun Tunichil Muknal cave system in the Tapir Mountain Reserve in Cayo District to see thousand-year-old Mayan burial remains. If circumnavigating rock pools and clambering over boulders sounds too strenuous, but you still have a taste for underground adventure, ask your hotel to arrange a guided canoe trip into Barton Creek Cave.

Shopping Saturday's popular open-air market in San Ignacio is is the place to stock up on bottles of chilli sauce, local honeys and jam. Find skin-softening natural glycerine soap and colourful embroidered huipiles textiles at Caesar's Place on the Western Highway – they make great gifts and souvenirs. Ambergris Caye island is the proud motherland of 'Pantyripper', an ominously named blend of pineapple juice and coconut liqueur – you can pick up a bottle at the Rum, Cigar and Coffee House on Pescador Drive (226 2020).

Something for nothing Belize is a bird-watcher's paradise. Providing 300 square miles of unspoilt places to perch, the Mountain Pine Ridge Forest Reserve attracts more than 500 species of feathered flutterer. Look out for keel-billed toucans, orange-breasted falcons and rare king vultures.

Don't go home without... a bottle of Marie Sharp's habanero sauce – widely available across the country, this potent concoction will give your food a Belizean zing for months after your return.

BEMUSINGLY BELIZE

Beach roulette – with chickens. Yes, you read that right. In San Pedro, Wednesday night is 'Chicken Drop' night. A giant bingo card is laid out on the beach with a wire mesh suspended above it. An inexplicably enthusiastic crowd each bets on a number, and a bird is set loose upon the 'board'. The pot goes to the one who has picked the square the chicken eventually chooses to 'drop' its droppings onto, and the lucky winner also gets to clean the board for the next round.

DIARY

February/March The whole of Belize celebrates Carnaval, but nowhere throws its heart into it quite like San Pedro. Costume parades cross the city, and people cover each other in coloured powder and lipstick. March 9 is Baron Bliss Day, featuring a regatta outside the Baron Bliss lighthouse in Belize City. **March/April** Easter Fair in San Ignacio is a family-fun festival, with music, games and sporting events. **August** The nine-day Deer Dance Festival in San Antonio, a hybrid of Christian and ancient Mayan culture involving ritualistic dance, a staged 'deer hunt' and greased pole climbing. **September** Independence Day is marked on the 21st with events nationwide. **October** Pan-American Day (or Columbus Day) on the 12th celebrates *mestizo* (Spanish/Mayan) culture with races, regattas and beauty pageants.

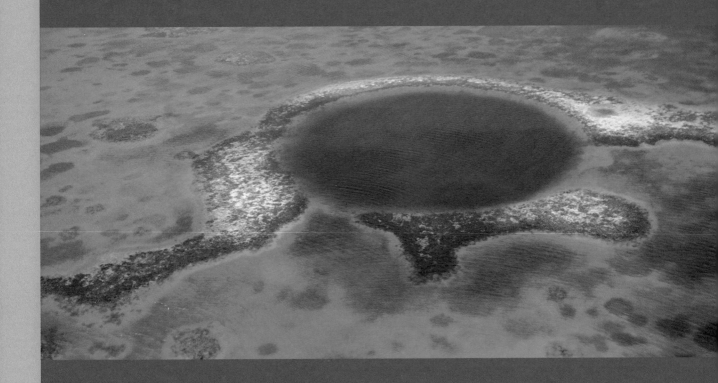

Blancaneaux Lodge

STYLE Coppola cabana
SETTING Majestic Mayan mountains
DESTINATION Belize

'The landscape has been primped
to perfection by legions of dedicated
gardeners. Nature is definitely
nurtured here, and it has been staged
and lit to Hollywood standards'

'I love the smell of habanero in the morning,' exclaims Mr Smith as he delves into a mountain of chilaquiles – tortillas scrambled with egg, chillies and cheese. It's one of Blancaneaux owner Francis Ford Coppola's favourite breakfasts, apparently. I look to the pine-swathed hills that steam as mist burns up in the morning sun, and smile at the hummingbirds that dart around the flamingo-pink bougainvillea. It's hardly *Apocalypse Now*, I think as we're handed two more cappuccinos.

Our location is a three-hour drive from Belize City airport, which, as we discovered when we arrived yesterday, culminates in a 50-minute jolt along a dirt track. As we turned into the lodge's hibiscus-lined driveway, and Mr Smith wondered aloud whether he'd ever sit down comfortably again, I happened to notice an airstrip. I'm all for authenticity and experiencing the thrill of the journey, but I'd have taken a flight in a five-seater Cessna any day.

How Francis found Blancaneaux has entered into lodge legend. We are told the story as soon as we arrive. The scene: Blancaneaux was left mouldering by its owner after the jaguars he was regularly shooting started to dwindle away. Strange that. Coppola was in Belize after the tribulations of filming Marlon and the boys in the Philippines and, while up to his beard in pine forest, happened across this abandoned wreck. He felt that, with its back-to-nature vibe, it was the ideal place to write; and, after a decade of doing it up, he opened it to visitors.

The combination of hills, waterfalls, woodland and gently ruffling foliage makes for a convincing jungle playground, though, in truth, it's a landscape that has been primped to perfection by legions of dedicated gardeners. Nature is definitely nurtured here, and it has been staged and lit to Hollywood standards. Standing on the wooden terrace of our cabana, I listen to a soundtrack of birdsong that's so loud it drowns out the nearby waterfall.

Our home for the weekend, built from local hardwoods and topped with shaggy palm thatch, is like a treehouse perched on the hillside. Inside it's as colourful as the orioles that flit around the roof. Striped woven hangings, which dangle down rough white walls, are echoed by the

huge rugs and vivid bedspread. It's the yellow and black carvings of beady-eyed jaguars skulking in the corners that give the space its real character, though. This is laid-back living, where sun-warmed breeze wafts through open doors and windows, softly blowing the fresh flowers on tables, and bringing in the scent of pine.

A short amble up to Big Rock Falls is as much as we can manage before dinner in the Montagna restaurant. The Italian-in-the-jungle idea is certainly unusual, and the pastas and wood-fired pizzas, supplemented by wines from Coppola's Californian estates, are intriguing. If the idea of air-freighted vegetables fills you with horror, fear not: the kitchen is supported by a lovingly tended organic kitchen garden. This means the restaurant is able to chalk a couple of Belizean dishes onto its specials board each night, and that Mr Smith and I can sample a delicious black bean and chicken stew.

I am woken the next day by a talking conch shell. 'This is your wake-up call!' it shouts as I jab blearily at Mr Smith's ribs. There's something surreal about being roused by a mollusc – the communications system is another of Coppola's idiosyncratic touches – but needs must. It's our own fault: after several glasses of Shiraz last night, we committed ourselves to an early horse ride through the rainforest. This seemed a better idea at 11pm yesterday than it does at 6am today.

In the afternoon, we canoe on the green waters of Barton Creek, and paddle deep into an enormous, stalactite-dripping cave to visit a Mayan sacrificial site. The bats that hang like leathery sacks from the cave ceiling squirm in the light of our super-powerful torches, and our guide suggests we turn off the beams 'for a moment of reflection'. All spiritual feelings evaporate for me when we are plunged into blackness. I sit rigid in the canoe, bracing myself for the first bat to tangle itself in my hair. It's thrilling, though.

That evening, Mr Smith and I sink up to our chins in a steaming hot pool and reflect upon what a wonderful couple of days we've had. Our fellow guests, with whom we commune over plantain chips in the Jaguar Bar, are in complete agreement. A collection of intrepid couples and adventure-hungry honeymooners, they have all fallen in love with the low-key atmosphere. We only wish that, like them, we were staying for longer.

It turns out a place aboard the five-seater Cessna is easily organised, so I book the plane to add some drama to our departure. After just two nights in this rainforest retreat, I leave the lodge feeling like the star of one of Mr Coppola's movies. We rise off the airstrip, leaving the dense, emerald-coloured jungle in our wake, and I swear I can hear Wagner's 'Ride of the Valkyries' resounding triumphantly in my ears.

Reviewed by Mr & Mrs Smith

'Our cabana, topped with shaggy palm thatch, is as colourful inside as the birds that flit around the roof'

NEED TO KNOW

Rooms 20, including six two-bedroom Villas, a Family Cabana, the Francis Ford Coppola Villa and a private cottage.
Rates Low season, $230–$1,200; high season, $285–$1,600, including Continental breakfast; excludes nine per cent tax and 10 per cent service charge. Enchanted Cottage rates include 24-hour butler service.
Check-out Noon; check-in, 3pm.
Facilities Stables, spa, two outdoor swimming pools, small library, free WiFi throughout. In rooms, iPod docks, 'shell phone' intercom system, handmade organic toiletries.
Children Sloping grounds and steps make it a tricky proposition for babies and the buggy-bound, but kids are welcome. Under-12s stay free, otherwise extra beds are $50 a night (excluding tax). Baby cots and babysitting can be arranged in advance.
Also If the bumpy three-hour drive from Belize City airport seems too much, you can charter a Cessna plane to zip you over the jungle canopy to Blancaneaux Lodge's own airstrip.

IN THE KNOW

Our favourite rooms Although Francis Ford Coppola's own villa is the largest, with a kitchenette and a vast open-air living room, we were taken with the Honeymoon Cabanas and their soft cream sofas and ornate beds. Number 5 has a secluded terrace with a sweeping waterfall view, as well as a private heart-shaped garden.
Hotel bar The ceiling fans in the Jaguar Bar are souvenirs from *Apocalypse Now*, and the hand-carved slate bar counter is decorated with glyphs of Mayan gods. Throughout the day, hummingbirds come to feed on the tropical flowers while Blancaneaux's guests sip hibiscus daiquiris or fruity Jaguar Juice rum cocktails.
Hotel restaurant The treehouse-like Montagna serves up the owner's Italian culinary favourites – the Belizean jungle is not where you'd expect to find a wood-fired pizza oven. At the poolside restaurant, Guatemaltecqua, you're more likely to savour authentic Mayan dishes featuring chillies, beans and tortillas.
Top table From the table on the far right of the wrap-around terrace, you can ogle jungle views in two directions, and, at breakfast, marvel at the birds and butterflies that fill the forest air.
Room service Meals, drinks and snacks can be brought to your cabana until 9pm.
Dress code Jungle casual, with a splash of glam by night.
Local knowledge Whether your preferred mode of transport is by foot, horse, bike or canoe, the Lodge is ideally placed for budding explorers to launch jungle expeditions. Deep in the Chiquibul rainforest, Caracol, the most extensive set of Mayan ruins in Belize, is a short 4x4 journey away.

LOCAL EATING AND DRINKING

The Lodge's remote location limits your culinary options somewhat, and the closest you're likely to come to 'eating out' is asking staff to pack you a picnic. However, if you find yourself in nearby San Ignacio, the choice improves, with a trio of simple, reliable and femininely named eateries: **Eva's** (824 2267) and **Hannah's** (824 3014) on Burns Avenue, and **Martha's** (804 3647) on West Street. Each serves authentic Belizean cuisine in humble but lively surroundings.

GET A ROOM!

To book this hotel, go to www.mrandmrssmith.com or ring our expert travel team on 1 800 464 2040. Activate your free membership online (see page 4) to qualify for the exclusive Smith card offer shown below when you book with us.

 SMITH CARD OFFER A 30-minute Thai-style massage each.

Blancaneaux Lodge Mountain Pine Ridge Forest Reserve, Cayo District (www.mrandmrssmith.com/blancaneaux-lodge)

Rio de Janeiro

BRAZIL

RIO DE JANEIRO
La Suite

RIO DE JANEIRO

CITYSCAPE Ocean, rainforest, and a cast of millions
CITY LIFE Booty-shaking beach parties

With its superabundance of natural beauty – mile-long tropical beaches, dramatic mountainscapes, lush jungle backdrop – Rio is one of the most attractive destinations on the planet. Add to that a population whose blazing spirit and passion are envied the world over: its glamorous citizens eschew conformity and dull days, and their energy enlivens every corner of this sprawling megacity-on-sea. From fashionable Ipanema to the arty, leafy community of Santa Teresa, the streets buzz with music, humour and the indefatigable Carioca spirit. Whether you're a VIP in Joa (Brazil's Beverly Hills), or a beach bum on Copacabana, life is lived at a hectic pace – dancing, flirting and posing are national pastimes. Caipirinhas, baile funk and bar hopping are all part of this electric 'carpe diem' culture, and never in more Technicolor glory than during Carnival, the tail-feathered, heart-racing, soul-uplifting celebration of life's pleasures.

GETTING THERE

Planes The international hub is Antonio Carlos Jobim airport, aka Galeão, 20km north of the city centre. The 40-minute taxi ride to the Zona Sul area should cost R$80.
Trains The metro system serves a limited area: Linha 1 runs through the centre down to Copacabana; Linha 2 goes to Zona Norte. Santa Teresa has trams (*bondinhos*) to hop on.
Automobiles Driving can be slow and/or scary: have a go if you think you're tough enough (the main thoroughfare isn't called Avenida Ayrton Senna for nothing). Traffic lights are often ignored. Buses are cheap, and fine for daytime trips.
Boats Ferries from Rio to Niterói leave from the quays near Praca XV; the hydrofoil is a bit faster.

LOCAL KNOWLEDGE

Taxis Affordable and plentiful. Unless you speak Portuguese, write down the address, and don't worry if the driver asks a fellow cabbie for directions. Make sure the meter is on.
Currency The Brazilian real (R$).
Dialling codes Brazil: 55. Rio de Janeiro: 21.
Tipping culture In restaurants, 10 per cent is usually added to bills. Apart from that, gratuities aren't the norm, though cab drivers and waiting staff will appreciate any gesture.

Siesta and fiesta Be ready to party late, especially during Carnival. Bar hours vary, but many keep it going till the last customer leaves. Most shops close at around 7pm.
Do go/don't go December to February is summer (high season), when the city buzzes with excitement during the Carnival build-up, and long days on the beach give way to party nights. Winter is cooler and calmer – but only just.
Packing tips Bring: teeny-weeny bikinis, dancing shoes, Carioca attitude, Astrud Gilberto CDs. If you're a hungry bug's dream come true, bring insect repellent as well. Leave behind: your best jewellery, inhibitions.
Recommended reads *A Death in Brazil: a Book of Omissions* by Peter Robb, an insightful, tightly written analysis of modern Brazil; funny and instructive, *The Scorpion's Sweet Venom: Diary of a Brazilian Call Girl* by Bruna Surfistinha is a suitably raunchy beach read; Priscilla Ann Goslin's *How to Be a Carioca* is a tongue-in-cheek guide to the city's people.
Cuisine Hard-partying Cariocas like their rocket fuel: strong, sweet coffee, plus exotic smoothies made with power-packed ingredients such as açaí, goji berries or guarana, which are ubiquitous and inexpensive. The main menu staples are rice and beans, and stews, such as

feijoada and moqueca; fresh fish is good, as are churrasco steaks, straight off the southern plains. There are plenty of contemporary and international restaurants in the Zona Sul, or you can share tapas (*petiscos*) at traditional *botequins*. Our favourite Brazilian export is cachaça, the sugar-cane spirit that puts the kick in your caipirinhas.

WORTH GETTING OUT OF BED FOR

Viewpoint Take a cable-car ride up to the granite dome of Sugar Loaf Mountain, 369m above Rio, to see a dazzling vista of the whole city and Guanabara Bay. Or, for the ultimate view, take a helicopter ride along the coast and around Christ the Redeemer (www.helisight.com.br).

Arts and culture Among Rio's state-funded theatres, the Teatro Nelson Rodrigues (2262 5483) is home to the brilliant Intrépida Trupe dance company. The Instituto Moreira Salles (www.ims.com.br) is among the city's most vital cultural centres, with excellent visual arts, music and film. There are countless venues where you can experience samba, that essential expression of Brazilian joie de vivre: in Lapa, try Carioca da Gema (www.barcariocadagema.com.br) for live music and sexy sambistas, or Clube dos Democráticos (2252 4611) on Rua do Riachuelo for Carnival pleasures in a 19th-century ballroom.

Activities Surf's up – try Leblon, Ipanema or Copacabana or, better, head to Prainha (ask at your hotel about the Surf Bus from Largo do Machado). Runners can hit the beach, too, for sand-enhanced workouts (try to avoid the 9am rush, though). Climbers are surrounded by tempting ascents, with 50 routes up the Sugar Loaf alone – Climb in Rio (www.climbinrio.com) can guide both beginners and rock-face veterans to their own cliffhanger moment. Contact Rio Hiking (www.riohiking.com.br) for all manner of outdoor adventures, from horse riding to hang-gliding.

Perfect picnic Assemble a feast at one of Rio's excellent farmers' markets (*feiras livres*) – try Praça Nossa Senhora da Paz in Ipanema on a Friday morning, or the gourmet market on Saturdays on Rua Frei Leandro in the Jardim Botânico (3874 1808; www.jbrj.gov.br). Take it to the beach (see below) or on a ramble through Tijuca Forest.

Best beach The city beaches are numbered, one to 12, and it's all very tribal: Posto 7 in Ipanema is surfer central; Posto 11 in Leblon is family- and couple-friendly. Posto 10 is a sporty spot; while Ipanema's Posto 9 is where the beautiful and the hip hang out. To escape the crowds, you'll have to make a sortie to Niterói and the gorgeous strands at Piratininga or Camboinhas.

Daytripper Head for the hills of Petrópolis, an hour's drive out of the centre, where well-to-do Cariocas escape at weekends for cool mountain breezes and general chilling out among leafy streets and moguls' mansions. While you're there, visit the Imperial Museum, or find cut-price cotton pieces at the textile factory outlets on Rua Teresa.

Walks Rio isn't short of green lungs. Open daily until 5pm, Parque da Cidade is set on the edge of Gavéa, extending up into the Tijuca Forest, 116 acres of green space networked with trails and paths. Around Lagoa de Freitas, Parque Cantagalo and Parque Patins are popular for strolling and jogging, with kiosks and live music at night.

Shopping The streets of Leblon and Ipanema are studded with scores of appealing shops; the best womenswear boutiques are on Rua Maria Quiteria and Rua Garcia d'Avila. In the Centro, the teeming Saara market, near Uruguaiana metro, is open for business every day except Sunday, with anything and everything for sale; even more enticing is the nearby Camelódromo market, a labyrinth of little stalls selling baile funk CDs, designer knock-offs and much more. Rua do Lavradio in Lapa is home to both antiques shops and contemporary furniture showrooms.

Something for nothing The Centro Cultural Parque das Ruinas (2252 0112), a cultural centre in a neoclassical mansion in Santa Teresa, has live jazz shows on Thursday nights. And, hey, a day on the beach costs *nada*.

Don't go home without... buying half a dozen pairs of Havaiana flip-flops, dancing all night to bossa nova beats and competing fiercely at beach football.

REALLY RIO

Floresta da Tijuca is the world's biggest urban rainforest, with hundreds of rare species of plants and wildlife. It is also full of historical attractions, from the obvious Cristo Redentor (Christ the Redeemer) atop Corcovado mountain to the gem-like Mayrink Chapel, adorned with murals painted by one of Brazil's best-known 20th-century artists, Candido Portinari.

DIARY

January Dia de São Sebastiao on the 20th sees a procession and a huge concert on Copacabana beach. **February** Carnival! Rio hosts the world's biggest party, no contest (www.rio-carnival. net). **June** Fiery, folkloric fun across the city for the Festas Juninas. **July** Arte de Portas Abertas, when the artists of Santa Teresa open their doors to the public (www.chavemestra.com.br). **September–October** Rio de Janeiro International Film Festival (www.festivaldorio.com.br), aka Festival do Rio, the most prominent movie mash-up in South America. **December** Reveillon: two million people dressed in white hit Copacabana beach for fireworks and New Year's Eve fun.

La Suite

STYLE Modernism outside, maximalism inside
SETTING Brazilian Beverly Hills
DESTINATION Río de Janeiro

'The hotel is styled with a unique
blend of contemporary LA chic and
classic Gallic elegance, imbued
with red-hot Brazilian passion'

T is the final weekend of a month-long trip through Brazil – a luxurious sign-off before returning to our real lives. As expectations go, ours are at 'ridiculously high'. Security guards set a VIP tone and motion our driver through to a quiet residential street. We fall out of our cab, dusty and travel-fatigued, in front of a large, faceless, nondescript grey door – disappointment looms.

Our casually dressed host, Rodrigo, opens the door and swiftly La Suite's seductive charm and sweeping sea views come to the fore. It's a clifftop villa in Joatinga – the Beverly Hills of Rio – where floor-to-ceiling windows and a huge grandstand terrace give way to a panorama of Brazil's high-drama megalopolis. To one side, the turquoise blue of the Atlantic encircling the Cagarras islands; to the other, a jungle-fringed swathe of Rio's trademark beaches – Leblon and Ipanema. Sugar Loaf Mountain with Christ the Redeemer is in the distance – Baz Luhrmann couldn't have created a more magical backdrop.

La Suite is a guesthouse rather than a conventional hotel, belonging to charming Frenchman François-Xavier Dussol and his Brazilian partner Rodrigo Harold. Dussol fell in love with Rio a decade ago and moved here permanently from

Paris to set up Rio's first boutique hotel, La Maison, and, more recently, La Suite. Both are styled with his unique blend of contemporary LA chic and classic Gallic elegance, imbued with red-hot Brazilian passion. Louis XV chairs in rich vibrant colours, a Murano-glass chandelier and local graffiti art add flair to this modern residence. What makes François and Rodrigo the perfect hosts is that they are as excited about their city and pool-party paradise as us newcomers. Between them, they know Rio's every secret – invaluable when you have only one weekend to get under the skin of this larger-than-life destination.

All seven of La Suite's guestrooms are themed by colour, and we've plumped for purple. Rodrigo shows us to our elegant, wood-floored suite; it's decorated in bold stripes, complete with walk-in wardrobe, antique French dresser and sumptuous pillow-covered king-size bed. All of this is almost eclipsed by the bathroom. Resplendent in opulent amethyst marble, it comes with a two-headed lovers' shower – though, in truth, it's so huge that any amorists in there might not even find each other in all that steam.

On François' recommendation, we take a cab along the coast to the city centre. We hop on a tram up cobbled streets to the bohemian hillside hangout of Santa Teresa – a maze of crumbling former colonial residences and favela-supplied arts and crafts boutiques. We're here outside of carnival season, but the bars and cafés are packed with locals and tourists spilling onto the streets, live music pouring from every window and doorway. A local band keeps the crowd on its feet – just a typical Saturday afternoon in Rio. We find a free table at Espirito Santo, and soak up the views of Lapa and Copacabana beyond before our next adrenalising activity. In any other circumstance, a soccer game would be the last thing optioned on a romantic getaway, but this is Rio: normal rules don't apply. We have tickets for Flamengo v Botafogo at the Maracanã stadium. We arrive having never heard of the teams but, after a dose of the samba drums, flares and fireworks – staple accessories at every Rio match – we leave hoarse, arm in arm with new *amigos*.

'A huge grandstand terrace gives way to a panorama of Brazil's high-drama megalopolis'

Rio has restaurants for every taste, but dinner back at La Suite is the most beguiling option. We cosy down on velvet sofas in the sitting room and Rodrigo brings us a couple of caipirinhas – Rio measures. We sip them, entertained by Jolie, the lady of the house – La Suite's pet dachshund. It feels as though we're staying with close friends, and dining here just reinforces that. You're simply asked if there's anything you don't eat (my list is extensive: allergic to this, intolerant of that) – and are served the most deliciously imaginative, tailor-made delights from La Suite's resident French chef. We tuck into salads of mixed greens, warm figs and strips of Parmesan (a real rarity in Rio), then fillets of mahi-mahi, topped with peppery shrimp pieces, and creamy mashed baroa potatoes. All is enjoyed at a private table on the deck overlooking the twinkling lights of Rio. There is no months-in-advance booking required and, even better, our bedroom is but a wobbly walk away.

Breakfast, eaten on our private terrace the following morning, is most soothing. Just-squeezed exotic juice, fresh fruit, cheese and cold cuts, home-made pastries and scrambled eggs – is this fair in the land of the world's skimpiest bikinis? After a dip in the Playboy-mansion-worthy circular pool (regulation swimming attire donned; tummies sucked in), we head for the beach. Posto 9 on Ipanema? That is *so* last summer – Joatinga beach is where those-in-the-know top up their perfect tans. It's only a 15-minute walk but our 'could he be more lovely?' host François insists on driving us.

Word-of-mouth exclusivity gives Joa an unspoilt charm and we skip over the rocks to the white sandy cove to join the only other person – an Adonis running lengths (no Rio beach is complete without one). We slap on the factor 20 and get supine. A word of warning – in our blissed-out state we didn't notice the tide coming in. Suffice to say, no one looks sexy in a too-small bikini, panicking, clambering from rock to rock with beach bags aloft. In the drama, we were hoping we'd miss our flight. No such luck. Like old friends, François and Rodrigo give us hugs goodbye with promises of an invite to their next pool party. We're back home saving up for our next trip already: they'd better have meant it.

Reviewed by Mr & Mrs Smith

Rooms Seven.

Rates €300–€450, including breakfast and tax.

Checkout Noon, but flexible on request (depending on subsequent bookings). Earliest check-in, 11am (though, as some flights arrive into Rio in the very early morning, the hotel will always do what it can to accommodate its guests).

Facilities Outdoor pool, infinity pool (as of late 2008), library of books, CDs and DVDs, WiFi, chauffeur service, and massages, manicures, hair stylist by arrangement. In rooms, air-conditioning, fully loaded iPods and iPod docks.

Children Under-fives stay free, with baby cots provided. Over-fives: €150 for an extra bed. A babysitting service is provided by the hotel maids (a small tip is suggested).

Also Pets are welcome at La Suite. Smoking allowed. The hotel also offers airport transfers for €60 each way, and an insiders' tour of Rio de Janeiro for €190. Oh, and it has its own helipad, too.

IN THE KNOW

Our favourite rooms The Black Suite has yards of windows, surrounding you with views of ocean, mountain and city, and two bathrooms. The Purple Suite is the most spacious, with an amazing marble bathroom and giant lovers' shower. The pretty Pink Room is ideal for a couple with a child, since the room is divided into two.

Hotel bar Exotic-fruit caipirinhas, taken on the terrace, are a speciality.

Hotel restaurant Chef Pascal Joly, former chef of the Plaza Athénée in Paris and second chef at Joël, is now responsible for the delectations served on the terrace or poolside, or in the dining room with its hip Seventies furniture if you choose.

Top table You can dine on your own private terrace; otherwise we love the views from the main deck.

Room service There's hot food (based on what's being prepared in the kitchen) and drinks available from 8am till late.

Dress code Slinky and stylish sunwear.

Local knowledge If you'd like a little respite from Rio's throbbing urban delights, then head up to Buzios – a beautiful and far less hectic section of the Brazilian coastline that's just a couple of hours north of the city. Quiet beaches, atmospheric coves and traditional fishing villages make this the weekend escape of choice for the chic Carioca.

LOCAL EATING AND DRINKING

Zuka (3205 7154) on Rua Dias Ferreira has marble walls and a sunken kitchen area in which food is grilled in front of your eyes, then doused in mouthwatering sauces. It also produces the best tortellini in the country, and a huge range of cocktails. The Japanese diaspora is big in Brazil, so competition among the finest sushi restaurants is stiff. The hugely popular **Sushi Leblon** (2274 1342), also on Rua Dias Ferreira, attracts a stellar clientele, so queues can be long, but it is worth the wait to sample its famous shrimp and foie gras. The charming pink and green **Zazá Bistro** (2247 9101), on Rua Joana Angélica in Ipanema, serves up excellent Brazilian dishes with oriental influences. It has a lovely outside terrace, which is quite rare in Rio. It may be a little off the beaten path, but the quirky, art deco **Restaurante Olympe** (2539 4542) in Jardim Botânico on Rua Custódio Serrão, is where French superchef Claude Troisgros conjures up Gallic cuisine using fresh Brazilian ingredients.

GET A ROOM!

To book this hotel, go to www.mrandmrssmith.com or ring our expert travel team on 1 800 464 2040. Activate your free membership online (see page 4) to qualify for the exclusive Smith card offer shown below when you book with us.

 SMITH CARD OFFER A bottle of champagne on arrival.

La Suite 501 Rua Jackson de Figueiredo, Joa, Rio de Janeiro (www.mrandmrssmith.com/la-suite)

Paris

Beaujolais

Dordogne

Southwest
Provence

FRANCE

BEAUJOLAIS
Château de Bagnols

DORDOGNE
Château les Merles

PARIS
Hotel Daniel

SOUTHWEST PROVENCE
Oustau de Baumanière

BEAUJOLAIS

COUNTRYSIDE A vine romance
COUNTRY LIFE Haute cuisine heaven

Prepare to have your tastebuds tantalised and your eyes amazed: with its distinguished wines, world-renowned cuisine and ornate châteaux of honey-coloured stone, Beaujolais is everything the committed Francophile dreams of. Located in the heart of France, this is a rural idyll of old villages, vineyards, lush farmland, forest and gentle hills, where the graceful Saône and Rhône rivers merge. At its core is the chic metropolis of Lyon, former capital of the silk industry and the first stop on any self-respecting gourmand's grand tour. A bright firmament of Michelin-starred restaurants dazzles discerning palates across the region, offering white-linened tables overflowing with Burgundy and some of the finest fine dining in France. Horse riding, ballooning and cycling will let you savour the rich landscape of Beaujolais, and even burn off a few calories after a night on the gastronomy.

GETTING THERE

Planes Lyon Saint Exupéry airport (www.lyonairport.com) sees plenty of short-haul action from across Europe and North Africa; fly to Paris or Nice for long-haul connections.
Trains High-speed TGVs connect Lyon to the rest of France and Europe. The station isn't central, but an efficient tram network will get you there. You could also take the Eurostar from London, via Lille or Paris (www.eurostar.com).
Automobiles A car is highly recommended if you want to visit the vineyards, châteaux and historic towns scattered throughout Beaujolais and Burgundy; a 30-minute drive from Lyon takes you into the heart of the region.

LOCAL KNOWLEDGE

Taxis In towns, pick one up from a taxi rank or hail one on the street. If you're travelling in remote areas, try to book a car in advance – or prepare for a long walk.
Currency Euro (€).
Dialling codes France: 33. Beaujolais and Lyon: (0)4.
Tipping culture Restaurant and café bills usually include a service charge (*service compris*) but it's customary to leave a small tip. For taxi drivers, add 10 per cent.
Siesta and fiesta Many restaurants close after 2pm and

reopen in the afternoon around 4pm; some are closed on Mondays and Tuesdays. Small shops also break for lunch, even in Lyon; most close on Sundays.
Do go/don't go Visit in May to see cherry blossom in bloom, or during the autumn harvest, when the turning leaves provide a spectacular display of colour. Summer in the city can be hot and humid, but never overwhelmingly so.
Packing tips Credit cards, for gourmet treats and shopping sprees in Lyon. A notebook for jotting down recipe ideas.
Recommended reads *French Women Don't Get Fat* by Mireille Guiliano (for the non-runners among you); Bocuse's *Regional French Cooking*, a culinary must-read by one of the country's foremost chefs; Tracy Chevalier's beautifully woven tale of tapestry, *The Lady and the Unicorn*.
Cuisine Haute! Haute! Haute! This patch of French soil has more (Michelin) stars than the Milky Way. Highly prized local ingredients include tender Charolais beef and excellent wines, including Chablis, Burgundy and, of course, Beaujolais. Vine and bovine are perfectly married in the region's characteristic boeuf bourguignon; coq au vin is another classic. Cheese lovers should try Epoisses, a pungent creamy number said to have been Napoleon's

favourite. Follow the chefs to Lyon's covered market, Les Halles, to sniff out what's cooking in a restaurant near you, from boudin noir to foie gras; or you may prefer to follow your nose on a countryside tour of wineries. And... The Pierres Dorées area of southern Beaujolais is named after the golden stone that gives the region's farmhouses and castles their distinctive charm.

WORTH GETTING OUT OF BED FOR

Viewpoint Look out across 'la Terrasse' on the climb to the Col du Fût d'Avenas for spectacular views over Beaujolais and, on a clear day, Mont Blanc. Beaujolais Vert's conifer-sprinkled hillsides have earned it the moniker Little Switzerland. Drive on to Juliénas for rewarding valley vistas.

Arts and culture If towers and moats light your fire, you've come to the right place: the region is renowned for its beautiful castles. The formal gardens of 17th-century Château de La Chaize (www.chateaudelachaize.com) in Brouilly – also a renowned wine estate – are breathtaking; Château de Cormatin (www.chateaudecormatin.com), between Tournus and Cluny, contains wonderfully opulent rooms; and the mediaeval villages of Jarnoiux and Oingt are presided over by turreted wonders. Cultured Lyon will keep arts buffs bamboozled with its bounty: the striking opera house on Place de la Comédie (www.opera-lyon. com) offers artistic excellence inside and out; and the masterpiece-packed Musée des Beaux-Arts (www.mba-lyon. fr) is Lyon's answer to the Louvre. Aspiring designers will love the Musées des Tissus et des Arts Décoratifs (www. musee-des-tissus), where displays include everything from ancient Egyptian tunics to Zaha Hadid silverware, via Marie-Antoinette's bedroom wall hangings.

Activities Snacking, sipping and snoozing are top of our to-do list, but there are plenty of ways to imbibe fresh French air: take a hot-air balloon flight (www.air-escargot. com), ramble vineyards and taste wines, and ride horses or bikes (not necessarily in that order). Hire two-wheeled or four-hooved transport locally; your hotel will have details. The Ecole Beaujolaise des Vins (www.beaujolais.com) in Villefranche offers wine-tasting courses and tours. Many local vineyards host cellar visits by arrangement; try Château de Vaurenard (www.chateaudevaurenard.com).

Perfect picnic Pack yourself *du pain*, *du vin*, some hunks of cheese and a saucisson sec (preferably gathered at an open-air market in one of Beaujolais' prettier villages), and head for the hills or the banks of the river Saône.

Daytripper The picturesque lakeside city of Annecy, 80 minutes' drive from Lyon, has a long history and an Alpine flavour: pretty canals, cowbells and bright red geraniums complete the picture. Browse the Wednesday morning market, then take to the clean, clear waters for a spot of waterskiing, windsurfing or wakeboarding.

Walks Lyon is a great place for pottering. Bring flat shoes for the cobbled streets of Vieux Lyon, then explore the labyrinthine *traboules* – the underground passages originally used by 18th-century silk-makers to carry their delicate fabrics from Silk Hill down to the river. The Resistance also used them for sneaking about during World War II.

Shopping There's a daily food market on Place aux Herbes in Mâcon (except Mondays), and on Saturday morning at Quai Lamartine. There's also a huge covered market in Villefranche on Sundays. Open-air markets on Croix-Rousse hill and Quai St-Antoine in Lyon are where you'll pick up local specialities like Saint-Marcellin cheese. Historic master pâtissier Pignol (04 78 37 39 61) on Rue Emile Zola sells delicate confections. The city rivals Paris for chic boutiques, particularly between Place Bellecour and Cordeliers in the Carré d'Or district; silk scarves are a top buy.

Something for nothing The cellars of Francisque Rivière in Bagnols are free to visit. At nightfall, 300 of Lyon's landmarks and monuments are illuminated by thousands of lights, creating a magical setting for an evening stroll.

Don't go home without... a few bottles of wine; take your pick of the local *vignerons*, or try superior grog shop Antic Wine (04 78 37 08 96), at 18 Rue du Boeuf in Lyon, for a grand selection of grands crus.

BEAUTIFULLY BEAUJOLAIS

Legend has it that Beaujolais' peaks were created by the giant Gargantua, emptying his shoes of troublesome stones (or drunkenly lobbing them, depending on who tells the story). Pick your way among them as you follow the wine route through the region, visiting the villages of Beujeu, Brouilly, Chénas, Saint-Amour, Fleurie, Morgon and Moulin-à-Vent.

DIARY

June–July Lyon's Roman amphitheatre hosts Les Nuits de Fourvière (www.nuitsdefourviere.fr), a month-long performing arts festival. **November** The third Thursday of the month sees Beaujeu's townsfolk flock to taste the year's Beaujolais Nouveau; the first barrel is pierced at midnight, after a procession of burning torches made from the dead vines – known as the Fête des Sarmentelles (www.rhonealpes-tourism.co.uk). **December** The Festival of Light is held just before New Year in Lyon, when windows are lit with candles and there is a lantern procession through the city. Concerts and operas are held at the same time (www.lyon-france.com).

Château de Bagnols

STYLE Five-star French castle
SETTING Vineyard-framed rural idyll
DESTINATION Beaujolais

'The rooms here are so exquisite
it is mad not to stay in for the evening
and do your own version of "You
be Louis and I'll be Marie-Antoinette".
Just don't lose your head'

For more than a decade, I had dreamt of Château de Bagnols. When I was editor of *Elle Decoration*, I saw incredible pictures that lodged in my imagination, images from childhood: *Beauty and the Beast*, *Bluebeard's Castle*, *The Princess and the Pea*... The extravagant interiors looked about as far from the usual idea of a boutique hotel, and from the modern design that filled the pages of my magazine, as was possible. Intensely beautiful, the pictures that struck me most were of the château's beds – insane four-posters piled high with mattresses and hung with heavy red-brocade drapes or antique silks – which I could hardly believe were real. This was the stuff of the films – of Sofia Coppola and Peter Greenaway. However, it was a dream, and I never went.

Now, finally, invited to review the hotel with my husband, it was time to visit Bagnols in the heart of Beaujolais. Would I be horribly disappointed? Were those pictures a stylised sham? As we arrived in the village of Bagnols, 12 miles from Lyon, and spied the extraordinary castle walls, the answer was, clearly, no. This is a really staggering building in a tiny village, its historic might absolutely apparent. Complete with moat, drawbridge and towers in the honey-coloured stone known as *pierre dorée*, the schoolbook stronghold is punctured by neat, cruciform arrow holes.

The interior of the château does not disappoint. It is the brainchild of a truly cultured woman, Lady Helen Hamlyn, who also owns the house by architects Mendelsohn and Chermayeff in Old Church Street, London – one of England's first modernist homes. The rooms in both the original 13th-century castle and the 'new' (15th-century, in other words) block are beautiful. Our bed was as sublime as I had hoped, decorated with fragile antique textiles and made up with tactile Swiss bedlinen (which you can buy there, too). Next to the bed, the water tumblers were made of silver, giving us a visceral introduction to what it must have been to be a French aristocrat. The bathroom was grand, too, with an antique marble bath and local products including a really, really strong lavender bath foam – the type that works against typhoid and tigers. We also had a huge sitting room, filled with bleeding-heart-coloured sofas, and another tiny room covered with early Renaissance frescoes. It blows your mind.

The kitchens are central to the building and, thanks to a clever sleight of design, you walk through them on your way to anywhere, past the teeming, steaming theatre of food preparation. The grounds are lovely, with dense borders of lavender and a formal garden where we took drinks before dinner. The swimming pool is round, with grass growing right up to its edge. Alas, all this whimsy and wonder has to fit into a 21st-century reality, and the food and service at Bagnols are of a very French kind, rather than matching, in my mind, with the beyond-beautiful environment. The human contact is formal and, operationally, the hotel deals in star ratings and status rather than princesses and peas.

Château de Bagnols is certainly the most beautiful hotel I have ever stayed in. To have a heavenly time, order room service (after all, how often do you have your own four-poster?). The rooms are so exquisite it is mad not to stay in for the evening and do your own version of 'You be Louis and I'll be Marie-Antoinette'. Just don't lose your head. We also dined in the very grand Salle des Gardes, where we had cherry clafoutis for pudding; in contrast, we lunched under the trees, on goat's cheese and red wine.

During the day, go out and explore, do your own thing; the château has bicycles you can go off on, for picnics and jaunts. We made use of its nicely produced book of trips that you can enjoy by bike or car, which took us to just the sort of places we love. We spent a morning at an over-the-top food market at Villefranche, where we did the rounds of the vast quantities of local produce. We bought huge bags and bundles to take home, including an array of fresh goat's cheese and a

sausage called Jésus (the old ladies laughed when I asked them why, leaving me none the wiser), as well as ogling all those great, artistically ordered piles of fruit and vegetables.

Hanging out in yeasty cellars and debating the relative values of 2004 and 2002 is very much our idea of fun, so we also enjoyed a visit to a much-awarded local winemaker, Alain Chatoux, who makes Beaujolais and some very decent white. If you think there is no significant difference between men and women, you might think again after a session of wine-tasting. Down in Mr Chatoux's chilly *cave*, we noted that Mr Smith preferred the powerful kick of a 2003 or a 2005 vintage, while Mrs Smith put her money on the lighter, chillable 2002 or 2004. An interesting experiment, and not one without its non-scientific compensations.

For a change of aesthetic, we drove an hour to see the modernist convent La Tourette by Le Corbusier. One of his last works, it is a building that expresses the interior life of man, and embodies his search for intensity and soul. Built around the progress of the sun, it allows light to enter in many different ways. Slits of sunbeam accompany you down corridors and altars are dramatically lit with wizard fingers of light. It is incredibly moving. We weren't sure how to follow that, except by plunging back into the brocade-draped, fresco-covered, sumptuous worldliness of our quarters at Château de Bagnols – from the sublime to the luxurious, you might say.

Reviewed by Ilse Crawford

'This is a really staggering building, its historic might – moat, drawbridge, towers and arrow holes – absolutely apparent'

NEED TO KNOW

Rooms 21, including eight junior suites, four suites and one apartment.
Rates €445–€915; Lady Hamlyn Apartment, €2,500; from €22,000 a night for exclusive occupancy. Breakfast, from €32.
Check-out Noon; check-in, 3pm, but flexible subject to availability.
Facilities Heated outdoor pool (May to September), library with internet access, spa and beauty treatments, hairdresser, bicycles to borrow. Free use of nearby tennis courts. Luxury chauffeured cars available for transfers and touring.
Children Welcome. English-speaking babysitters can be booked on request, there's a children's menu, and extra beds (at €105 a night) are a possibility in some rooms.
Also Guided tours, hiking, horse riding, golf, hot-air ballooning, cookery classes and wine tasting can be arranged. Small dogs are permitted in the hotel. Smoking is allowed on request.

IN THE KNOW

Our favourite rooms All rooms are lovingly restored and furnished with dramatic antiques (and historical anecdotes). Previously a chapel, Room 8 has curved walls and an arched ceiling, 18th-century frescoes and a gilded four-poster bed; Room 1 has a tower bathroom and a handsome crimson-hung four-poster bed; and Mrs Smith likes to pretend she's Madame de Pompadour on the primrose-yellow damask canopy bed in Room 6.
Hotel bar There's a small bar on the first floor, which stays open until the last guest leaves.
Hotel restaurant Michelin-starred La Salle des Gardes serves Modern French cuisine, as well as traditional regional dishes and spit-roasted meats and game, in the former guards' room and on the south-facing terrace. There is, of course, an excellent list of Beaujolais grands crus and Burgundies. Lunch is served from noon until 1.45pm; dinner, 7.30pm–9.45pm.
Top table Dine by the fire in winter; outside on the terrace under the century-old lime trees in summer.
Room service 24-hour service, with a reduced menu after 10pm.
Dress code No jeans: châtelaine chic for her; jacket for him.
Local knowledge Arrange a wine-tasting session in the Château's splendid Cuvage, set around the lower courtyard, then spend the rest of the afternoon wandering the castle grounds, planted with cherry orchards, long avenues of clipped yews, blooming lilacs and hazelnut trees.

LOCAL EATING AND DRINKING

There are a dozen Michelin-starred French restaurants within an hour of the château, including: **L'Auberge de l'Ile** (04 78 83 99 49) at Place Notre Dame on L'Ile Barbe, just north of Lyon, a 17th-century house surrounded by wooded gardens; silk-adorned **Guy Lassausaie** (04 78 47 62 59) on Rue de Belle Cise in Chasselay, with a contemporary atmosphere and good-value set menus; and **L'Auberge du Pont de Collonges** (04 72 42 90 90), the triple-starred Paul Bocuse restaurant with a gypsy caravan-coloured exterior and refined dining rooms. **Le Vieux Moulin** (04 78 43 91 66), on Chemin du Vieux Moulin in the village of Alix, is a relaxed country inn where you can fill up on rustic French fare. For livelier evenings, you'll have to head into Lyon: **Le Caffé Milano** (04 37 28 97 98) on Rue de l'Université is a fun New York-style bistro; **Bus Café** (04 72 74 40 91) on Quai Général Sarrail is a crowd-pleasing, cocktail-shaking DJ bar in a converted bus station.

GET A ROOM!

To book this hotel, go to www.mrandmrssmith.com or ring our expert travel team on 1 800 464 2040. Activate your free membership online (see page 4) to qualify for the exclusive Smith card offer shown below when you book with us.

 SMITH CARD OFFER Wine tasting at a local vineyard (or a bottle of Brouilly – a grand cru – during the harvest). Those staying two nights or more in a Suite or Apartment receive a three-course lunch (excluding drinks).

Château de Bagnols 69620 Bagnols, Beaujolais (www.mrandmrssmith.com/chateau-de-bagnols)

DORDOGNE

COUNTRYSIDE Bucolic backwaters
COUNTRY LIFE Wine, woods and winding rivers

In the warm valleys of southwestern France, where the Dordogne, Isle and Lot rivers wriggle their way down towards the rugged Atlantic coast, the lush landscape, sunny days and mild temperatures combine to produce perfect conditions for growing grapes and nurturing truffles. Happily for us, these are also ideal surroundings in which to linger and enjoy the world's finest wines and the region's culinary specialities (preferably while soaking up a stirring view of hill and horizon). The photogenic mediaeval towns, pretty villages and towering châteaux of the Périgord region have names that will be instantly recognisable to oenophiles and gourmets: Bergerac and St Emilion are synonymous with their eminent vineyards; and Périgueux calls to mind market stalls laden with truffles. Here, time is measured in vintages and happiness comes by the glass. Santé!

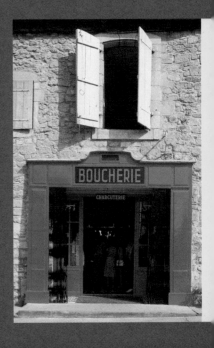

GETTING THERE

Planes Connect with one of Europe's low-cost airlines to fly into Bergerac airport (www.bergerac.aeroport.fr), just outside the town centre. There's a greater choice of international flights to Bordeaux (www.bordeaux.aeroport.fr), 120km east of Bergerac.
Trains The TGV from Paris to Bordeaux takes three and a half hours (it's about eight from London via Eurostar); the train from Bordeaux to Bergerac takes one hour.
Automobiles A car is indispensable for exploring the vineyards and countryside; there are various car-rental companies at the airports, but it's best to pre-book.

LOCAL KNOWLEDGE

Taxis There's no chance of hailing a cab out in the sticks. In Bergerac, call 05 53 23 32 32 to reserve your ride; a taxi from the airport into town will take five minutes and cost around €8. Or burn off those foie gras calories with some pedal power: hire bicycles from Apolo (05 53 61 08 16; www.apolo-cycles.com). It also rents out scooters and motorbikes, if bicycle clips aren't your style.
Currency Euro (€).
Dialling codes France: 33. Bergerac, Dordogne: (0)5.

Tipping culture Service charges are always added to restaurant bills, but a few extra euros will be appreciated.
Siesta and fiesta Shops tend to shut 12.30pm–2.30pm. Restaurants are often closed on Sundays and Mondays outside the summer months.
Do go/don't go Spring is sunny but changeable, with May and June absolute perfection. Summer is busy but ideal for canoeing on the Dordogne. September and October see fine weather and the all-important grape harvest (known as the *vendange*). Winters are usually wet and mild.
Packing tips A corkscrew, wine guide and pinafore for wannabe chefs; panniers for pedal-powered picnics.
Recommended reads Edmond Rostand's play *Cyrano de Bergerac* tells of the beak-nosed swordsman and his love for Roxane; Soil Association founder member Philip Oyler relives the good old days of Dordogne valley farming in *The Generous Earth*.
Cuisine The Périgord conjures up gastronomic dreams of wine, walnuts, mushrooms and truffles, not to mention the ducks and geese reared to produce foie gras. A Périgord speciality is confit de canard (duck legs, cooked and preserved in their own fat), usually served with

Salardaise potatoes (sautéed in duck fat) and a nice fresh salad of frisée or endive. If you can possibly eat any more, and your arteries aren't irredeemably hardened, try some tiny little cabécou (a goat's cheese), or walnut tart with wild strawberries, served with a chilled Monbazillac dessert wine. Find regional recipes at www.pays-de-bergerac.com.

WORTH GETTING OUT OF BED FOR

Viewpoint The village of La Roque-Gageac, near the charming mediaeval town of Sarlat, clings to the cliffs overlooking the Dordogne valley. The most striking view is from the ruins of the 12th-century troglodyte fort, reached via a precarious-looking wooden staircase. Afternoons can be busy in season; go early to avoid traffic.

Arts and culture The Dordogne is dotted with castles, fortified bastides and châteaux. Two of the best are the Renaissance Château de Puyguilhem (05 53 05 65 65) at Villars, and the very grand garden-enhanced Château de Hautefort (05 53 50 51 23; www.chateau-hautefort.com), northeast of Périgueux. Just south of Bergerac, Château de Monbazillac (05 53 63 65 00; www.chateau-monbazillac. com) – which gives its name to the area's dessert wine – is a gorgeous eyeful of 16th-century castle, with the added bonus of a lovely terrace and wine shop. You can also tour its modern wine cellars, two kilometres away.

Activities There is good clean canoeing fun to be had on the Dordogne between Argentat and Beynac; Copeyre (05 65 32 72 61; www.copeyre.com) in Souillac hires out kayaks and mountain bikes. It would be a crime to visit the Bergerac area without doing a little wine tasting; go to www.vins-bergerac.fr for more details. We love the stylish but unstuffy wine boutique and tasting bar L'Essentiel (05 57 24 39 76; www.essentiel-vin.com), on Rue Guadet in St Emilion. Alternatively, hike across the St Emilion region, tasting as you go, on a guided walking tour (05 57 55 28 28; www.saint-emilion-tourisme.com). There's a challenging but relaxed nine-hole golf course at Château les Merles (www.lesmerles.com).

Perfect picnic You've riverbanks and hillsides aplenty to pick from in the Dordogne; hit a local market in the morning to source farm-fresh cheese, warm bread, pastries, juice and sun-ripened tomatoes (and a bottle of something suitable for drinking in a field). Note: morning really does mean morning in France; the markets will be over by noon.

Daytripper Book two weeks in advance to visit the wine cellar of Château Margaux (www.chateau-margaux.com), north of Bordeaux. The neoclassical castle and its estate produce some of Médoc's finest wines. The cellars are closed in August and during the harvest.

Walks Head to the delightful listed gardens of Château Marqueyssac (www.marqueyssac.com) near Vézac, where six kilometres of walking paths wind through whimsically trimmed boxwood hedges. For added romance, go after dusk on a Thursday in high summer, when musicians play until midnight among the thousands of candles lighting the paths.

Shopping In Bergerac, La Bille de Bois (05 53 63 14 87) at 6 Place du Docteur Cayla turns out enough old-fashioned wooden toys to put Santa's elves out of a job. There are markets in Bergerac and Périgueux on Wednesdays and Saturdays, Lalinde on Thursdays (a particularly picturesque one), Libourne on Fridays and Sarlat on Saturday. Bergerac also hosts a fantastic fleamarket selling antiques and bric-à-brac on the first Sunday of the month.

Something for nothing The suitably haughty figure of Cyrano de Bergerac takes pride of place in Bergerac's Place Pelissière. The statue's famously protruding nose is often stolen. In summer, there are free jazz performances in the cloisters of La Maison des Vins every Wednesday night. For details of more events in Bergerac, go to www.bergerac-tourisme.com.

Don't go home without... a superior bottle of wine – there are so many fabulous local labels to choose from; try a velvety Monbazillac, a sweet white wine often drunk to mark special occasions.

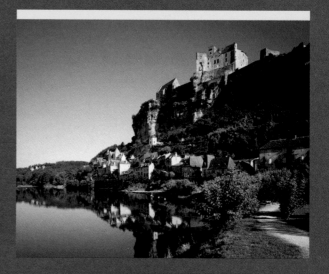

DELICIOUSLY DORDOGNE

Périgord 'black diamond' truffles are famed for their earthy taste and aphrodisiac qualities, and can cost up to €900 a kilo. They grow well in the Dordogne (although hot, dry summers don't do them any favours), and the main markets during the harvest season of December to early March are Périgueux, Sarlat and Brantôme. Out of season, look for preserved black winter truffles.

DIARY

May The châteaux of St Emilion open their wine cellars for the season; some offer free samples. **Late June** A 90-minute drive from Bergerac, Bordeaux holds its four-day Fête le Vin (www.bordeaux-fete-le-vin.com) every two years – including 2008 – with wine tasting, concerts and auctions on the banks of the Garonne. **July** Bergerac's magnificent four-day food and wine festival kicks off around Bastille Day (14 July); there'll be dining in the streets and music everywhere – go to www.pays-de-bergerac.com for details. **September** The start of the wine harvest is announced on the third Sunday of the month from the Tour du Roi in St Emilion, accompanied by parades (www.saint-emilion-tourisme.com). **October** The serious business of determining the best nut-swinger in France begins in earnest on the first Saturday of the month at the French Conkers Championships in Abjat-sur-Bandiat (www.ffconkers.org).

Château les Merles

STYLE Neoclassical winery
SETTING Bergerac's route des vins
DESTINATION Dordogne

'Black satin slippers lay next to our bed in special boxes, and a silver bowl of cherries from the château's organic garden was waiting for us'

'We're definitely coming back,' I said to Mr Smith as we parked the hire car and walked, just after midnight, into the white, pebbled, candlelit courtyard of Château les Merles. A long table of late diners were finishing off their puddings underneath the stars. 'Hang on – we haven't even checked in yet,' he pointed out, as we sat down in a pair of white-upholstered Philippe Starck chairs and were immediately brought welcoming glasses of champagne and a plate of canapés. (These included specialities of the Dordogne region: we pounced on foie gras, tomato tartlets, and deliciously crisp radishes and endive.) Within seconds, the cares of the day, the plane delays and the car-hire queue were distant memories.

The air, scented with the lavender and thyme that border the courtyard, further aided our relaxation. The 17th-century château was breathtaking in the crescent moonlight. After checking in, without actually having to get up from our table, we were shown to our suite. It was decorated in a style I am christening 'convent de luxe': dark wood, antiques, lots of white upholstery, crisp snowy linens and huge windows everywhere. 'Who's hidden the nuns?' I asked. But any concealed nuns were sybarites, too: black satin slippers lay next to our bed in special boxes,

and a silver bowl of berries from the château's organic garden was waiting for us. There were two parallel white sofas in the little sitting room, and a dark-velvet chaise longue for stretching out and reading and chatting on, side by side. In the gleaming black and white bathroom we found a similar blend of monochrome luxury and simplicity.

Even if our beds were of that silly Siamese-twin configuration (locked together but made up separately), it wasn't the end of the world, as they were extremely comfortable, and we couldn't have had a more delightful awakening in the morning. Manic birdsong roused us and I pulled back the shutters to reveal the hotel's swimming pool sitting picturesquely in the lush gardens. Fear of missing breakfast prevented us from taking a quick dip there and then and, instead, we returned to the courtyard restaurant to sample the château's morning delights.

A table inside was spread with garden fruits, home-made bread, viennoiserie, cheeses and hams, and other local delectables. I've never eaten a dish of freshly picked blackcurrants for breakfast before, but I can recommend it. We sat for ages, eking out the meal with supplementary cappuccinos and croissants, basking in our new setting.

As breakfast drew to a close, our thoughts turned naturally to lunch, so we got into the car and drove to the local town of Bergerac, about 10 minutes away. We wandered round the narrow streets of the old town, buying hats, looking at antiques and hunting slightly obsessively for some pink and gold dessert plates while dodging statues of Cyrano, the town's most famous romantic hero and, along with goose liver, the region's most celebrated export.

Lunch, at the hotel's recommendation, was at the excellent (and modestly named) L'Imparfait in a quiet back street, where we feasted in a shady courtyard on sea bream and lamb shanks. They were both exceptional. After some light shopping (more local wine, foie gras, some candlesticks), we made our way back to the hotel and stretched out on the sunloungers, coming to every now and then to summon some drinks via the phone, which was conveniently situated right by the pool.

I couldn't imagine any possible improvement on the scene, but Mr Smith, post-swim, was nursing a very understandable complaint. He wistfully mentioned to staff that he was going to miss an important football game. A huge projector screen was instantly rigged up in an empty upstairs ballroom, and cold beers (and kir royales for me) were delivered to us throughout the match. So much more civilised than our local pub, we observed, looking up at the chandeliers.

Evening came, and all the corridors became crowded with small girls in tutus. The local ballet academy, it transpired, was putting on its end-of-term gala at the hotel. We watched from a nearby bench, drinks in hands, as the tinies performed before us, overseen by their stern 'Mamzelle'. Then we dined in the courtyard where a special buffet had been prepared. The local wine and produce were just delicious, and I felt so happy I genuinely contemplated joining the dancers for their *Swan Lake* finale. Mr Smith, however, kept a firm hold of my elbow, distracting me with spoonfuls of chocolate mousse, until the dangerous moment had passed. Lead us not into temptation, as any good concealed nun would no doubt say...

Reviewed by Susie Boyt

'We couldn't have had a nicer awakening. Manic birdsong roused us and I pulled back the shutters to reveal a picturesque pool'

NEED TO KNOW

Rooms 15, including two suites and one apartment.

Rates €120–€295. Breakfast, €15.

Check-out 11am, but late check-out is sometimes available. Earliest check-in, 3pm.

Facilities Swimming pool, tennis court, golf course (though this is definitely *not* a golf hotel), complimentary WiFi, massage and other treatments on request, laundry service. In rooms, satellite TV, DVD player.

Children Warmly welcomed. Pre-booked day-care facilities are available for €10 an hour. An extra bed costs €15.

Also The château has a narrow, challenging nine-hole golf course (you can hire clubs). Horse riding can be organised with the local stables.

IN THE KNOW

Our favourite rooms Suite 7 is spacious and has a fine view over the Dordogne valley. Suite 8 has high ceilings, classical styling, and views over the swimming pool and golf course.

Hotel bar The Bistrot is an informal lounge bar with a light menu of tasty and unfussy dishes. You can try wines from the château's own vineyards, as well as a large selection of renowned local wines.

Hotel restaurant La Bruyère Blanche at Château les Merles serves excellent New Périgordine cuisine, with a strong emphasis on fresh and seasonal local ingredients. Opt for the chef's garden menu of the day, which is a constantly changing, five-course delight. The château sources all its wines locally from the Bergerac region.

Top table Out in the courtyard on a summer's evening; by the fireside in winter.

Room service Breakfast is available from 8.30am–10am. An imaginative 'world food' menu is available from 10.30am–7pm.

Dress code Campagne chic: informal with a splash of style.

Local knowledge Historic Bergerac, just a 10-minute drive from the hotel, is the scene of one of France's best markets on Wednesday and Saturday mornings (there are less spectacular ones held daily). The mediaeval centre fills with stalls showcasing the finest regional produce – including foie gras, truffles and local wines – so take a *grande* shopping bag with you. Alternatively, sip a café au lait at an outdoor table while you watch all the bustle with an air of Gallic detachment.

LOCAL EATING AND DRINKING

In Bergerac, **L'Imparfait** (05 53 57 47 92) on Rue des Fontaines serves a short, seasonal menu, which changes every day according to what's good and fresh at the market that morning. **L'Enfance de Lard** (05 53 57 52 88; closed on Tuesdays) on Place Pélissière is renowned for its delicious meat dishes – try the duck-heart kebab if you're feeling brave. Its open fire creates a cosy atmosphere in the cooler months. **Le Repaire de Savinien** (05 53 24 35 46) on Rue Mounet Sully has simple decor and an excellent French and international menu. In St Emilion, **Le Clos du Roy** (05 57 74 41 55; closed on Tuesdays and Wednesdays) on Rue de la Petite-Fontaine has inventive fish and seafood dishes, and a bulky wine list. In Tremolat, a 10-minute drive from Château les Merles, **Le Vieux Logis** (05 53 22 80 06) is one of the area's gastronomic highlights, in which gourmet Périgordine cuisine is served in an old tobacco-drying room set in beautiful gardens.

GET A ROOM!

To book this hotel, go to www.mrandmrssmith.com or ring our expert travel team on 1 800 464 2040. Activate your free membership online (see page 4) to qualify for the exclusive Smith card offer shown below when you book with us.

 SMITH CARD OFFER A glass of champagne each, a selection of regional amuses-bouches and a bottle of wine from the vineyards of Château les Merles.

Château les Merles Tuilières, 24520 Mouleydier, Dordogne (www.mrandmrssmith.com/chateau-les-merles)

PARIS

CITYSCAPE Boulevards and brasseries
CITY LIFE Born to be bon vivants

Paris is a dream project for pedestrians, with endless secrets hidden away from all the wonderful clichés. There aren't many cities that conjure up a sense of nostalgic romance and timeless elegance as readily as the French capital; whether you're at the top of Montmartre or the bottom of the Eiffel Tower, in the Louvre or on the Left Bank, it's chic to its bones and still pushing style frontiers. Between the Gothic cathedrals and grand neoclassical avenues are timely flashes of futuristic bravura: La Grande Arche, the Pompidou Centre and L'Institut du Monde Arabe all proving that Paris' revolutionary spirit is still very much alive and kicking. Hold hands in a fleamarket, hunt down fashion and foodie delicacies in the Marais, pay tribute to couture pioneers from Coco Chanel to Jean Paul Gaultier, then, when you've filled your boutique boots, head to Belleville or Oberkampf for a shot of gritty realism.

GETTING THERE

Planes A taxi from Charles de Gaulle international airport to the centre costs about €50; buses and trains run regularly into town for a fraction of the cost. Orly airport, southeast of Paris, handles short-haul flights.
Trains There are six main stations in Paris, all central and linked to the fantastic Métro underground system (www.ratp.fr). Eurostar trains arrive into Gare du Nord.
Automobiles Parking can be a challenge in Paris, and pricey; you're better off without a car. Instead, rent Vélib pushbikes from the 24-hour self-service stands (www.velib.paris.fr).

LOCAL KNOWLEDGE

Taxis Can be hailed in the street if you're more than 100 metres from a rank (these are all over Paris and have phones if no taxi is waiting).
Currency Euro (€).
Dialling codes France: 33. Paris: (0)1.
Tipping culture In bars, leave small change amounting to about 10 per cent. Restaurants usually state *service compris*; but it is polite to leave a few coins.
Siesta and fiesta Parisians hit their favourite cafés and patisseries around 7am for breakfast; shops are usually open 10am–7pm; restaurants get busy around 9pm; and clubs often keep the tunes playing till dawn.
Do go/don't go Paris grinds to a halt in August, the national holiday. We love springtime, when the blossom is out and the light is beautiful, and crisp autumn days.

Packing tips Sunglasses, silk scarf, cigarette holder, Edith Piaf CD. Maps: taxi drivers can be uncertain sometimes. If you don't speak French, a phrasebook is indispensable.
Recommended reads *Down and Out in Paris and London* by George Orwell sees the streets from a different perspective; Ernest Hemingway details 1920s Parisian life in his memoir, *A Moveable Feast*; and Geoff Dyer updates Hemingway for Generation X in *Paris Trance*.
Cuisine If you only do one thing in Paris, let it be sipping a crème or a pastis at a boulevard bistro: whatever your wont (still-walking steak, croque monsieur, rillettes, warm chèvre salad or tarte tatin), it will taste immeasurably

better eaten at an alfresco table on a cane chair. Paris is also renowned for its dainty tea houses and French fancies – by which we mean mouthwatering millefeuilles, melting macaroons and buttery pastries. Ladurée is beloved of fashionistas for its pretty pastel confections; Mariage Frères is one of the finest tea rooms; and you'll often see a scrum queuing outside haute pâtissier Pierre Hermé (01 43 54 47 77) on Rue Bonaparte in St Germain.

WORTH GETTING OUT OF BED FOR

Viewpoint Crowded but irresistible, the Eiffel Tower is open 9.30am–11pm (midnight in high season); the city panoramas from the top are breathtaking. If all that steel doesn't take your fancy, visit L'Institut du Monde Arabe (www.imarabe.org): as well as an incredible façade and Islamic art exhibitions, its top-floor terrace offers great views across the Seine to Notre Dame and Ile de la Cité.
Arts and culture The Louvre (www.louvre.fr) is vast; avoid the conveyor-belt effect by visiting in the late afternoon, and lavishing attention on just one or two of its wings. The Musée National d'Art Moderne is on level four of the Centre Pompidou (www.centrepompidou.fr), Richard Rogers' radical insides-outside exhibition space. Musée National Picasso Paris (www.musee-picasso.fr) occupies an old house in the Marais, and is full of the artworks Pablo couldn't bear to part with; and the Musée d'Orsay (www.musee-orsay.fr) is a converted train station packed with artistic treats. Visit Musée Carnavalet (01 44 59 58 58) on Rue de Sévigné for an engaging history of Paris.
Activities The Seine's open-top Bateaux-Mouches riverboats are a popular way to see the sights; most depart from Pont de l'Alma. Stick to a one-hour trip and give the touristy dinner cruises a miss. Ramp things up a notch on a private lunch cruise down the St Martin canal aboard *La Coda*, a small Dutch barge (www.parislacoda.com); or sweep your Mr or Mrs off their feet and arrange dinner for two on a sleek Yachts de Paris cruiser (www.yachtsdeparis.fr). Fat Tire Bike Tours (www.fattirebiketoursparis.com) will guide you round the sights on Schwinn bikes, Segways or your own two feet; the night-time tours are fun.
Perfect picnic Grab a bottle of champagne from the minibar and some pastries, smoked salmon baguettes or tarts from Gérard Mulot (01 43 26 85 77) at 76 Rue de Seine, and enjoy them in the Jardin du Luxembourg on the Left Bank. Another good green grazing spot is the Jardin des Tuileries near the Louvre: get gourmet snacks at Fauchon or Hédiard on Place de la Madeleine.

Daytripper Live out your Louis XV/Madame de Pompadour/Marie-Antoinette/Sun King fantasies (delete as applicable) at the incomparable Château de Versailles (www.chateau versailles.fr), just outside Paris. The palace interiors are spectacular, the gardens sprawling and manicured, and the palpable sense of history makes you long to don a powdered wig and swish about in raw silk and stockings.
Walks Chic St Germain is an edifying place for a stroll, with plenty of shops, cafés and culture to keep you occupied; the area has historically been the haunt of artists, poets and intellectuals, and there are still plenty of great bookshops and galleries to help kick-start your grey matter.
Shopping Rue du Faubourg Saint-Honoré is chock-full of designer boutiques; our favourite is Colette (www.colette.fr), a celebrated lifestyle store with fashion, books and a café. There are quirky independent shops, cafés and bars in the trendy Marais district, aka quartier Juif – it's also the only area largely open on Sundays. Porte de Clignancourt market is a huge fleamarket for clothes and antiques, open Monday–Saturday until 7pm. If you're a sucker for department stores, hit Le Bon Marché on Rue de Sèvres.
Something for nothing Follow in the footsteps of *Amélie*, wandering through Montmartre (the bohemian hill streets that saw the birth of the can-can), and up to the Sacré-Coeur for more resplendent city panoramas.
Don't go home without... getting lost – Parisian delights are more often found off the beaten path: musicians practising in a leafy square; buying *cartes postales* at a little stationery shop; or stumbling on an open art studio.

PERFECTLY PARIS

Admire Paris' unique layout from atop the 200-year-old Arc de Triomphe, the epicentre of bravura city-planner Baron Haussmann's star of boulevards; it's worth clambering up its many internal stairs to peer down the Champs-Elysées and enjoy pleasingly photogenic views down to Place de la Concorde and up to La Défense. Open daily, 10am–10.30pm (11pm in summer).

DIARY

May St Germain's Jazz Festival (www.festivaljazzsaintgermainparis.com) gets the Rive Gauche tapping its Louboutin-clad toes. **May–June** The French Open tennis championship brings grand-slam glamour to the City of Lights (www.fft.fr/rolandgarros). **June** La Fête de la Musique (www.fetedelamusique.culture.fr) on the 21st celebrates the start of summer and sees the streets lined with stages for live bands. **June–July** Paris Jazz Festival – free weekend concerts in Parc Floral (www.parcfloraldeparis.com). **July** Bastille Day on the 14th, a public holiday with a huge military parade down the Champs-Elysées and fireworks over the Eiffel Tower, is followed by the opening of Paris Plage, the summer's temporary urban beach. **August–September** Open-air Classical Music Festival in Parc Floral. **October** Paris stays up all night for the nocturnal arts party dubbed Nuit Blanche (www.smith52.com).

Hotel Daniel

STYLE 18th-century exoticism
SETTING Chic Champs-Elysées
DESTINATION Paris

'Here at last is a hotel both classy
and feminine, but which also
appeals to my decadent side'

Our room is as cosy as the inside of a sewing box, with billowing curtains in old gold and jade-green wallpaper painted with pretty blossoms. This is an exception, though, as the Daniel's rooms are generally covered with a sort of 18th-century toile de Jouy featuring Chinese kite-fliers, swirling ferns, exotic tropical trees or picturesque expeditions by elephant. If you fancy a snug green boudoir, or rich red walls decorated with whimsical images suggesting dalliance, it's worth mentioning your preferences on booking, as every room is very different. The Eastern theme continues in a cavalcade of bamboo-framed desks, inlaid tables, entertaining curios and butterfly-covered lamps. The bedsheets feel as smooth as cream.

Within minutes, a welcome pot of green tea arrives. It's served in a delightful basket with willow-pattern cups, and accompanied by a plateful of colourful macaroons from Ladurée. Mrs Smith purrs with approval. Here at last is a hotel both classy and feminine, but which also appeals to Mr Smith's decadent side. The bathroom comes with a big jar of Dead Sea bath salts and a full-length mirror; the hairdryer resides in a sweet little hamper and the wardrobe shelves are lined with broderie anglaise runners. Marie-Antoinette would be very happy here.

It's a sign of the times that the first squeal of delight the Hotel Daniel inspires in Mrs Smith comes from the news that it offers free WiFi. Being a Eurostar regular with a vintage couture business straddling London and Paris, madame is always looking for romantic little hotels in which she can happily mix work with pleasure (otherwise known as Mr Smith).

In this respect, the Daniel is a classic example of that petite discovery you really don't want to tell anyone about. Well, there are only 26 rooms, including nine suites, and it would be very tiresome if your friends snapped them all up. Tucked away in the well-heeled streets of the Eighth, the hotel rises up over six floors, two of which offer rooms with balconies. It's part of the hotel circuit that attracts guests who know they are assured of refined comforts and intelligent service, but a commendable panache is also much in evidence thanks to its Lebanese owners, who own the elegant Hotel Albergo in Beirut, too.

Now that we're *bien installés*, it's time to enjoy the City of Light. Stepping out, we find the Daniel surrounded by inviting restaurants that range from simple bistros to the two-Michelin star Apicius, just across the street. Walk south and you hit the grand runway of the Champs-Elysées, which these days is just too tacky and congested to be endured for long. Head north and there's the oh-so-Paris Parc Monceau, its benches filled with well-turned-out mothers, nannies and *enfants*. Our preference, though, is to stroll east along Rue du Faubourg Saint-Honoré, which gradually builds to a frenzy of window-shopping delights. First up is gourmet food emporium Dalloyau, then comes that famous fashion-house parade that kicks off with Christian Lacroix and Pierre Cardin.

As it's a Wednesday, we take advantage of the late-night opening of the Louvre, heading straight for the exquisite ethnic sculptures in the little-visited galleries devoted to the arts of Africa, Asia, Oceania and the Americas. A few days before, Mrs Smith called to book dinner at nearby Le Fumoir, an untouristy restaurant with slick service and a cosy library at the back. Afterwards, French taxis being up there with the most useless in the world, we whizz back by Métro.

Breakfast the next morning is delivered to our room on a white linen-covered trolley, a harmonious still life of coffee, newspaper and delicious what-the-hell pastries. Mrs Smith has work to do that day, and when her Parisian business

'The Eastern theme continues in a calvacade of entertaining curios and butterfly lamps'

partner walks into Hotel Daniel's lounge, which brims with plush cushions, Chinoiserie and gorgeous orchids, she can't help but cry 'Ooh là là!' It's the ideal setting to discuss their new website over an open MacBook and *deux coupes de champagne* while Mr Smith gets a few work-related errands in the bag before lunch.

The restaurant at the Daniel is archetypally small and intimate, with silky banquettes and wall cabinets filled with dainty coloured glasses. We felt it would work equally well whether you were there for a high-powered business meeting or a sexy assignation. Chef Denis Fetisson pops out of the kitchen to discuss our preferences from a menu featuring Roquefort soufflé, ravioli filled with anchoyade and foie gras, and far too many *desserts onctueux*. The next day, our request for a late check-out is instantly granted, and when the breakfast order gets delayed due to an oversight, all relevant charges are immediately waived. This is a hotel that genuinely cares about the time you spend within its exotically decorated walls – whether you're checking in with a laptop, a lover, or maybe both.

Reviewed by Nigel Tisdall

NEED TO KNOW

Rooms 26, including nine suites.
Rates €350–€760. Breakfast: Continental, €24; American, €34.
Check-out 11am, but can be extended to 6pm at a half-day rate (subject to availability).
Facilities Concierge service, PCs and mobile phones to borrow on request, complimentary WiFi, air-conditioning, laundry service. In rooms, minibar, LCD TV, Molton Brown toiletries, soft bathrobes, slippers, newspapers with breakfast.
Children Extra beds in suites cost €75 a night; children under 12 stay free. Babysitting starts at €47 for three hours.
Also Guests can visit l'Espace Payot spa and hammam at a specially reduced half-day rate. Teatime is a chic affair at Hotel Daniel, with loose-leaf teas from Mariage Frères: try a delicate Ceylan Orange Pekoe. Leave tired Louboutins out overnight and they'll reappear – buffed to perfection – the next morning. Smoking and non-smoking rooms are available.

IN THE KNOW

Our favourite rooms All the Deluxe rooms are on the sixth floor; 602 has a large bathroom with a spectacular view of the Parisian rooftops. You can enjoy breakfast on your balcony in most of the suites and watch the sun set over the tip of the Eiffel Tower from the Daniel Suite. The Paris and Daniel Suites are the most romantic.
Hotel bar Sip a Kir Royale while nestling among the sumptuous satin cushions in Le Lounge bar, open until 1am.
Hotel restaurant Restaurant Daniel serves an eclectic feast of tasty morsels. Talented chef Denis Fetisson creates unique gourmet dishes from fresh local produce. A reduced bar-style menu is available in Le Lounge for guests at the weekend, and there's a summer menu from 25 July to 25 August, when the restaurant is closed.
Top table Cosy up at one of the elegant recessed banquette tables, for an intimate *dîner à deux*.
Room service 24 hours; hot food until the restaurant kitchen closes – after that, it's cold dishes until breakfast.
Dress code Vintage couture; sleek cheong-sams; nifty tailoring.
Local knowledge There are several obvious reasons to get out of bed when your hotel is in such a prestigious location: shopping, shopping and more shopping – the Eighth arrondissement is a style-tracker's dream hunting ground, with upscale outlets galore. Make sure you head into the Second, too, to visit the elegant and beautiful Serge Lutens-designed Les Salons du Palais Royal on Rue de Valois. You'll never want to buy your perfume from anywhere else again.

LOCAL EATING AND DRINKING

You won't have to walk far to find a café or bistro you like the look of, but chocolatier and tea shop **Ladurée** (01 40 75 08 75) at 75 Avenue des Champs-Elysées is loved for its melt-in-the-mouth macaroons, fancy-sandwich brunches and sugar-coated high teas. A gateau's throw from Hotel Daniel on Rue d'Artois, **Apicius** (01 43 80 19 66) has two Michelin stars and a loyal clientele, drawn to dine at the 18th-century townhouse by Jean-Pierre Vigato's elegant Modern French menu. On the same street, **Bocconi** (01 53 76 44 44) is an informal Italian trattoria. You're also close to the triple-starred restaurant of **Pierre Gagnaire** (01 58 36 12 50) on Rue Balzac, which has a fabulous seasonal menu of boundary-pushing cuisine. Chic club and eatery **La Cantine du Faubourg** (01 42 56 22 22) serves Asian fusion in a stylish lounge-bar setting at 105 Rue du Faubourg St-Honoré – ideal for a pre- or post-prandial drink.

GET A ROOM!

To book this hotel, go to www.mrandmrssmith.com or ring our expert travel team on 1 800 464 2040. Activate your free membership online (see page 4) to qualify for the exclusive Smith card offer shown below when you book with us.

 SMITH CARD OFFER Mariage Frères tea for two served with Ladurée's famous macaroons (when available) or other sweet treats.

Hotel Daniel 8 Rue Frédéric Bastiat, Champs-Elysées, 75008 Paris (www.mrandmrssmith.com/hotel–daniel)

SOUTHWEST PROVENCE

COUNTRYSIDE Scenes from Van Gogh
COUNTRY LIFE Whole lotta rosé

This is a land of light and colour, where the languid river Rhône winds its way through fruit orchards and bright fields of lavender before melting into the watery maze of the Camargue. On the Mediterranean coast, cowboys, white horses and neon-pink flamingos roam the dunes and marshes; upriver and inland, atmospheric Arles and its laid-back neighbour Nîmes in Languedoc-Roussillon offer a beguiling blend of Roman ruins, rustic cuisine, café culture and sun-dappled boulevards. Provence's patchwork history and pivotal position on the ancient trade route between Italy and Spain mean you can admire aqueducts before your aperitifs, and order paella after pastis. And in the vertiginous village of Les Baux, teetering high among the olive groves, vines and craggy uplands of the Alpilles, you can gaze upon fields of vivid sunflowers and dine alfresco on starry, starry nights.

GETTING THERE

Planes There are regular flights to regional airports Marseille (www.mrsairport.com) and Montpellier (www.montpellier. aeroport.fr). Nîmes has links to various European cities with budget carriers such as Eurociel and Ryanair, but your best bet from beyond Europe is to travel via Paris.
Trains We heart high-speed TGVs: they'll zip you from Paris or Lille to Avignon and Nîmes in three hours; Eurostar operates services to Provence from London via Paris from July to September, and TGV Med links Avignon to Marseilles, Montpellier and Geneva. For tickets and information, see www.raileurope.co.uk.
Automobiles Inter-city transport is good, and town centres are often pedestrianised, but a car is useful if you want to explore the countryside and its remote villages.

LOCAL KNOWLEDGE

Taxis In larger towns, use a taxi rank – or have your hotel order a cab. Prices are cheaper here than on the nearby Côte d'Azur, but there may be a charge for luggage.
Currency Euro (€).
Dialling codes France: 33. Provence: (0)4.
Tipping culture Restaurant and café bills must include the service charge by law, normally about 12–15 per cent of the total; extra tips are not expected, but it's usual to leave a few coins as well.
Siesta and fiesta Businesses are normally closed from noon till 2pm. Banks close at 4.30pm. Restaurants get busy after 9pm and often close Mondays and Tuesdays.
Do go/don't go The Mediterranean climate is mild, but the famously fierce Mistral wind can be a misery. Spring brings carpets of flowers; summers are long and hot. September, when France has gone back to work, is perfect.
Packing tips Take cobble-friendly sandals rather than stilettos; binoculars and bug repellent for the Camargue; and paints and a sketchbook to act on any inspiration.
Recommended reads It's Provençal paintbrushes at dawn in Martin Gayford's *The Yellow House: Van Gogh, Gauguin, and Nine Turbulent Weeks in Arles*; Romans and romance in *Caesar's Vast Ghost: Aspects of Provence* by Lawrence Durrell; and classic countryside capers in *Letters From My Windmill* by Alphonse Daudet.
Cuisine Provence is the perfect place to get your head around the concept of *terroir*: every mouthful of the land's culture-crossing *cuisine du soleil* and Côtes du Rhone

wine is bursting with baked-in sunshine, aromatic herbs and earthy rusticity – the refreshing rosés are particularly typical. Taste temptations include red-wine stews known as daubes; Camargue's red rice and salt-cod brandade; Marseille's famous bouillabaisse; saucisson d'Arles; and herb-liqueur-laced Papalines d'Avignon – go to Pâtisserie Mallard (04 90 82 42 38) at 32 rue des Marchands in Avignon to sample the best of these sweet morsels. Tapas fans can get their fill in Spanish-influenced Nîmes.

WORTH GETTING OUT OF BED FOR

Viewpoint There's a wonderful vista towards the Camargue from the battlements of the fortress in Les Baux de Provence. In summer, go early to avoid the crowds.
Arts and culture Hum the tune and dance the dance 'Sur Le Pont D'Avignon'; behave with more decorum at the monumental, mediaeval Palais des Papes (www. palais-des-papes.com). Marvel at ancient sites including the 20,000-seat Roman amphitheatre in Nîmes, which doubles as a bullring and performance space; check events listings with the tourist office on Rue Auguste (www.ot-nimes.fr). Nîmes' Maison Carrée temple occupies the site of the old Roman forum, and is beautifully reflected in the glass façade of Sir Norman Foster's contemporary gallery, the Carré d'Art. Arles has an equally impressive amphitheatre, Les Arènes (www.arenes-arles. com), home of the famous Easter Féria bullfights.
Activities This is a great place to hike and bike, but if it's warm, cool off as you kayak down the Gardon river to the Pont du Gard from Collias with Kayak Vert (04 66 22 80 76). On calm days, float around in a wicker basket propelled by fire: a one-hour hot-air balloon flight costs €220 a person with Les Montgolfières du Sud (04 66 37 28 02). Taste organic local wines and hand-harvested olives in the cellars of Mas de la Dame (www.masdeladame.com), on the southern flanks of the Alpilles. Paragliding is on offer in the village of Seynes (www.parapentesud.com).
Perfect picnic Find a spot among the sunflowers and vines of the Alpilles, and enjoy the landscapes that inspired Cézanne and Van Gogh. Other options include the grand Jardins de la Fontaine in Nîmes, or Parc du Duché in Uzès.
Daytripper Montpellier is one of France's most energetic and prosperous cities. The sprawling Place de la Comédie is a good starting point for an exploration. Relish the sea-salty flavour of Bouzigues oysters slurped on the spot at the morning market before exploring the boutiques and cafés of the old town; book a table at Michelin-starred Le

Jardin des Sens (04 99 58 38 38) for a restorative *repas*.
Walks Visit Mas Sainte Berthe and follow the 30-minute circuit around its vines and olive groves beneath the looming rocks of Les Baux; then reward yourself with some of the delicious local produce – including tapenades, olive oil and wine – on sale in the vineyard's boutique (04 90 54 39 01; www.mas-sainte-berthe.com).
Shopping There's no greater shopping pleasure to be had in Provence than on market day, when squares and streets become a rainbow of colours from tomato to lavender. Aix-en-Provence holds a fantastic daily market on Place Richelme; pop into the design boutiques lining Rue Fabrot while you're there. Uzès has a Saturday market selling home-made goodies from honey to linen; delve into the streets near Place aux Herbes for art and antiques. Rue de la Madeleine in Nîmes is great for boutique browsing and grazing; buy dentally challenging slabs of nougat, croquants and sweet pastries at Maison Villaret (04 66 67 41 79).
Something for nothing Vincent Van Gogh churned out more than 200 canvases during the 14 months he spent in Arles. Many of the spots where he worked are marked by yellow panels: begin at Place Lamartine, site of *The Yellow House*, and finish on the Place du Forum at *A Café Terrace at Night*. Perhaps cheat a bit and buy an aperitif while you're there.
Don't go home without... seeing Pont du Gard, the famed triple-decker aqueduct built by the Romans near Remoulins to deliver drinking water through the hills of the Uzège to Nîmes (it's now a Unesco World Heritage site).

PERFECTLY PROVENCE

The Camargue is a coastal wilderness of marshes, dunes and flamingo-specked salt flats, with whitewashed houses and gypsy villages. *Gardians* (the Camargue cowboys) watch over the region's famous herds of black bulls and white horses; to get a real flavour of the region, explore the beaches and marshes as they do, on horseback (www.promenadedesrieges.com).

DIARY

March/April Toreadors congregate at the Arènes d'Arles for the cape-tastic celebration of tauromachy that is Easter Féria (www.arenes-arles.com). **May** More bull action, plus plenty of street parties, at the Féria de Pentecôte in Nîmes (www.ot-nimes.fr). Gypsies from all over Europe gather in Saintes-Maries-de-la-Mer from 24–26 May to pay their respects to St Sarah, the Black Madonna (www.saintesmaries.com). **June–July** Open-air arias at the Festival d'Aix (www.festival-aix.com), a month of song days for world-class opera stars. **July–August** Horns of the jazz variety lock at Avignon's annual Tremplin Jazz Festival (www.trempjazz.com). **Early September** With paella, sangria and bull-running, the Rice Festival in Arles has a decidedly Spanish flavour (www.tourisme.ville-arles.fr). **November** The Festival d'Abrivado – a gathering of *gardians* at Saintes-Maries-de-la-Mer – sees devil-may-care cowboys charge across the beach.

Oustau de Baumanière

STYLE Chic country retreat
SETTING Rocks and ruins of Les Baux
DESTINATION Southwest Provence

'Handmade wood-block furniture and
a 10-foot satin chaise longue are pure
design-museum pieces. French doors
open out onto a view of verdant grounds,
then olive groves and vineyards'

I met Mrs Smith at the airport and off we soared to Marseille. In my pocket were the spider-scrawl directions to the hotel I'd taken down over the phone that early and bleary morning. The weather was spectacular, so at the airport we coughed up the extra few euros and upgraded from a rental car that looked like as though it should have been reserved for Fred and Wilma Flintstone to a sporty convertible.

Now, be warned: Oustau de Baumanière is hidden away in an obscure part of southwest Provence. It's a good hour's drive from Marseille, if you know where you're going, and an infinite puzzle if you don't. So, lost and tetchy, somewhere between Nice and Barcelona, we bought a map ('une carte' *en Français* – something I discovered it was worth knowing).

Having put away my smudged scribblings and given Mrs Smith a speed lesson in navigation, I made steady progress towards Oustau de Baumanière. When you peel off the highway, the world changes. The drive takes you between Salon and Arles, and every town looks as though it's straight out of *Jean de Florette* or one of those vintage French films. We resisted the temptation to join in a communal summer party at a village along the way, and continued towards our destination; the hot, moist air making a giant herbal humidor of olive, garlic and rosemary. We wound our way up a small mountain, crossing the castle ruins of Château des Baux. Rolling down to our final target was like descending into Shangri-La.

I find carparks give a fair indication of a hotel's calibre, and this one screamed 'understated' and 'high-end'. The pristine gravel path crunched beneath our tyres as we slid in between our car's rich relations. There is a huge emblem projected onto the rocks above that looks Egyptian or Masonic. The light flattered the exquisite architecture of this 30-roomed hotel and the majestic cliffs behind. It might just as well have read 'class'.

A garçon appeared from nowhere, welcoming us by name. This exquisite cordiality continued into the tiny high-polished hardwood and limestone check-in, and as we travelled in the crocodile-skin lift up the single floor to our bedroom. Our room looked just superb: it gave us a warm glow that lingered for days. Spacious, lofty and slightly asymmetrical, it matched 17th-century origins with modern-day, surround-sound extras. The creative lighting design supplied switches ready to match any mood.

Handmade wood-block furniture and a 10-foot satin chaise longue were pure design-museum pieces. The dull stuff (minibar, safe) was hidden behind a false wall. French doors opened out onto a view of the verdant grounds, then olive groves and vineyards. The bathroom held its own, too. I spent a foolish few seconds pressing a jade pebble on the wall in an effort to turn the lights on, only to discover that the walls were embossed with seashells and stones. The bath was bigger than the Flintstones car we nearly hired.

A patio in front, protected from any light drizzle by a canopy of fig trees, is where Baumanière guests eat some

of the best food in France. A glance at the prices might shave the edges off your appetite, though we opted for just the one course, while I kept an eye on everything served around me as it either burst into flames or was cut from its bone with a hiss of Sabatier. The wine list arrived, the size of a pantomime fairytale book, and after struggling like a nine-year-old with the Sunday papers, I let our waiter select something with the decimal point nearer the front end of the price. The chef meekly approached us and asked our opinion; I told him it was excellent and with reassured strides he bowled back to a hot kitchen. We ended on a shared crêpe Suzette and some crystallised local fruits, and retired to bed trying to pretend this was the sort of place we come to all the time.

The next day we took a little sun in the beautiful grounds and a dip in the icy-cold Twenties pool, then walked up to the castle carved into the mountain. The Château des Baux is touristy without being tacky; the ancient alleyways of the town are lined with shops full of local products, and the bars and cafés are cheap and friendly. A steep walk up to the remains of the fortifications rewarded us with a wondrous view; I wondered whether it was that great artists were drawn here or if reasonable artists were just blessed with great things to paint. Down the hill, on the way back to the hotel, we came across Cathédrale d'Images, a huge cave that hosts sound-and-light shows, with locally inspired masterpieces projected onto its walls.

As our farewell to this fine land, we took the car for a spin around some of the local towns; then, after getting utterly lost for a final time, we headed back for a few nightcaps at the hotel. Thrusting my hand in my pocket, I came across the directions I had scrawled down the other day. I took them out, screwed them up and threw them in the ashtray. I now know where Oustau de Baumanière is: it's in Provence, pretty close to perfection.

Reviewed by Nick Moran

'Spacious, lofty and slightly asymmetrical, our room matched 17th-century origins with modern-day, surround-sound extras'

NEED TO KNOW

Rooms 30, including 11 suites.

Rates In low season, €230–€440; high season, €260–€555, including tax and service charge. Continental breakfast, €22.

Check-out Noon. Check-in, 3pm.

Facilities Extensive grounds with outdoor pool, terraces, tennis court and car park; WiFi. In rooms, flatscreen TV, CD/DVD player, minibar, safe, hairdryer.

Children Welcome; extra beds can be added to rooms for €30 (free for under 12s), and babysitting can be arranged locally from €10 an hour.

Also Spa Baumanière offers massages, facials and other pampering treatments. It also has a Turkish bath and sensory pool.

IN THE KNOW

Our favourite rooms Interiors marry mod cons with period details and quirky design touches, particularly the large rooms in the main 16th-century Oustau (Room 63 has an indoor tree). The five rooms housed in the Provençal mas, La Guigou, have a farmhouse feel; and the remaining 14 in the yellow Manoir are all about low-key country-house chic. We love the Junior Suites at the front of the manor, with soothing views over its flower-scattered terrace and the swimming pool.

Hotel bar Drinks are available from the restaurant from 9pm until midnight. The cellar has a stupendous collection amounting to some 100,000 bottles. If Château Guiraud or Pétrus don't appeal, try Domaine de Baumanière's own wine, Affectif, made from biodynamically grown Grenache grapes.

Hotel restaurant With two Michelin stars, the restaurant at Oustau de Baumanière is world-renowned. The menu, overseen by chef-patron Jean-André Charial, features top-quality caviar, foie gras and a dazzling array of premier grand crus. It features plenty of locally sourced fresh fruit and vegetables, too. Lunch is served 12.30pm–2pm; dinner, 7.30pm–10pm.

Top table Near the window, overlooking the terrace and garden.

Room service A room-service menu is available from noon until 3pm, and again between 7pm and 10pm.

Dress code Refined sophistication.

Local knowledge Cooking lessons and wine-tasting seminars can be arranged at the hotel. Just outside Les Baux de Provence, Cathédrale d'Images (www.cathedrale-images.com) is a huge cave in which famous artworks related to the area are projected onto the walls.

LOCAL EATING AND DRINKING

For lighter snacks and drinking, head to alleyways around the Château des Baux in nearby Les Baux de Provence, and see which of the little bars and cafés take your fancy. Many have terraces and wonderful views over the surrounding countryside. **La Cabro d'Or** (04 90 54 33 21), located on the Baumanière estate, offers dining on the wonderful tree-shaded patio during the warmer months. Most ingredients among the fish, shellfish and meat dishes are sourced locally, including vegetables and olive oil from the estate. In nearby Eygalières, **Chez Bru** aka **Le Bistrot d'Eygalières** (04 90 90 60 34) is another Michelin-starred honeypot for gourmets. In Maussane-les-Alpilles, **La Place** (04 90 54 23 31) on Avenue Vallée des Baux, an excellent bistro run by the same people as Oustau de Baumanière, does wonderful Alpilles lamb dishes.

GET A ROOM!

To book this hotel, go to www.mrandmrssmith.com or ring our expert travel team on 1 800 464 2040. Activate your free membership online (see page 4) to qualify for the exclusive Smith card offer shown below when you book with us.

SMITH CARD OFFER A recipe book by Jean-André Charial, Oustau de Baumanière's Michelin-starred chef-patron.

Oustau de Baumanière 13520 Les Baux de Provence, Bouches-du-Rhône
(www.mrandmrssmith.com/oustau-de-baumaniere)

Berlin

GERMANY

BERLIN
Lux 11

BERLIN

CITYSCAPE Soviet so-cool republic
CITY LIFE Louche and lowdown

Willkommen to perhaps Europe's most fascinating city. Flying in the face of stuffy German stereotypes, famously liberal and fun-loving Berlin has long been a magnet for pleasure-seekers. Lines of bars and clubs, blaring out rock, techno and everything in between, have now replaced the famous Berlin wall, and are testament to the city's resilience and upbeat character. Indeed, the collapse of the Iron Curtain has allowed its dormant creativity to flourish. Art galleries have sprung up in almost every vacant warehouse space, theatre and cabaret venues continue to pack them in, and awe-inspiring buildings such as the metal-and-glass Reichstag have brought iconic design to the Soviet-era cityscape. Add to this a vibrant culinary scene, offering everything from traditional würst to elaborate Asian fusion, and this city is one you'll never want to leave. Berlin? It'll take your breath away.

GETTING THERE

Planes There are three airports in Berlin. Berlin International, better known as Tegel, is the most likely arrival point for visitors from the US. It's about six miles north of the city centre, and is well served by transport links. Schönefeld and Tempelhof are equally easy to get to and from. For information, go to www.berlin-airport.de.
Trains Deutsche Bahn (www.bahn.de) is Germany's national rail service, and operates cross-country links, as well as routes to other European cities. Berlin's metro system – the U-bahn – runs from the early hours of the morning until just after midnight; and all night at weekends.
Automobiles Don't bother. Parking places in central Berlin are difficult to find, and very expensive when you do...

6.30pm. The city goes a bit quiet on a Sunday. Bars tend to close between 1am and 3am in the week, and stay open till 5am at the weekends. Clubs can go on all night.
Do go/don't go There's never a bad time to visit Berlin. In the balmy summer, there are all kinds of alfresco delights to indulge in; in winter, it may be cold and up-to-your-knees snowy, but it's also incredibly atmospheric. And there's glühwein on sale everywhere to warm you up.
Packing tips A portable DVD player on which to watch brilliant Berlin-set films – take your pick from *Metropolis*, *Good Bye Lenin!*, *The Lives of Others*, *Cabaret*, *Downfall* and, um, *Octopussy*, among others.

LOCAL KNOWLEDGE

Taxis You'll find taxi ranks all over the city, and you can also call Taxi Fon (0800 8001 1554) to get one sent to you. When you get into a cab, the meter will always be set to €2.50. Expect to pay €1.50 a kilometre after that.
Currency Euro (€).
Dialling codes Germany: 49. Berlin: (0)30.
Tipping culture Restaurant bills include service, but it is usual to add five to 10 per cent on top of this. Add about 10 per cent to your taxi fare and five per cent to your bar bill.
Siesta and fiesta Berlin shops are legally allowed to open around the clock, which makes for erratic opening times – though you're unlikely to find anything closed before

Recommended reads Christopher Isherwood's *Goodbye to Berlin* chronicles the decadence of city life in the years just before World War II. *The Spy Who Came In From The Cold* by John Le Carré is a snapshot of Cold War espionage. *Russian Disco* by Wladimir Kaminer is a collection of tales about 'everyday lunacy on the streets of Berlin'.

Cuisine Though most dishes on Berlin menus are of the rib-sticking variety, the city serves up plenty of lighter fare. Splendid Delikatessen (9212 7247) on Dorotheenstrasse sells artisan honey, organic vegetables and salads alongside the meatloaf. There's a strong eco movement here, too, so good vegetarian food is easy to find. Germany is justly famous for its beers, and Berliners adore weizenbier (made with wheat). The country's wines, especially Riesling and Müller-Thurgau, are well worth checking out, too.

And... Enjoy the quintessential Berlin musical *Cabaret* amid the art nouveau splendour of the Bar Jeder Vernunft theatre (www.cabaret-berlin.de).

WORTH GETTING OUT OF BED FOR

Viewpoint Built by the Communists to loom over free West Berlin as a symbol of Soviet might, the Fernsehturm (television tower) in Alexanderplatz is the tallest structure in the city at 368m. Take a lift up to its viewing platform. From here, you can see the entire city spread out beneath you. For information, go to www.berlinerfernsehturm.de.

Arts and culture When the Cold War ended, artists from all over the world flocked to Mitte, in search of low rents and the creative vibe. The area is still home to plenty of quirky galleries specialising in experimental art. Try Eigen + Art (280 6605) on Auguststrasse, or Tacheles (282 6185), an artists' collective in an old department store on Oranienburgerstrasse. The latter regularly hosts impromptu parties and gigs. For art from the ancient Greeks to the 20th century, head to the Alte Nationalgalerie (2090 5577) in Mitte and Tiergarten's Gemäldegalerie (266 2951).

Activities Berlin Zoo (254 010), right in the city centre, is home to Knut, probably the world's most famous polar bear. Swimming is extremely popular in Berlin, and the city has many beautiful, Soviet-era *schwimbads*. Stadtbad Mitte (3088 0910), close to Lux 11, comes with heated tiles, a criss-cross beamed glass roof and stained-glass windows picturing proud workers going about their toil.

Perfect picnic Stock your picnic hamper in the food hall of department store KaDeWe (21210) and then take the S1 train from Schöneberg to Wannsee, two linked lakes in the southwest of the city, and dine on the shores.

Daytripper Just half an hour outside Berlin, Potsdam, former seat of the Prussian royal family, is a refined alternative to the bustle of the German capital. Based around the rococo Schloss Sanssouci, the town is famed for its ornate gardens and lush parkland.

Walks New Berlin Tours (5105 0030) and Original Berlin Walks (301 9194) will both lead you expertly through streets that were at the forefront of one of modern European history's most turbulent periods.

Shopping If you're looking to update your look, then you won't go far wrong in Mitte. Walk along either Alte or Neue Schönhauser Strasse, and you'll find all manner of designs you won't see anywhere else. Women should pack their men off in the direction of clothes store Respectmen (283 5010) and music Mecca DNS Recordstore (247 9835), and then spend a leisurely couple of hours browsing the innovative creations at Claudia Skoda (280 7211) and vintagewear at Sommerladen (177 299 1789), or trying on the beautiful shoes at Calypso (2854 5415).

Something for nothing The city's four Weinerei bars (www.weinerei.com) are a blessing for visitors struggling to adapt to the soaring rate of the euro. Simply pay a €1 deposit to get a glass, then help yourself to as much wine as you like. Pay as much as you think fair – and maybe treat yourself to one on the house...

Don't go home without... sampling currywürst, sliced wiener sausage slathered in thick spicy sauce and sprinkled with curry powder, from the famous Konnopke's Imbiss snack bar (442 7765) in Prenzlauer Berg.

BRILLIANTLY BERLIN

See the city as those who lived behind the Iron Curtain did, and drive a Trabant – the tiny tin box on wheels that the State decreed suitable for East German citizens – around East Berlin's Communist-era landmarks. A Trabi-Safari guide will take the lead in another car and provide commentary via radio. For more information, call 2759 2273 or go to www.trabi-safari.de.

DIARY

June The city's biggest gay carnival (and, believe us, there are quite a few), the Christopher Street Day Parade, sees more than 400,000 take to Berlin's streets in all manner of flamboyant costumes. Expect lots of piercings. **October** Commemorating the day in 1989 when the wall finally tumbled, the Day of German Unity on 3 October sees street parties being held throughout Berlin. **December** Christmas markets spring up throughout the city – pretend to do your shopping whilst joining the locals in getting subtly sloshed on schnapps and glühwein.

Lux 11

STYLE White lines blowin' through my mind
SETTING Mittel Mitte
DESTINATION Berlin

'The corridors seem to have been designed for Liberace. Softly lit in hot pink, these dark passageways are part dungeon, part club VIP area: totally Berlin'

spend a few moments trying to distinguish the flat-capped and duffel-coated dummies in one huge plate-glass window from the flat-capped and duffel-coated hotel clientele in the other. It's like watching a film of Berlin Fashion Week on an outdoor cinema screen.

Reception resembles what people in the Sixties thought the future would look like — angular, white, uplit desk; spotless white walls; severe black-bordered doors — but beyond, Lux 11 feels more like the 19th-century building in which it is housed. A glass lift glides up to thick wooden doors that look as though they belong in a financial institution. If these were designed for the State Bank, however, the corridors leading to the rooms seem to have been designed for Liberace. Softly lit in hot pink, these dark passageways are part dungeon, part club VIP area: totally Berlin.

Our room, the executive suite, is so clean, so white, so geometric, that to enter it is akin to walking onto a squash court. Mrs Smith, after a quick round of sofa-sitting and kitchenette cupboard-opening, declares it's like a particularly comfortable studio flat. The shower, however, is big enough to sub-let on its own.

We pull back the curtains and lean out of our third-floor windows to inhale snow-tinged air and survey the Soviet-era architecture of East Berlin around us. Those neon displays atop brutal grey edifices are fooling no one. We've gone back in time to 1984, and Cold War paranoia is palpable. Even the ozone-piercing Alexanderplatz television tower to our right, an enormous Marxist middle finger pointing right at West Berlin, blinks menacingly.

We head down to the bar for a pre-dinner drink. Everything around us is white — the tables, the walls, the linen, even the staff uniforms — and we, Mrs Smith in a burnt-orange dress, me in a green shirt, feel like blots on a pristine landscape. Seated in the centre of the buzzing Shiro i Shiro restaurant, surrounded by stylish English- and French-speaking couples, we share a selection of freshly cut sashimi, sliced in the corner sushi bar, before indulging in a platter of scallop and yellow-fin tuna rolls. Mrs Smith, who was sceptical about finding anything for vegetarians in meat-loving Mitteleurope, is in piscivorous heaven.

I'm fully aware of Berlin's louche reputation, but this is ridiculous. There's a sex shop in the airport. Not tucked away discreetly, but bang opposite the arrivals gate, so it's the first thing you see when disembarking. Mrs Smith, in one of those skittish moods that comes as a result of having to catch a flight a couple of hours before most milkmen would think about getting out of bed, finds it hilarious, but not as funny as she finds my subsequent attempt to telephone Lux 11 for directions, and speak to the staff in their native language. 'Go on,' she says enticingly. 'Do your German face — your eyes screw up when you try to think of the words.'

Our taxi driver seems to have no problem understanding me, and, after a drive through Berlin's sprawling outskirts — past the Reichstag, Brandenburg Gate and over where the wall once stood — we are dropped outside the hotel. At first, it's hard to tell where its façade begins and the next-door clothes boutique ends, and Mrs Smith and I

The next morning, we head out for a walk. Just a few metres from Lux 11 we find another porn shop. Good grief; what's going on? It's as though sex was banned under the Communists, and everyone's peeling off their party-issue overalls and making up for it now. We go for a decidedly non-erotic breakfast of omelettes and potatoes, where Mrs Smith notices we're the only customers in the café not drinking alcohol. It's 10am. Groups of friends are chatting over glasses of schnapps, and hausfraus gossip with foaming beer steins before them. This city is making me feel positively puritanical.

'Reception resembles what people in the Sixties thought the future would look like'

So, at Gendarmenmarkt Christmas market, Mrs Smith and I head straight for the glühwein stall, and purchase steaming mugs of hot, spicy wine that warm our bellies and fill our heads with wooziness. We shuffle around the faux-Alpine huts, and browse selections of everything from rails of dirndls to gingerbread hearts saying 'Ich liebe dich'. The air is thick with the smell of food; sausages sizzle next to molehill-sized piles of onions and cabbage on giant griddles, and meat of all shapes and sizes smokes away on barbecues. I treat myself to the Berlin speciality of currywürst – a sliced frankfurter smothered in curry sauce.

Back at the hotel, wrapped up in bedclothes with a bottle of champagne open on the bedside table, we watch a Chevy Chase film dubbed into German on the flatscreen TV. We've barely scratched the surface of this sin city – indeed the naughtiest thing I've done is unwittingly eat a casserole of baby deer in a traditional restaurant – but we're both desperate to come back and plumb new depths of depravity. And, having spent two nights in the harmonious, all-white environs of Lux 11, Mrs Smith and I wouldn't dream of cleansing our sordid souls anywhere else.

Reviewed by Mr & Mrs Smith

NEED TO KNOW

Rooms 72, including 16 suites.

Rates €165–€295, including breakfast. There is an additional charge of €15 a night for stays of less than three nights.

Check-out Noon, though this can be extended to 2pm on arrangement; earliest check-in, 4pm.

Facilities Aveda hair salon and spa, garage, laundry. In rooms, kitchenettes, flatscreen TV, DVD player, fax machine, WiFi.

Children Welcome: baby cots are available, and extra beds can be added to rooms for €25 a night. Lux 11 works with a nanny service to provide babysitting, from €16 an hour.

Also If you suddenly get cold feet about the outfit you've chosen to wear to dinner, fear not. The apartments are part of a building that also contains the Ulf Haines store, home of some of Berlin's most stylish fashion collections.

IN THE KNOW

Our favourite rooms Executive suites 317 or 417, with their surfeit of windows looking out over the famous Alexanderplatz television tower, are the ones to ask for. Both come with their own living area and sizeable kitchen.

Hotel bar Set at one end of Shiro i Shiro, the bar is an elegant counter around which are set high stools – the ideal vantage point for watching impossibly good-looking barmen mix martinis.

Hotel restaurant Shiro i Shiro, though not strictly the hotel's in-house restaurant (Lux 11 bills itself as an 'apartment house'), can certainly be considered as such – it's to one side of reception and your Continental breakfast buffet is served here in the mornings. With its white, minimalist interior, it is up to the kitchen to provide the colour, which it does with aplomb. Choose sushi – freshly prepared by knife-wielding Japanese chefs at a corner counter – or delicious Modern European cuisine.

Top table Go for an alcove at the back of the restaurant. Sit on your curved blue-velvet banquette and peer out at fellow diners through the diaphanous drapes.

Room service As Lux 11 is essentially an apartment building, no room service is offered.

Dress code Elegant black for him; Astrid Kirchherr crop for her.

Local knowledge The darker side of Berlin's past is acknowledged by the spectral Holocaust Memorial (www.holocaust-mahnmal.de), just around the corner from the Brandenburg Gate. Made up from thousands of concrete blocks it looks, at first glance, like a giant cemetery; walk amongst the stones, though, and you will find yourself drawn down into a disorienting maze-like structure in which time eerily appears to stand still. It's an incredibly moving experience.

LOCAL EATING AND DRINKING

Alpenstück (2175 1646) on Gartenstrasse serves up hearty southern German cuisine such as sausages, sauerkraut and schnitzel in a stylish environment. **Brecht's** (2859 8585), a bistro-style restaurant down by the river on Schiffbauerdamm, has a more Austrian bent. Try its veal sausages or gnocchi in a creamy cheese sauce. Young Michelin-starred chef Michael Hoffman does astonishing things with seafood at **Margaux** (2265 2611) on Unter den Linden. **Susuru** (211 1182), just along Rosa Luxemburg Strasse, is an excellent Japanese noodle bar with chic decor. Its udon selection makes for a good lunch option. Drink in the evening at **Altes Europa** (2809 3840) on Gipsstrasse. It's an atmospheric café bar with an old-fashioned ambience that's frequented by Berlin's beautiful people.

GET A ROOM!

To book this hotel, go to www.mrandmrssmith.com or ring our expert travel team on 1 800 464 2040. Activate your free membership online (see page 4) to qualify for the exclusive Smith card offer shown below when you book with us.

 SMITH CARD OFFER A bottle of wine from a renowned vineyard. Up to two discounted beauty treatments or massages. VIP entrance to the hotel's favourite nightclubs and lounges on selected days.

Lux 11 9–13 Rosa Luxemburg Strasse, D-10178 Berlin (www.mrandmrssmith.com/lux-11)

How to...

mix a
minibar
cocktail

With a little imagination and a decent selection of ingredients, you should be able to blend more from the minibar than just beer and lemonade. These cocktails are perfect for impromptu parties in your room or to surprise your other half in the bath.

Preparation is the key. Cocktails must be cold, so a full-sized champagne bucket filled with fresh ice is paramount. You'll also need a few lemons and limes, a couple of oranges, a sharp knife and some appropriate glassware. Check that you have lots of white sugar-cubes and sachets, and that you have change to tip room service. Minibars are not well-known for their vast array of choice, but here are a few great classics and a couple of contemporary cocktails that can be made easily from the basic ingredients. Cheers...

TOM COLLINS

The long, refreshing gin-based classic. Squeeze the juice of half a lemon into a tall glass. Dissolve four sachets of sugar into the juice and add a mini bottle of gin. Top up the glass with ice and sparkling mineral water or soda water. Stir well. If you have any lemons left over, garnish the drink with a wedge.

CUBA LIBRE

Basically a dressed-up rum and Coke – but it comes from Cuba, so it must be cool. Take a tall glass and fill it with ice cubes. Pour in a mini bottle of rum (aged, if you have it) and fill with Coke. Then take a lime, cut it into wedges, squeeze them all into the drink and drop them in. Give it a good stir.

SUITE SANGRIA

It feels as though you're achieving some kind of greatness if you can knock up an impressive bedroom sangria. This is enough for two or three people. You will need to pour the following ingredients into an ice bucket: a small bottle of red wine (or two, ideally); half a brandy miniature; half a Cointreau miniature; the juice of half an orange; three to five sachets of sugar (to taste). Make sure all the sugar has dissolved by stirring, then add ice if you want it cold; otherwise just serve it with slices of lime or orange.

GODFATHER

This is perfect after a satisfactory three-courser, and it couldn't be easier to make. Add half each of a mini bottle of whisky and a mini bottle of Amaretto to a tumbler half full of ice cubes, then stir.

CHAMPAGNE COCKTAIL

If you manage to score some Angostura bitters from room service to make this glamorous classic, all the better. First, take a sugar-cube and rub it firmly on the skin of an orange until the cube turns slightly yellow (picking up all those lovely bitter orange oils from the peel). Then place it in the bottom of a champagne flute and dash two drops of bitters over it. Pour half a mini bottle of brandy over the sugar and slowly top up with champagne.

DANDY SHANDY

A contemporary take on the beer/lemonade combo: a classic. Add half a mini bottle of Cointreau to a large glass full of ice cubes, then top it up with equal measures of lager and lemonade. Cut half a lime into wedges; squeeze and drop them into the drink. Stir well.

BLOCKBUSTER

Dead simple to make, and even easier to drink. Pour a mini bottle of rum into a tall glass full of ice cubes, almost topping it up with equal measures of Coke and ginger beer (ginger ale is a good second-best). Then squeeze the juice of a lime into the glass and stir.

DIRTY MARTINI

If you've got a jar of olives and some elegant glasses handy, this is a sophisticated tipple for two. Empty a gin miniature into a large glass or jug, and add a handful of ice and a splash of the brine from the olives. Give it a good stir and strain (perhaps with the aid of a fork) into the glasses. Pop an olive into each.

GIMLET

A refreshing alternative to the good old gin and tonic, perfect for a hot-climate sundowner. Stir together two parts gin to one part lime juice or lime cordial; serve on the rocks with a splash of soda water.

MRS SMITH'S TEA-PUNCH

Designed for larger social shenanigans, this refreshing punch will serve up to four people. It is tricky but rewarding to make. Measure two highball glasses of water into your kettle, and boil. Pour over two teabags in an ice bucket, and leave to steep for a minute. Take out the teabags and squeeze in the juice of a lemon, then add two mini bottles of gin and a dozen or so sachets of sugar. Fill with ice to cool it down, and serve in small glasses garnished with slices of lemon.

RUSTY NAIL

One for the retro-lover, if you're lucky enough to find Drambuie in your minibar. After putting ice in two glasses, empty one whisky mini into each, then divide the Drambuie between them. Add a twist of lemon.

Grenada

GRENADA

GRENADA
Laluna

GRENADA

COASTLINE Verdant spice island
COAST LIFE It's a rum do

Piece of advice: go to Grenada, before the rest of the world does. Somehow, this nutmeg-flavoured island has remained untouched by time and tourism, and retains the genuine kick-back-and-unwind vibe that's been lost elsewhere in the Caribbean. Weekends here are about cricket on the parish green and snoozing on the porch. With no tourist-tramped heritage trails to spoil the peaceful atmosphere, visitors are free to explore the lush rainforest and waterfalls of the interior, 45 heavenly beaches, and the pastel-hued, horseshoe-shaped harbour of St George's. The colonial buildings and community feel are the stuff of nostalgic fantasy: white-gloved policemen direct traffic, and schoolchildren in starchy pressed uniforms walk home together along the side of the road in the afternoons. Like them, Grenada – with its light muscovado beaches and cinnamon-scented fields – is made of sugar and spice and all things nice.

GETTING THERE

Planes Point Salines International Airport (444 4101), 11km from St George's, receives flights from the UK and the US. Most journeys will require a stop on one of the other Caribbean islands. There's a local departure tax of $20.
Automobiles If you want to rent a car for exploring, have the hotel organise one; that way, it'll be delivered and collected. If you get lost, stop and ask a local – it's no generalisation to say everyone's extremely friendly.
Boats Osprey Lines ferries (www.ospreylines.com) will take you to the neighbouring island of Carriacou in 90 minutes; there are also services from Petite Martinique.

rainy season is June–December, but showers are brief.
Packing tips Bring your snorkel, but leave your watch at home and go with the flow.
Recommended reads *Tide Running* by Grenadian resident Oonya Kempadoo provides a thrillingly sensual taster of Caribbean life. *Spice: The History of a Temptation* by Jack Turner turns the spice-trade race into a gripping yarn.
Cuisine There's fresh fish and seafood in abundance, with bananas, mangoes, coconuts and roti filling in the gaps; dishes on this spiciest of islands exhibit a fascinating blend of Creole, Indian and African influence. Grenada's national dish is known as 'oildown'. Adored by islanders,

LOCAL KNOWLEDGE

Taxis Ask the hotel to arrange airport pick-ups. Brightly coloured water taxis can shuttle you between St George's and Grand Anse Beach for about EC$10 a couple.
Currency East Caribbean dollar (EC$); the US dollar is also accepted in most places.
Dialling codes Grenada: 1 473.
Tipping culture A 10 per cent service charge is added to the bill at most restaurants. Any further tips are up to you.
Siesta and fiesta If you pitched 'siesta' and 'fiesta' against one another in Grenada, they would both just lie down and have a nice long nap. Even the airport shuts at 11pm. Shops close at 4–5pm Mondays–Fridays; Saturdays, 1pm.
Do go/don't go The average year-round temperature is around 25°C, with tropical breezes to keep you cool. The

the coconut-laced meat and dumpling stew gets its name from the way the coconut oil sinks to the bottom during cooking. Fish Friday is a weekly festival in Gouyave, when locals hang out from 4pm, often with live music and entertainment, until the fish, rum and beer run out. As well as various dark and white rums, the island also produces a nutmeg liqueur, La Grenade (www.delagrenade.com). And… Grenada lies below the hurricane belt and tends to miss out on scary storms, though it was devastated by hurricanes Ivan and Emily in 2004 and 2005 respectively.

WORTH GETTING OUT OF BED FOR

Viewpoint As you drive north through lush rainforest along the road from St George's, stop just before you arrive in St Andrew's, at the peak of the hill, to look back on Grenada's capital harbour city.

Arts and culture A tour of the Dougaldston Estate, 10 miles north of nutmeg capital Gouyave, where bananas, coconuts and spices are processed, is a suitably aromatic substitute for the usual museum schlep. Another unusual way to learn about Grenada's folklore and history involves snorkelling or diving at the world's first underwater sculpture park – think Anthony Gormley meets *Pirates of the Caribbean* (www.underwatersculpture.com). Get an insight into rural life at 300-year-old Belmont Estate (442 9524; www.belmontestate.net), a former sugar mill in St Patrick – it has lovely views and walking trails.

Activities Grenada offers some of the best diving in the Caribbean, with 50 sites to explore, including the biggest shipwreck in the region – the ocean liner *Bianca C*; Aquanauts (444 1126; www.aquanautsgrenada.com) will kit you out and take you down. Then there's fishing, or dolphin- and whale-watching trips (www.catamaran chartering.com). Alternatively, hike along gorgeous trails in the Grand Etang National Park (440 6160), or head into the rainforest for some rubber-tubing along Balthazar River. Adventure Jeep Tours (444 5337; www.grenada jeeptours.com) will take you trekking, biking or to secluded beaches for snorkelling.

Best beach A white-sand idyll on the northeastern tip of the island, Bathway Beach is a lovely spot with a natural lagoon, perfect for a lazy day of swimming and a picnic of barbecued chicken. Try Magazine Beach for snorkelling. Closer to St George's, Grand Anse is beautiful but busier.

Daytripper Take the ferry across to one of Grenada's satellite islands, Carriacou or Petite Martinique, where there's fantastic snorkelling and dreamy beaches – Paradise

Beach on Carriacou is a superb stretch of powdery white sand, but you might prefer to charter a boat and play Robinson Crusoe on one of the uninhabited outlying islets.

Walks Follow in the footsteps of Grenada's own Indiana Jones, the machete-wielding hiking hero Telfor Bedeau (442 6200), and trek to Concord Falls or Seven Sister Falls. His challenging day-long hikes will take you through the rainforest (wear anti-scratchy-plant jeans and trainers).

Shopping In St George's, browse the Market Square (busiest on a Saturday morning) for local produce and spices, and the Esplanade Mall on Melville Street for local arts and crafts – Figleaf (435 9771) has a nice selection. Keep your eyes peeled for delicious organic chocolate bars made by the Grenada Chocolate Company (so good it's stocked by Rococo Chocolates in London); lots of shops in St George's sell it. The islanders' favourite rum is Clarke's Court Rum (which they claim leaves them hangover-free), produced at the Grenada Sugar Factory in St George's (www.clarkescourtrum.com).

Something for nothing Inhale and be hearty: the very air you breathe has aromatherapeutic properties, with cloves, nutmeg, cinnamon, ginger, bay leaves and turmeric lacing the salty tropical breeze. Make time to chat to people – there's no point in rushing about here, and Grenadians are renowned for their fantastic sense of humour.

Don't go home without… ordering the Grenadian version of rum punch: lime juice, sugar syrup, dark rum and ice, with a generous spinkling of nutmeg – go on, you know you want to…

GROGGILY GRENADA

The River Antoine Estate, in the parish of St Patrick's at the north end of the island, is home to the oldest water-propelled rum distillery still functioning in the Caribbean. Here, River's Royale rum of astonishingly high alcohol content is made from fermented sugar cane in astonishingly basic surroundings. Islanders recommend you 'sit down' while drinking it (lest you become astonishingly legless, we assume).

DIARY

January Men grapple with huge fish during the Spice Island Billfish Tournament (www.sibt grenada.com) – 2009 is the 40th anniversary. Heave to for the Grenada Sailing Festival (www. grenadasailingfestival.com) at the end of the month. **February** Grenada's Independence Day on the seventh is a public holiday celebrated with pomp and parades. Carriacou Carnival kicks off the weekend before Lent – don't miss the Shakespeare Mas, where gaily garbed performers engage in a battle of wits. **May** The totally banging Drum Festival (www.spiceisle.com/drum krumah) and totally exhausting International Triathlon (www.grenadatriathlon.com). **June** Fisherman's Birthday, Gouyave's all-day celebration of patron saint St Peter. **August** Spice Mas Carnival (www.spicemasgrenada.com): calypso, jump-ups, Devil Mas bands and DJ trucks.

Laluna

STYLE Balinese-boho beach cottages
SETTING Green hills, white sand
DESTINATION Grenada

'Sunset over the Caribbean is followed by
the illumination of tiny lights across the
hotel grounds, greeting the rising of
the moon that gives the hotel its name'

decks and Asian-influenced furniture, and a soothing colour palette of mottled ochres and muddy blues, it ticks all the right boxes. So far, so upmarket boutique hotel. But it's a laid-back Caribbean vibe that sets it apart. We've arrived at lunchtime and because our room isn't ready, we're relieved of our bags and ushered straight into the restaurant. Here we're handed menus that perfectly encapsulate Laluna's effortless cool. No more than a folded piece of corrugated cardboard containing a two-page list held together by a length of string, the menu couldn't be simpler – but still it achieves design class and confident sophistication.

This mood continues in the hotel's simple layout: a central, open courtyard edged by a dining room, open bar and discreet reception area. There's an infinity pool in the middle and a beach on the fourth side. The 16 rooms stack up the hillside behind reception; they're only seconds away, but you'd never notice them unless you looked up. It is neat, clever and intimate, and you never, for a second, feel as though you're in a resort – or a hotel for that matter.

In the restaurant, the fare is simple Italian (the chef is Calabrian) – pasta, pizza and fish of the day, plus some regional standards. I start with prosciutto and melon, and follow it with a pumpkin and asparagus pizza. Mrs Smith opts for the gazpacho and pappardelle with mushrooms. We wash it down with deliciously chilled bottles of Italian rosé and San Pellegrino. We could have been in Tuscany but for the sparkling Caribbean Sea barely 10 yards away.

By the time Mrs Smith is mopping up the last of her sauce, our cabana is ready. After a 30-second check-in, we're given our key and asked if we want to be shown to the room or find our own way there. Given that it is barely 15 yards away and visible from reception, we choose to strike out on our own. This kind of service – casual and laissez-faire, but clearly intended for people who want to do things their way – is typical of Laluna. 'The bar's there, you don't need to book the restaurant, the beach towels are there, the sea is there, suit yourself,' we are told by staff.

The concrete cabanas, topped with wooden-tiled roofs, may have all been constructed in the same way, but they're decorated individually. Painted in an imaginatively

Mrs Smith and I have a thing about small hotels, having long since fallen out of love with all those enormous resorts, with their Wednesday night buffets and inevitable queues for reception. Hotels, for us, have to provide intimacy as well as character, and we are always on the lookout for originality.

As regular visitors to Grenada, we're keen to see whether this 16-cottage retreat lives up to its excellent reputation. The journey there doesn't bode well. As we bump our way along a potholed track, I can't help but think that Laluna seems to be hiding itself from all but the most determined visitors. However, when we finally turn into Morne Rouge Bay, and find ourselves driving through colourful cabanas sitting on a sea-facing hillside, I silently give thanks that this road will have deterred the tourist hordes.

On first sight, Laluna, situated in a cove surrounded by high cliffs, certainly looks the part. With its dark-wood

conceived range of washed-out colours, with decks dotted with teak day beds, giant beanbags, canvas awnings and plunge pools, they sit at least 15 yards apart from each other. Screens of mature foliage guarantee privacy.

Inside, the cabins are dark and cool, with welcoming king-size four-posters, polished concrete floors and textured walls. Once again, every stick of furniture, from the cushion-strewn bench seat to the minimal bathroom fittings, feels individually

'Painted in washed-out colours, the cabanas are protected by screens of mature foliage'

sourced and completely at home in its eclectic setting. Nothing feels mass-produced or formulaic. We kick back and chill for half an hour before heading to the beach for a late-afternoon swim.

Sitting on our deck before we head down the hill to dinner, we watch what we soon discover is Laluna's nightly light show. Sunset over the Caribbean is followed by the illumination of a thousand tiny lights across the hotel grounds, greeting the rising of the moon that gives the hotel its name. The plethora of carefully positioned wall lamps, hidden spots, candles and lanterns casts a visual spell that reinvents every area as a sophisticated and magical nocturnal space.

It's an apt metaphor: Laluna is a shining light amid the dull lustre of the Caribbean's many mega resorts. The staff are friendly but unintrusive, the facilities completely wonderful. If you want to relax and combine the beauty of the region with a little southern European sophistication, you'll love it. We came looking for style and character, and found it in spades.

Reviewed by Mark Joy

NEED TO KNOW

Rooms 16 cottages.

Rates Low season, $390–$650; high season, $730–$1,050, excluding tax and service at 18 per cent. American breakfast, $25.

Check-out 1pm; an even later check-out is possible, depending on subsequent bookings.

Facilities Pool, spa, small gym, library, video/CD selection, free WiFi throughout, spa and wellness centre (opening late 2008). In rooms, TV, VCR, CD player, Bellora bedlinen, monk-made Italian toiletries.

Children Over-14s are welcome, but pay the full adult rate.

Also The hotel is largely open to the air, so smoking is allowed throughout.

IN THE KNOW

Our favourite rooms High on the hill, cottages 11 and 12 afford spectacular views of the crystal waters of the bay below. Lower down, Laluna's beachfront cottage is just 40 feet from the water's edge, meaning that you can start each day by sauntering from your floaty-draped four-poster bed to the sea. All cottages come with plunge pools on their veranda.

Hotel bar Shaded by a thatched roof, the Sunset Bar by the beach is a chilled Balinese living room affair, with day beds aplenty and sofas galore. Its predominantly Italian wine list is impressively extensive. Last orders, 11pm.

Hotel restaurant A handcrafted Indonesian-style roof of woven palm fronds caps the open-air dining area, propped up with rough-hewn tree-trunk beams. The hotel's Calabrian owner imports fresh food and wine from his native Italy, meaning there are always olives, prosciutto, gnocchi and their ilk on offer.

Top table Secure a table for two in the corner nearest the pool and the ocean, where you can feel as though you've got the whole place to yourselves.

Room service Snacks, drinks and meals can be brought to your cottage from 8am until 9pm.

Dress code Star-spangled glamour: an assortment of A-listers have holidayed here.

Local knowledge Strike out for the Grand Etang National Park in St Andrew and trek through the Grenadian rainforest to the Seven Sister Waterfalls, a series of seven grab-the-camera beautiful falls, with huge pools to bask in. Laluna can arrange a picnic and guide to see you through the three-hour yomp. Non-jungle lovers have the option of diving, golfing, snorkelling, kayaking or fishing off Morne Rouge's peaceful beaches.

LOCAL EATING AND DRINKING

If you would like a change from Laluna's Italian menu, you can titillate your tastebuds with local West Indian fare at **La Belle Creole** (473 444 4316) at Grand Anse's Blue Horizons resort, or with freshly made sushi and sashimi at **Carib Sushi** (473 439 5640) in the Marquis Complex. Gary Rhodes has a popular outpost – **Rhodes Restaurant** (473 444 4334) – at the Calabash Hotel in St George's, which serves predictably delicious seafood, including swordfish and barracuda. For lighter bites (including sublime curried conch and nutmeg ice-cream), try the **Nutmeg Café** (473 440 2539), overlooking the harbour in St George's.

GET A ROOM!

To book this hotel, go to www.mrandmrssmith.com or ring our expert travel team on 1 800 464 2040. Activate your free membership online (see page 4) to qualify for the exclusive Smith card offer shown below when you book with us.

 SMITH CARD OFFER A 30-minute massage each and a bottle of prosecco.

Laluna Morne Rouge, St George's (www.mrandmrssmith.com/laluna)

County
Meath

IRELAND

COUNTY MEATH
Bellinter House

COUNTY MEATH

COUNTRYSIDE Fresh Eire
COUNTRY LIFE Fast horses and slow rivers

As the seat of the legendary High Kings of Ireland, the deep green pastures of this northeastern county are the ancient royal heartlands of the aptly named Emerald Isle. Although close to the city thrills of bustling Dublin, Meath has an enchantingly relaxed pace all of its own. The racecourses may occasionally thunder under the fleet hooves of Irish thoroughbreds, but time – like the silvery rivers teeming with trout and salmon – flows softly through this land. You can explore the ageless charm of the Royal County on foot, on horseback or by hot-air balloon; browse the stalls of farmers' markets groaning with fresh organic produce; or happen upon ancient, myth-rich Celtic hill forts. And, once you've allowed the slow pulse of Meath to seep into your veins, there can be nothing more pleasurable than luxuriating with a summer picnic on the banks of the Boyne, under the long shadows of mighty Trim Castle.

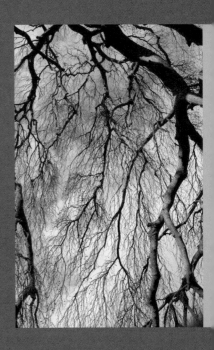

GETTING THERE

Planes The town of Navan in the heart of County Meath is just 33 miles – half an hour's drive – from Dublin International Airport (www.dublinairport.com). Dublin city centre is 45 minutes from the airport by Air Coach (www.aircoach.ie); a taxi costs about €35 (www.cabhire.net).
Trains The main coastal line between Dublin and Belfast passes 30 minutes of your time on its run through County Meath to Drogheda via Laytown (www.irishrail.ie).
Automobiles A rental car is the easiest way to make the most of your stay in this region. From Dublin, drive along either the M1 motorway, the N2 or the N3 – they all travel north through County Meath.

LOCAL KNOWLEDGE

Taxis Minicabs are your only option here: Navan Free Phone Cabs operates 24/7 and can be contacted locally on 1800 313233. Otherwise, ask your hotel to book transport.
Currency Euro (€).
Dialling codes Ireland: 353. Navan: (0)46. Slane: (0)41.
Tipping culture About 15 per cent will go down well in restaurants, but service is sometimes already included in the bill, so check how much you leave.

Siesta and fiesta This part of the world is not exactly the throbbing heart of the universe: the pace of life is gentle, with corresponding opening times. Restaurants and pubs will generally have closed their doors by 10pm or 11pm.
Do go/don't go There are only two important seasons: the Flat season and the National Hunt season. Rainfall is high, but makes the countryside luminous green – when the sun does shine, you'll realise why it's called the Emerald Isle.
Packing tips Bring your riding and fishing gear: Meath is famous for both activities, and it's claimed that steeds run faster and jump higher here. Local legend also has it that the fish in the county's rivers can talk. Blarney, no doubt.
Recommended reads The Complete Poems of Francis Ledwidge – the poet hailed from Slane. Or tuck into a book by an author who lived in Meath: Lord Dunsany's The Gods of Pegana, or Mary Lavin's The Shrine and Other Stories.
Cuisine The wild brown trout, salmon and sea trout from Meath's rivers are delicious; tasty Dublin Bay prawns are actually a species of lobster. Try Irish soda bread, perhaps with a hunk of Glebe Brethan cheese from Tiernans farm in Dunleer (www.glebebrethan.com), or the county's whiskey-laced fruitcakes. Purists may prefer to drink the

whiskey itself – the Cooley distillery, along the coast in Dundalk, produces both Connemara and Knappogue Castle (www.cooleywhiskey.com).

And... Amble over to Trim Castle's Norman fortifications: you may recognise them as one of the film sets used for *Braveheart*, and they're worth a visit, if only to imagine lusty men brandishing broadswords.

WORTH GETTING OUT OF BED FOR

Viewpoint Also known as the Hills of the Witch, the Loughcrew cairns near Oldcastle are a series of tombs dating back at least 4,000 years. The trek up is steep, but the views from the top are breathtaking – that's if you have any breath left to take. Around the spring and autumn equinoxes, the sun illuminates the central chamber of the largest tomb.

Arts and culture Traditional Irish music and dance abounds; catch a formal performance or an exuberantly informal pub gig; see www.comhaltas.ie for listings. The Snail Box (www.snailbox.ie) near Slane and Brogans (046 943 1237) in Trim both host regular evening shows. For insights into the Celtic past, visit the Brú na Bóinne Centre (041 988 0300) near Donore to see the eerie megalithic tombs of Newgrange; it's very popular in summer, so go early to avoid the crowds.

Activities Get over to Rathe House (046 905 2376) in Kilmainhamwood for a clay-pigeon shoot, off-roading or rafting. According to folklore, County Meath held its own Olympics long before the Greeks; chariot racing might be a bit tricky to organise, but horse riding is still an option; try the Kells Equestrian Centre (046 924 6998). While you're in Ireland, take advantage of 'the Mulligan' – a discretionary free stroke – at the Navan Golf Club (046 907 2888) or on the Royal Tara course (046 902 5508). Alternatively, soar above the ruins of Trim Castle with Irish Balloon Flights (046 948 3436).

Perfect picnic Head for the banks of the Boyne; we love the view from the fields across the river from the ruins of Trim Castle. Pick up freshly baked bread and sweet picnic treats at George's Patisserie (041 982 4493) in Slane.

Daytripper Dublin is only a short drive from Meath, and one of its most famous treasures hails from the Royal County. So, in between indulging in the shoppers' delights of Grafton Street and enjoying the city's pub scene, why not take a quiet moment in Trinity College Library to contemplate the artistic marvel that is the Book of Kells? Some 1,200 years old, it's reckoned to be the finest illuminated manuscript of the Western world (www.tcd.ie).

Walks The Boyne Ramparts Walk runs from Navan along the River Boyne to Stackallen Bridge; it's a beautiful five-mile stroll (ring the Solstice Arts Centre on 046 909 2300 for details). There are lovely forest walks at Mullaghmeen and Deerpark a few miles outside Oldcastle; the area has plenty of fine picnic spots, too.

Shopping Dublin's boutique shopping is hard to beat, but there are some excellent craft and artisan studios in County Meath. We particularly like Thomas Diem Pottery (01 835 9083; www.diempottery.com) in Ashbourne and Seamus Cassidy's woodturning studio in Navan (041 982 5032). If you want to sample some of the delicious local produce, Oldcastle has a farmers' market on Fridays, while Kells holds its market on Saturdays.

Something for nothing The Hill of Slane is where St Patrick is said to have lit a holy fire to burn the snakes out of Ireland. There are the dramatic ruins of a Franciscan monastery on the hilltop and, if you can climb your way up the twisting staircase in the bell tower of St Patrick's church, you'll be rewarded with one of the best views in the county.

Don't go home without... putting some money on the horses. There are some fantastic racecourses in County Meath, including Bellewstown (www.bellewstownraces.ie) and Fairyhouse (www.fairyhouseracecourse.ie), the home of the Irish Grand National on Easter Monday. At the annual Laytown meeting, the horses actually race along the beach (041 984 2111).

MAJESTICALLY MEATH

The Hill of Tara has huge historical, spiritual and mythical significance. Although its history spans four millennia, all that remains of the royal fortress (apart from heart-stopping views) are its mighty earthworks and the Lia Fáil or 'Stone of Destiny'. The stone is said to be magical, and will apparently roar if the rightful king of Ireland puts his feet on it. Well, it's worth a try...

DIARY

Easter Monday The Irish Grand National is run at the Fairyhouse Racecourse in Ratoath (www. fairyhouseracecourse.ie). **May** The Drogheda Arts Festival (www.drogheda.ie/artsfest) brings five days of street theatre, song and dance to town. The Tattersalls International Horse Trials (www.tattersalls.ie) sees Ireland's finest bloodstock on show. **July** Le Chéile Festival (www.le cheile.com) in Oldcastle is a small yet hugely rich celebration of arts and music. The Midlands Music Festival (www.midlandsmusicfestival.ie) is a showcase for rock, pop and folk. **August** The biggest live gigs in Ireland are held at Slane Castle (www.slanecastle.ie); the Rolling Stones played in 2007. **September** The autumn equinox is marked by druidic ceremonies at ancient sites, particularly the Hill of Tara; similar events take place on the summer solstice in June.

Bellinter House

STYLE Urbane Palladian mansion
SETTING Rolling riverside parkland
DESTINATION County Meath

'As we swish up the drive, the 18th-century mansion looms ahead, all twinkly and inviting. It feels as though we're in a Jane Austen novel, arriving at a much-anticipated ball hosted by the local catch'

The period-drama spectacle continues inside – as finding our room involves an expedition up a cantilevered staircase and along an opulently plastered landing, beneath an elaborate, oval-domed ceiling that's propped up by slightly bonkers Doric columns. Those Georgians certainly never stinted on their proportions. Our room has the requisite high ceilings, floor-length sash windows and impressively heavy shutters that come as standard issue in country piles. Apparently Bellinter takes its name from the Irish words *Baile* and *Saoir*, which means 'home of the carpenter' and, judging by the wood panelling that's everywhere, the place has evidently kept many a craftsman busy over the years.

Despite the grand lines, there's still something refreshingly up-to-date about Bellinter House. With modern art on the walls, contemporary furniture dotted about and some very non-18th-century fabrics fulfilling the soft-furnishing function, it's more like hanging out in the country pad of a design-savvy, modern-day squire than being trapped in a stuffy museum. There's even technology that's so complicated I can't manage to switch the lights on. Luckily, Mr Smith has more perseverance with that sort of thing and, before long, he's cracked it – and is happily reassessing the mood and readjusting accordingly (on what seems like an hourly basis).

A quick glance at the clock stirs us into action and we rush down for a pre-dinner livener, keen not to miss last orders. I needn't have bothered, as the barman tells me that they only really close when the last guest drifts off to bed. Now that's my kind of watering hole.

Our table awaits and, after a quick aperitif, we head for Bellinter House's Eden Restaurant – which is the sister establishment to the award-winning Dublin eatery famous for its seasonal Irish menu. Danny had mentioned something about Smokies, which we notice on the starter menu. The smoked haddock, spring onion, crème fraîche and melted cheese combination makes me wish I'd paid more attention to his recommendations, because it's absolutely delicious. As is the hearty beef and Guinness stew (when in Ireland and all that), which comes with earthy wild mushrooms and a creamy mash. We haul

'It's a grand place you're headed,' says Danny Fitzpatrick in as fine an Oirish accent as can be heard. Danny, our driver from Dublin airport to Bellinter House, County Meath, hasn't so much kissed the Blarney Stone as settled in for an all-night love-in, judging by the rich, anecdote-filled commentary he provides as the lush countryside rolls by. It has been a hard week. So, we can't think of a better way to start the weekend than to sit back and let Danny's lilting soundtrack waft over us, while we gaze out at the luminescent green fields, and the watery sun sets through the mist. I was too whacked even to ask the origins of an anomalous herd of buffalo.

As we swish up the long drive towards the Palladian splendour of our boutique stay, Bellinter House, the 18th-century mansion looms ahead, all twinkly and inviting. It feels as though we're in a Jane Austen novel, arriving at a much-anticipated ball hosted by the local catch. All that's missing is the carriage and an empire-line frock.

ourselves back upstairs and tumble onto a springy marshmallow cloud of goose down and crisp white bedlinen. And, with those sturdy shutters blocking out the big bad world, our sleep is long and tranquil.

The next morning, I pull back the shutters dramatically, inviting in the kind of rural Irish view that stars every colour under the sun (as long as it's green). In the far distance, the river Boyne winds languidly through our framed picture, adding focus to the composition. Happily, Bellinter House is not the kind of hotel where the breakfast service is always ending just as you're heading down for it. We're able to indulge in a deliciously lazy full Irish breakfast in bed. It could be early afternoon for all we know. Not that anybody would care if it was.

With so much scenic action happening out the window, we're drawn from our cocoon to go and explore. There's a selection of wellington boots in all sizes, which is handy – who'd ever think to bring their own? We grab a pair each and meander through lush meadows along the banks of the Boyne, wading through long grass and over fields dotted with nonchalant cattle, before resting up by the river's edge, allowing the countryside's natural powers to work their restorative magic.

Funny how time flies when you're busy not doing much at all. Not that there isn't plenty to occupy restless spirits. For anyone who wants to curl up with a good book, the library's packed: with everything from a Joan Collins biography to Irish artists from the 1600s. Then there's a games room and fishing, golf, horse riding and clay-pigeon shooting for the energetic. But after our extensive walk, I'm more in the mood for a lie-down. And there are worse ways to fill a few hours

than to visit the Bathhouse spa, where a seaweed bath and body wrap leaves my skin feeling velvety, dewy and soft – a description equally germane to the Meath landscape.

We retire to the forest-toned drawing room where, gazing at the pretty plasterwork, I'm reminded of an ornately frosted wedding cake. As if on cue, afternoon tea arrives and we settle back on an elegant sofa. Other guests congregate and soon we're chatting about life and love, and wondering why we don't do this sort of thing more often. Maybe it's the fine food and favourite tipples. Or the promise of a comfy bed and a sound sleep. Perhaps it's the soothing emerald tones. Whatever. Danny Fitzpatrick was right: 'It's just grand.'

Reviewed by Serena Rees

'It's like hanging out in the country pad of a design-savvy, modern-day squire'

NEED TO KNOW

Rooms 34.

Rates Sunday to Thursday nights, €200–€320; Friday and Saturday nights, €260–€360, including breakfast.

Check-out Noon; check-in, 3pm.

Facilities Gardens, library, games room, indoor pool, spa, sauna, steam room, hot tub. In rooms, minibar, flatscreen TV, DVD player, Bose sound system, mood lighting, underfloor heating, Voya organic seaweed toiletries.

Children Welcome, with advance notice. Baby cots and foldaway beds provided; babysitters can be arranged. The split-level, beamed duplex rooms in the Stable Block, with beanbag-strewn living rooms, are ideal for small families.

Also Designed by Richard Cassels, 18th-century architect of the Irish Parliament, Bellinter House is of significant historical interest; the grounds and building are therefore open to the public daily from noon until 4pm.

IN THE KNOW

Our favourite rooms Main House rooms have high ceilings, huge bathrooms and cracking views; Main House 1 has a tub for two. For a peaceful, pampering-focused stay, rooms in the Ruin are tranquil, secluded and close to the spa; Ruin 3 has a copper bath, Ruin 4 a roll-top tub. Rooms in the East and West Pavilion are smaller and less dramatic, but they're still charming, with lovely views.

Hotel bar In the Bellinter Bar, pints are pulled perfectly and cocktails are cunningly crafted (we defy you to dislike the honey-sweet Bees Knees martinis); oenophiles could spend a happy day tasting their way round the Wine Bar's impressively stocked cellar.

Hotel restaurant Eden, set in the bright, vaulted basement, is where chef Gary Stinson conjures up Modern Irish bistro fare from fresh seasonal ingredients. All-day grazing and knock-out afternoon teas are served in the grand Drawing Room.

Top table A corner table by the wine-rack wall. On sunny days, on the terrace; or order a pre-packed picnic (complete with wine, champagne and blanket) and roam the gardens until you spy the perfect spot.

Room service Home-made soups, snacks and more substantial fillers are available 8am–11pm.

Dress code Tongue-in-cheek tweeds and cosy cashmere.

Local knowledge The countryside here is rugged and gorgeous – explore on foot in a pair of Bellinter House's loaner wellington boots, or on horseback from one of the five local equestrian centres. The hotel can make arrangements.

LOCAL EATING AND DRINKING

A mere moment from Bellinter, atop the historic Hill of Skryne, **O'Connell's** (046 902 5122) – affectionately known to locals as Mrs O's – is an authentic Irish country pub with buckets of charm. In Navan, get a caffeine fix or wholesome lunch at **Chekhov's Coffee House** (046 907 4422) on Bakery Lane – the home-made desserts are lovely. Informal **Hudson's Bistro** (046 902 9231) on Railway Street has an eclectic Irish menu with Thai, Cajun and Italian flourishes. **The Loft** (046 907 1755) on Trimgate Street is a popular dinner spot, beloved for its crab claws and Boyne salmon; it also has a sleek, buzzy tapas bar.

GET A ROOM!

To book this hotel, go to www.mrandmrssmith.com or ring our expert travel team on 1 800 464 2040. Activate your free membership online (see page 4) to qualify for the exclusive Smith card offer shown below when you book with us.

 SMITH CARD OFFER A Voya seaweed bath for two in the Bathhouse spa; there are two baths, so couples or friends can bathe side by side.

Bellinter House Navan, County Meath (www.mrandmrssmith.com/bellinter-house)

Venice

Florence

Tuscany

Rome

Puglia

Sorrento

ITALY

FLORENCE
Gallery Hotel Art

PUGLIA
Masseria Torre Coccaro

ROME
Portrait Suites

SORRENTO
La Minervetta

TUSCANY
Castello di Vicarello

VENICE
Ca Maria Adele

FLORENCE

CITYSCAPE Rich Renaissance tapestry
CITY LIFE Shopping and strolling

For a city boasting more past glories than the average continent, the capital of Tuscany is excitingly forward-looking. A love affair between culture, commerce and good living, Florence has long been celebrated as the most aesthetically pleasing city in all Italy, if not the world. Between the fairytale squares, centuries-old churches and sprawling palaces run streets alive with sociability, style and irresistible shopping. It's luxury goods a-go-go on roads such as Via Tornabuoni, traditional artisan jewellers on the mediaeval Ponte Vecchio and irresistible deli fare everywhere – the riches on offer are enough to tempt even the toughest of anti-capitalists out of their hair shirts. The city centre is architecturally breathtaking, and compact enough to stroll in an afternoon; follow heart-stirring glimpses of the gingerbread-hued Duomo and its frosting-pale Campanile down narrow streets, and eat Italian soul food in a simple trattoria.

GETTING THERE

Planes Florence airport (www.aeroporto.firenze.it) is a 20-minute drive from the centre of town. A taxi costs about €25. You can also fly into Pisa airport, from where a direct train takes 45 minutes and costs €5.
Trains The main station (Firenze SMN) is behind Piazza Santa Maria Novella, with high-speed connections to other cities in Italy and Europe (www.trenitalia.com).
Automobiles Having a car in Florence can be a hindrance – in fact, it's next to pointless – but a vehicle is essential if you want to explore the surrounding Tuscan countryside.

LOCAL KNOWLEDGE

Taxis You can't hail the metered white taxis in the street; go to a designated *fermata di taxi*. The major ones are manned 24 hours a day; most operate 7am–1am. Socota is one of the city's biggest cab firms (055 4242).
Currency Euro (€).
Dialling codes Italy: 39. Florence: 055 (always dial the '0').
Tipping culture Most restaurants add a cover charge that includes service. Locals leave a little small change in bars.
Siesta and fiesta Florentines are early risers. The main museums open at 8.15am (presumably the extra quarter

hour allows everyone to enjoy a civilised espresso en route) and close at 7pm or shortly before; some close on Mondays, so plan your cultural forays accordingly.
Do go/don't go Florence is packed throughout the summer, when it's also very humid; go in early spring or autumn.
Packing tips Aside from a sketchbook, a sunhat and sensible shoes, pack light: modern Florence is a shopper's paradise.
Recommended reads Even the title of EM Forster's *A Room with a View* conjures up piazza-perfect imagery; Giovanni Boccaccio spins 100 mediaeval yarns in *The Decameron*; and anyone who fancies themselves as a Renaissance muse should read Sarah Dunant's *The Birth of Venus*.
Cuisine If Florentines have a mantra, it's 'Give us this day our daily bread': they are fanatical about their filone, a salt-free loaf so beloved that its stale remnants are used to pad out dishes from ribollita (a hearty bean, vegetable and black cabbage soup) to pappa con il pomodoro (bread and tomato soup). If you like your bread salty, go for schiacciata, an oil-drizzled crusty focaccia. Other Florentine favourites include thick grilled Chianina steaks (bistecca alla fiorentina), pasta e fagioli (pasta with beans), cold cuts and game, all washed down with glasses of Chianti.

And... Take a wrap if you're going to peek inside churches; bare shoulders (and shorts) are frowned on. Binoculars are handy for neck-craning views of ceiling frescoes.

WORTH GETTING OUT OF BED FOR

Viewpoint Climb the 414 steps to the top of Giotto's Campanile, or up Brunelleschi's Duomo itself for 360-degree city views (www.duomofirenze.it). Alternatively, drive up to Fiesole and look down across the entire town; if you have time to linger, take lunch on the loggia of Villa San Michele (055 567 8200) and gaze across the Arno valley.

Arts and culture Sixty per cent of the world's most important works of art are housed in Italy – and half of these are in Florence. You'd have to try very hard to have a bad time just following your feet, but there are a few things you won't want to miss. The Cathedral of Santa Maria del Fiore, aka the Duomo, was built in 1434, and its dome is a celebrated feat of engineering. The castellated Bargello palace contains an unrivalled collection of Renaissance sculpture. The famous Uffizi Gallery houses breathtaking Botticellis, Michelangelos and Leonardos. Book museum tickets ahead if you can: ring 055 294 883 or visit www.polomuseale.firenze.it for details.

Activities If you feel overwhelmed by the amount of sights to see, hire an expert: Camilla Baines at Bellini Travel (www.bellinitravel.com) can get you private viewings; and Florence Guides (335 807 1180; www.florenceguides.com) are knowledgeable and entertaining, and can create personalised tours. Or see it all from the water as you're punted down the Arno in a traditional barchetto, with Florence River (0571 501366; www.florenceriver.it). Exercise-hungry desperados could go for a jog in Cascine Park (also a lovely place for a riverside stroll, hack, cycle or swim). Speed freaks head to Mugello (055 849 9111; www.mugellocircuit.it), an hour from Florence, to watch Ducatis, Aprilias and Ferraris scream round the race track.

Perfect picnic The historic *centro* is more blessed with piazzas than parks: find yourself a little enoteca (not Enoteca Pinchiorri, though, unless you're in the mood to splash out €12,500 on a bottle of Pétrus), and linger alfresco over a glass of good wine and a snacking plate of cheese or cured meats. Alternatively, take your pasta-à-porter to the lawns of Cascine Park or to Piazzale Michelangelo for a heart-stirring view of the city.

Daytripper Rent a vintage car and explore the hills (0578 263298; www.zephyrus.it). Spend a romantic day in San Gimignano, famous for its fortified towers, cobbled streets and sweeping views; or Siena, a perfectly preserved mediaeval city set on a round square (the campo). Pisa, home to the improbably leaning tower, is also not too far.

Walks Behind the Palazzo Pitti, the beautiful Boboli Gardens offer meandering walkways, shady arbours and statue-littered lawns – and provide the template for almost every noteworthy formal garden in Europe.

Shopping The Mercato Centrale in San Lorenzo is a huge covered food market crammed with every kind of local speciality. The market on Sundays around Piazza San Lorenzo can be disappointing; try hunting for antiques at the Piazza dei Ciompi fleamarket instead. There's a huge market at Cascine Park on Tuesday mornings. For designer clothes, Luisa Via Roma (055 217 826) on Via Roma is a high-fashion multi-designer boutique; Via Tornabuoni is luxury-label heaven. Universo Sanchez (055 288 244) on Via Il Prato is a lifestyle shop with clothes, a bar and a barber. Poke your nose into Farmacia Santa Maria Novella (055 216 276) on Via della Scala for the finest handmade fragrances.

Something for nothing Stroll across the Ponte Vecchio and spend a morning on the Oltrarno (the other side of the river): browse the antiques shops on Via Maggio; peek at the high Renaissance and baroque altarpieces in Brunelleschi's Santo Spirito church; and hang out in the shady piazza afterwards.

Don't go home without... deciding which piece of art you'd like to sneak back home in your suitcase. No cheating – you can only pick one!

FABULOUSLY FLORENCE

Michelangelo's pert-bottomed *David* has symbolised Florentine civic pride for over 500 years, but the five-metre-high nude hasn't always had an easy ride: he's been struck by lightning, had his toes hammered off, and his left arm was smashed by an airborne bench. Now, he's attracting too much attention, and moves are afoot to shift him away from the city centre to diminish the crush of adoring tourists (the real statue in the Accademia is visited by 1.3 million people every year).

DIARY

March/April Blowing up a wooden ox cart (*scoppio del carro*) outside the Duomo is the explosive way Florentines celebrate Easter. **May–June** Maggio Musicale Fiorentino (www.maggio fiorentino.com) is one of Europe's oldest music festivals. **Late June** Festa di San Giovanni around the 24th honours the city's patron saint; highlights include a regatta near Ponte Vecchio, a fashion show, and fireworks in Piazzale Michelangelo. **Early September** Children, lanterns, processions, street performances and parties: it's all going on for Rificolona on the 7th. **Late November** High-speed sightseeing in shorts at the Firenze Marathon (www.firenzemarathon.it).

are all stylish but solid, eschewing gimmicks or novelties. It's through a heavy door that we enter our room. The colour palette is cream, silver and dark wood – and the feel is contemporary but classical. Comfort isn't sacrificed in order to accommodate whimsical design. As tempting as it is to stall here and savour our surrounds, the sound of live music lures us down to dinner.

The only public outdoor space at Gallery Art is a delightful little terrace leading out from the bar and restaurant. If you don't manage to grab an alfresco spot, inside is also appealing, whether you sit at the bar, on a sofa in the corner or at a table for two next to the wall. Peopled by young and old, dressed-up and low-key, its biggest surprise isn't the clientele or the decor, but the Italian, French and Japanese fusion cuisine – best illustrated by the test tubes of flavoured oils and soy sauce on each table. Mr Smith congratulates the wine waiter on the way his recommended red harmonises with the tender fillet; such is the Italian love of food, our sommelier says, in earnest: 'This is a beautiful moment for you.'

The windows in our bedroom block any sound from outside, blinds stop the Tuscan sun from rousing you prematurely and you can programme your desired temperature. The value of a room in which you can have such a wonderful night's sleep should not be underestimated. And breakfast is just how it should be: a spread of fantastic pastries, hams and cheeses – we could happily stay a few hours grazing, especially as, in the library-style lounge and dining area, there is no clue that an outside world exists.

The queues for all the major sights are so enormous on this scorching day that we can't face broiling in a line only to be jostled along with a herd, however world-famous the art. You're guaranteed a fix of one masterpiece at least – a copy of Michelangelo's *David* is considerably placed outdoors for all to see at their leisure – so after a look at him we escape the crowd and head, predictably, to Boboli Gardens, south of the river, past Palazzo Pitti. They are deceptively enormous, and we get lost in lush green foliage.

F lorence can coax amazement out of the most jaded traveller. Snooty voyagers who've been known to snigger at the more naive tourist's awed remark about how old everything is will find this is one place where they can't help but share those sentiments.

We are delighted to discover that our very chic boutique hotel, which comes courtesy of the Ferragamo family, is seconds from the 14th-century Ponte Vecchio. It's the stuff fairytales are made of: tiny jewellery shops line the narrow cobblestoned bridge. As do tourists. Happily, in a city teeming with sightseers, the Gallery Hotel Art is all calm.

Modern lines and a minimalist-inclined decor contrast with the flagstone streets and centuries-old architecture outside. The overriding impression of the Gallery Hotel Art is one of impeccable quality; furniture and fittings

We're grateful for the workout we get from the steep inclines, in anticipation of the mountains of pasta we plan to consume at lunch. Our destination for doing just that is at the other end of town, but Florence doesn't take long to traverse. It also gives us the opportunity to get some first-class window-shopping done en route. Prada, Salvatore Ferragamo, Gucci and Hermès line our path, and then appear again on the next street. Markets overflow with handbags, belts and jewellery. If you're someone who shares the sartorial sensibilities of Donatella Versace, you're especially in luck; glittering tassels and animal prints abound. So if you want to give Carmela Soprano a run for her money, you know where to head.

'Contemporary but classical, the hotel rooms don't sacrifice comfort for whimsical design'

It may only be a step up from Michelangelo mousepads in the tourist stakes, but we take a walk from the Duomo, round to Santa Croce, past the Uffizi and the Palazzo Vecchio. Despite the fact that the sun is nowhere near the yard-arm yet, and our lunch is barely digested, Florence is home to such quality comestibles that we can't help thinking about our next meal. We pause for thought, and a glass of Chianti. Italians won't neglect any opportunity to feed or be fed; so antipasti are on offer where you'd be lucky to get a bowl of peanuts back home.

After peeking in a few venues attempting contemporary cool, we settle on family-run trattoria Buca Mario, where there are plenty of locals, affording us the best of both worlds: food that tastes homemade, and waiters well-practised in playing both server and entertainer to English speakers. We end our night with an animated 'chat' with the matriarch of the trattoria; the fact that she speaks as little English as we do Italian doesn't impede our merry conversation over a limoncello. It's the fitting finale to a whirlwind stay at Gallery Hotel Art, into which we've still squeezed all we craved. Rather like the power generation of drinks and medicines that fuels us these

NEED TO KNOW

Rooms **74, including 14 suites.**
Rates **€290–€1,500, including breakfast. Excludes 10 per cent tax.**
Check-out **Noon. Earliest check-in, 2pm.**
Facilities **Library, laundry service, limousine, use of a nearby golf course. In rooms, free broadband internet access, satellite TV, minibar.**
Children **Though the hotel is not geared towards children, it does welcome families. Children under three stay free, and extra beds can be provided for older children. Babysitters are available with 48 hours' notice.**
Also **Smaller pets are welcome, and the hotel staff are happy to help with sourcing anything you might need – from emergency collars to squeaky toys.**

IN THE KNOW

Our favourite rooms **Three penthouses on the seventh floor have amazing views over the skyline of this most atmospheric of cities; 701 has two terraces (with a super-comfy lounger on the deck); and 707 and 708 have terraces and a river view.**
Hotel bar **For the best cocktails in town, cosy up in the trendy Fusion Bar – all big windows, exposed brickwork and bustle – or take your drinks out to the decked terrace. Last orders vary.**
Hotel restaurant **(The Fusion Bar) Shozan-Gallery – it shares space with the bar, hence the name – serves up a unique blend of excellent Mediterranean/Japanese cuisine. Expert sommeliers will happily suggest wines to accompany each course.**
Top table **Go alfresco on the terrace when it's warm.**
Room service **7.30am–11pm. Snacks are available until noon, after which you can select dishes from the restaurant menu.**
Dress code **The clientele is as eclectic as the fusion on the menu; you'll fit in whatever your style.**
Local knowledge **Everyone knows about the Uffizi – that's why the queues to get in are so long. Get your fix of Renaissance art while wandering in the tranquil, sculpture-filled Boboli Gardens (055 238 8786) instead. The adjacent Palazzo Pitti (055 294883) is home to works by Raphael, Botticelli and other great 16th-century artists.**

LOCAL EATING AND DRINKING

Cantina Barbagianni (055 248 0508) on Via Sant'Egidio is in an ancient cellar; ideal for dinner à deux or a great-value two-course lunch. **Cibrèo** (055 234 1100) on Via dei Macci may be the most famous trattoria in Italy; it's formal and glamorous. Michelin-starred **Enoteca Pinchiorri** (055 242 777) on Via Ghibellina is set in a Renaissance palace, where Giorgio Pinchiorri himself helps you choose from his 150,000-bottle cellar. Make sure you book; jacket and tie required. **Buca Mario** (055 214 179) on Piazza degli Ottaviani is an excellent family-run trattoria preparing traditional Tuscan dishes, including delicious steak alla Fiorentina with cannellini. **Olio & Convivium** (055 265 8198) on Via Santo Spirito is a delicatessen and restaurant specialising in olive oils, native wines and local cheeses. **The Lounge** (055 264 5282) on Piazza Santa Maria Novella, with its terrace opening onto the piazza, is a see-and-be-seen environment for an aperitivo, a mojito or delicious Tuscan cuisine. The decidedly sexy **Pink Room** downstairs is great for cocktails.

GET A ROOM!

To book this hotel, go to www.mrandmrssmith.com or ring our expert travel team on 1 800 464 2040. Activate your free membership online (see page 4) to qualify for the exclusive Smith card offer shown below when you book with us.

 SMITH CARD OFFER **A gift from the luxurious Lungarno Details bath and beauty range, and a bottle of wine.**

Gallery Hotel Art 5 Vicolo dell'Oro, 50123 Florence (www.mrandmrssmith.com/gallery-hotel-art)

PUGLIA

COUNTRYSIDE The shapely heel of Italy
COUNTRY LIFE *Trulli*, madly, deeply

Located in Italy's sunny south, Puglia has a unique character and charm that's relatively unknown to outsiders; the holidaymaking Italians who flock here in the summer keep this laid-back playground of blue sea, golden sands and olive groves strictly a family affair. As at all good Italian get-togethers, food takes centre-stage: fresh fish, melons, figs, olive oils and wines keep those alfresco tables piled high with pretty provisions. Puglia also produces almost all of the country's – in fact almost all of Europe's – pasta. Despite this region seeming Italian down to its boots, the heel of Italy has a very cosmopolitan past. Greek, Spanish and Norman settlers have all paid visits, leaving behind a quirky mishmash of architectural heirlooms from Baroque churches and Romanesque cathedrals to whitewashed fishing villages and the conical stacked-whorl rooftops of Puglia's iconic *trulli*.

GETTING THERE

Planes Between them, Puglia's airports at Bari and Brindisi (www.aeroportidipuglia.it) handle regular flights to other Italian and European cities – including Rome, Venice, Barcelona and London – for US connections. Trains Puglia's main towns and cities are connected by train, but local services are often slow (albeit scenic). Fast trains from Rome or Milan are operated by TrenItalia (www.trenitalia.com). To visit remoter areas, such as the 13th-century Castel del Monte, you'll want wheels. Automobiles Car rental is absolutely essential if you really want to explore – it's the only way to get from A to B; pick one up at the airport when you arrive. Chancing upon tiny, ancient villages as you drive along is all part of the fun.

LOCAL KNOWLEDGE

Taxis Trying to hail a cab on the street won't get you anywhere; go to a rank or ask your hotel to ring and order one for you. They are metered and levy small extra charges for luggage and after 10pm.
Currency Euro (€).
Dialling codes Italy: 39. Bari: 080; Brindisi: 0831; Lecce: 0832. Leave in the 0, even when dialling from abroad.

Tipping culture A service charge is usually added to bills, but it is customary to tip an extra five or 10 per cent.
Siesta and fiesta Shops open early and close late, with long lunch breaks. Most close on Sundays and Monday mornings, except in resort areas. Banks also break for lunch, reopening at 3pm for an hour. Restaurants only start to fill at 9pm.
Do go/don't go Fine, sunny weather starts in spring and lasts well into autumn this far south; if you don't fancy sweltering-hot weather and busy beaches, visit in early or late summer for milder conditions and the chance to bag a decent spot on the sand.
Packing tips Summer wardrobe staples – think laid-back southern style, not chichi Capri – and a good roadmap. Recommended reads Francesca Marciano traces a family's past as they pack up their Puglian home, *Casa Rossa*; follow Charles Lister's footsteps as he journeys *Heel to Toe*; taste the Puglian countryside that inspired London's River Café chefs Rosie Gray and Ruth Rogers in *Italian Two Easy*. Cuisine *La cucina Pugliese* is about full, fresh flavours and robustly rustic recipes: grilled swordfish with sprigs of oregano and a squeeze of lemon; and antipasti such as

roasted aubergines and marinated peppers. Head down to Cisternino in the Itria Valley, and take in its colourful Monday morning market – a fabulous source for the ingredients that make Puglia's antipasti dishes truly sumptuous. Wander through the stalls hung with slender salamis and heavily laden with pungent blocks of pecorino, creamy balls of burrata, fresh capers, neon-bright lemons and plump scarlet tomatoes; there'll be a natural abundance of sun-ripened fruit and vegetables, and delicious olive oils. Definitely try the native pasta, orecchiette, or 'little ears'. The region's wine ain't bad, either: Salice Salentino, a visceral red, is one of the best.

WORTH GETTING OUT OF BED FOR

Viewpoint The hilltop mediaeval town of Locorotondo on the Murge plateau gives panoramic views of the sprawling Itria Valley; Selva di Fasano also offers surround-vision eyefuls of fields, woods and Adriatic coast. Arts and culture Make sure you make time to see the *trulli*; the Itria Valley is home to thousands of these circular limestone dwellings, with beehive-shaped roofs and whitewashed walls, particularly around Alberobello, where the settlements have earned Unesco World Heritage status. Puglia's towns are perfect for cultural grazing: Lecce (aka Salento) is known for its splendid baroque architecture; Bari and Otranto have impressive cathedrals; and Taranto's Museo Nazionale Archeologico (www.museo taranto.it) has a dazzling display of Hellenistic jewellery. Activities The region's flat terrain and grove-lined country roads are ideal for cycling; pugliainbici.com (340 264 4128) will deliver bikes to you, as well as helmets and other gear. The gentle coastal route from Bari to Monópoli offers a taste of Puglia's varied scenery. Stop for an ice-cream at Il Super Mago del Gelo on Piazza Garibaldi in clifftop fishing village Polignano a Mare. Alternatively, swap wheels for waves and charter a boat to follow the same route, finding private coves along the way. Rent clubs and tee off at the San Domenico golf course (www. sandomenicogolf.com) near Savelletri. Learn to whip up delicious Puglian dishes or traditional pasta with a local chef: Masseria Torre Coccaro offers cookery classes. Best beach The beaches on Puglia's Adriatic coast are pine-fringed and gorgeous, interspersed with hidden bays and sheltered lagoons. The village of Torre Canne has a long stretch of soft sand and shallow water for cooling off toes after working on the tan – it'll be crowded in August. Daytripper The Parco Nazionale del Gargano, in the north

of Puglia, juts out like the spur on Italy's boot, and contains the deep, dark Foresta Umbra (Forest of Shadows). These 11,000 hectares of pine, oak and beech are the last remnant of an ancient forest that once spread over most of Puglia (www.parks.it). Gather picnic ingredients en route and find a shady spot to spend the afternoon. Walks Puglia was once a Greek colony, and nowhere is this heritage more obvious than in Ostuni, where gorgeous whitewashed houses gleam against the cobalt sky and sea. Go along later in the day to join the locals on their *passeggiata* – the see-and-be-seen evening stroll. Shopping Bari's Via Sparano is the place to go for fashionable boutiques. Bari also has some excellent delicatessens: De Carne (080 521 9676) on Via Calefati is popular for local meats and cheeses. Almost every town in Puglia has its own market day, when, in addition to fruit and vegetables, you can find handicrafts such as terracotta pottery and embroidery; Ostuni's is on Saturday. Lecce's historic centre is a handy place to pick up crafty souvenirs. Something for nothing The shopkeepers in the *trulli*-town of Alberobello pride themselves on their hospitality and their wares. Many offer free wine-tasting in their shops. Don't go home without... dining at Grotta Palazzese (080 424 0677) at 59 Via Narciso in Polignano. This hotel restaurant is worth visiting for its unusual location – carved into a sea cliff. Traditional Puglian dishes are served with Adriatic wines inside a cave that has been used for entertaining since the Duc de Leto first converted the grotto into a hall in the 18th century.

PERFECTLY PUGLIA

Puglia produces some 70 per cent of Italy's olive oil. There are many different varieties, each with its own unique flavour, depending on the production method and harvest time: cold-pressed extra-virgin oils in particular develop distinctive aromas and delicate fragrances. The olive press of Il Frantolio di D'Amico Pietro near Cisternino (080 444 4671; www.ilfrantolio.it) offers tours and gourmet tastings – great for wine buffs looking for a new challenge.

DIARY

June One of the oldest motorcar races in the world, the Rally del Salento (www.rallydel salento.com), takes place in Lecce; it's a nail-biting event characterised by its sharp turns.
July The Festival della Valle d'Itria (www.festivaldellavalleditria.it) – a three-week event in the town of Martina Franca, with opera, classical and jazz performances – starts tuning up around the 20th of the month. **September** Jazz in Puglia (www.jazzinpuglia.it) brings international artists to Lecce for an all swinging, all dancing festival of soul, blues and syncopation.

Masseria Torre Coccaro

STYLE Refined fortress
SETTING Sun-baked and sea-scented
DESTINATION Puglia

'We stroll through the hotel's gardens and orchards. Arched windows smile among trailing plants and fragrant climbing honeysuckle; we're tempted to tarry by carved recesses with padded seating'

There's nothing like letting your imagination run a little wild to kick-start a sojourn in Puglia. The wedding guests were dancing the tarantella, a dance that originated in the Middle Ages in nearby Taranto as a means of treating the sickness, melancholy and madness brought about by the venomous bite of the tarantula.

On a terrace adorned with large wicker baskets and buckets of red, pink and orange flowers, a team of bustling waiters brought us menus, an amuse-bouche of mango-wrapped salmon mousse, and a dish of fresh organic vegetables served with a bowl of olive oil and balsamic vinegar. I ordered oysters (served with Parmesan to enhance their taste) and spaghetti, black with squid ink, while Mrs Smith settled for carpaccio with slices of deep-red wild strawberry. As we sat sipping grappa – and seven able-bodied men carried the grand piano back to its home in one of the several public lounges (all of which exhibit works of art from the local galleries) – we had a rare moment of total agreement: it was the best food we had ever eaten.

Our room, an old hayloft, was exquisitely furnished, with linen bedding, silky sofas, large baroque mirrors and antique furniture from the local markets. Much to Mrs Smith's delight, every current English and Italian magazine lay on the wooden desk. In the cave-like bathroom, a giant showerhead presided over a square stone bath surrounded by jars of blue bath salts and indulgent body-moisturising creams, lotions, shampoos and conditioners.

The next morning saw us strolling for a sumptuous breakfast through the hotel's formal gardens and orchards. Arched windows smiled among trailing plants and fragrant climbing honeysuckle; we were tempted to tarry by carved recesses with padded seating built into the thick whitewashed walls and wooden benches in the garden. A lake-style pool sloped down from the outdoor restaurant to a subterranean Aveda spa offering a vast selection of massages, and therapies in hot and cold pools. Not suffering from stress or tension, we drove off down the coast in search of Italy's best seafood restaurant instead.

Extending as far as the heel of the Italian boot, Puglia has a relieving lack of tourist-friendly features. The road signs

The night sky sparkled with stars as we watched the massive electric entrance gates to Masseria Torre Coccaro swing open. A long drive, flanked by rows of flickering candles in terracotta dishes and lanterns, led us to a car park containing at least a hundred cars. Having expected a small place with just 30 rooms, we walked timidly towards the warmly welcoming reception area. An open 17th-century chapel beamed out light and revealed crucifixes, while white tuxedo-clad men and elegantly dressed Italian models crowded around the massive grand piano that dominated a fairy-lit courtyard.

The hotel was hosting a full-scale wedding. Couples whirled rapidly in a clockwise circle around the courtyard, accompanied by the hectic rhythms of tambourines and mandolins. Then they suddenly stopped and whirled anticlockwise for a while, before changing direction again. 'That's the dance they did in *The Godfather*,' said Mrs Smith. 'It must be a Mafia wedding. How exciting!'

are confusing, and it was proving impossible for either of us to tell if the arrow directing us was pointing down the road or to the right. Whichever option we took, we inevitably arrived at either a *zona industriale* or a forlorn housing project on the edge of town. We had to weave through a formidable number of one-way streets to get back onto yet another country lane. We got lost, but deliciously so. Puglia is perplexing. Even the shabby and dishevelled look of the countryside's olive groves, ruined walls, and scruffy caper and cacti fields is misleading: the region's volcanic soil, reliable

'Our room, an old hayloft, was exquisitely furnished, with linen bedding, silky sofas, large baroque mirrors and antique furniture from the local markets'

sunshine and gentle winter rain produce two-thirds of Italy's olive oil, one-tenth of Europe's wine, and fruit and vegetables that taste as they did when we were children.

Polignano a Mare's Ristorante da Tuccino rises abruptly from the coast. Old men in vests watched their families dive from the rocks or sunbathe like lazy lizards on the craggy promontories, while posh yachts and speedboats ploughed through the bright-blue mottled sea. A mixed clientele of peasants, yuppies and kids in shorts tucked into enormous platters of fishy and crustacean delights. Wisely, we left the ordering to the head waiter.

Hours later, satisfied, full, but surprisingly refreshed, we drove back along the coast to Torre Coccaro to drink and swim at the hotel's private beach club before being swallowed by our bed. Unless one is a strict dieter, Torre Coccaro provides authentic hospitality at its very best. We left, swamped with reluctance and wishing we weren't already married.

Reviewed by Howard Marks

NEED TO KNOW

Rooms 37, including six suites.

Rates €262–€1,272, including breakfast and taxes.

Check-out Noon, but may be extended on request (subject to availability); earliest check-in, 2pm.

Facilities Aveda spa with small indoor pool, Turkish bath, Jacuzzi and gym (shiatsu, ayurvedic and reflexology massage are available, as are yoga and qi gong classes), bike hire, horse riding, hair stylist, nine-hole golf course. In rooms, TV/DVD player, free WiFi.

Children Under-twos stay for free. Children aged between two and 12 are charged at €80 a night. Baby cots, high chairs and car seats are available, as well as armbands for water babies. Babysitters can be arranged for €15 an hour.

Also Masseria Torre Coccaro's beach club, with a restaurant and private 14-metre yacht for guests' use on request, is five minutes away. The hotel also runs a cookery school.

IN THE KNOW

Our favourite rooms Room 35 is a junior suite in an ancient tower, with beautiful sea views and cosy fireplace. Room 6 is the Orange Garden suite, set into the bedrock, with large dining area, private garden and Jacuzzi. Room 16 has a private patio and a beautiful vaulted ceiling.

Hotel bar Set in one of the towers, the atmospheric bar is the perfect place for a pre-dinner cocktail – enjoy it in the evening sunshine on the garden terrace.

Hotel restaurant Egnathia restaurant is set under the star-shaped vaults of the old stables and serves organic Puglian cuisine. The beach-club restaurant specialises in sushi and fish dishes.

Top table Under the pergola with a view of the pool.

Room service Call for food between 7am and 2am. A snack menu is available when the restaurant kitchen is closed.

Dress code Floaty and breezy.

Local knowledge Hire bikes from the hotel, and pedal out into the Puglian countryside (not forgetting your sunhat). The fascinating Roman harbour of Egnatia, close to Masseria Torre Coccaro, was the embarkation point on the ancient route to Byzantium, and its ruins are well worth a visit.

LOCAL EATING AND DRINKING

In the neighbouring fishing village of Savelletri, **La Marea** (080 482 9415) has a simple ambience and does excellent seafood, including oysters and sea urchins. Try the gilthead in a salt crust. In the historic centre of Ostuni, **Osteria del Tempo Perso** (083 130 4819) on Via G Tanzarella Vitale serves delicious local recipes, such as spigola cartoccio con vongole and puréed fava beans. **Chichibio** (080 424 0488), in the pretty village of Polignano a Mare, offers exquisite grilled fish, seafood pasta and home-made lemon ice-cream. Nearby **Ristorante da Tuccino** (080 424 1560), which has a terrace overlooking the Adriatic, does fabulous seafood platters. We also like the family-run **Il Poeta Contadino** (080 432 1917) in Alberobello, which teams fine Puglian dishes (pork with smoked Scamorza cheese, monkfish in a potato crust) with a wonderful wine cellar.

GET A ROOM!

To book this hotel, go to www.mrandmrssmith.com or ring our expert travel team on 1 800 464 2040. Activate your free membership online (see page 4) to qualify for the exclusive Smith card offer shown below when you book with us.

 SMITH CARD OFFER A one-hour massage each in the spa.

Masseria Torre Coccaro 8 Corso da Coccaro, 72015 Savelletri di Fasano, Puglia
(www.mrandmrssmith.com/masseria-torre-coccaro)

ROME

It's true: Rome wasn't built in a day – and almost every moment of its lengthy and splendid history is still visible in some form. Parts of the city are perfectly mediaeval; classical columns rise from paved piazzas; Renaissance and Baroque buildings soar skyward, and breathtaking sculpture assaults your senses at every turn. With the Vatican in town, Easter and Christmas are highlights on Rome's calendar, but pilgrims of a more artistic persuasion flock to the tiny city state all year round to adore Raphael and Michelangelo's Sistine Chapel frescoes. Rome is also about the art of life – food, fashion and fun are enjoyed with religious zeal in this most sensual of European capitals. To get the best from this cultural Goliath of a destination, live *la dolce vita* as the locals do: colonise a café in the Campo de' Fiori; linger longer over rustic pasta in a traditional trattoria; let your feet wander and your eyes roam.

GETTING THERE

Planes Rome is served by two airports: Fiumicino and Ciampino (www.adr.it). A cab from Fiumicino will set you back €60 (it should be less on the way back, though). From Ciampino, the 15km taxi ride to the city centre costs €30.
Trains Stazione Termini is the main station, providing express city connections to Florence, among others (www.trenitalia.it). The Leonardo Express to Fiumicino airport departs every half an hour and takes 35 minutes.
Automobiles Driving in Rome is not for the nervous and, unless you want to venture further, a car will be more of a pain than a pleasure. You can park in blue zones for €1 an hour; the daily rate for carparks is around €25.

LOCAL KNOWLEDGE

Taxis Hail one anywhere, or ring the number displayed at ranks. Avoid unlicensed taxis, especially for airport rides – if in doubt, get your hotel to arrange transport.
Currency Euro (€).
Dialling codes Italy: 39. Rome: 06 (you must still dial the initial '0' of the area code when dialling from outside Italy).
Tipping culture A 15 per cent service charge is usually included on restaurant bills; leave small change for drinks.

Siesta and fiesta Romans holiday en masse in August, so shops and restaurants may be closed: ring ahead to check opening times. Some businesses also close for lunch.
Do go/don't go In summer, the city gets sweaty; you may prefer spring or autumn, but winter is the quietest. One of the pleasures of a visit to the Eternal City is exploring its countless lesser-known treasures at random; Rome's museums are often surprisingly uncrowded.
Packing tips Rosary beads; a pick and shovel to unearth ancient artefacts lurking beneath the streets (the reason the city's metro system has never been completed); footwear that can handle marching up Roman roads.
Recommended reads Edward Gibbon's *The Decline and Fall of the Roman Empire* is *the* history book; HV Morton's 1950s memoir *A Traveller in Rome* is absorbing and evocative; Anthony Capella's lit-rom-com *The Food of Love* is peppered with mouthwatering culinary descriptions of life in the city.
Cuisine The foundation of Roman food is *cucina povera* (rustic cooking); much of it focuses on working-class staples and offal, such as trippa alla Romana (tripe with tomato ragù) and baccalà (fried salt cod), but there are plenty of less challenging delicacies, such as saltimbocca

(veal rolls with sage) and rigatoni all'amatriciana (pasta with tomato and pancetta sauce). Testaccio, where the city's stockyards once were, is still the preserve of Rome's butchers, and there are dozens of traditional trattorias and delis, including Volpetti (06 574 2352) at 47 via Marmorata. Rome has a vibrant café culture, so join locals for a piazza-view coffee. Tasting note: no self-respecting Roman would order a milk-laden cappuccino after mid-morning; go for a high-octane ristretto instead.

WORTH GETTING OUT OF BED FOR

Viewpoint Piazza del Campidoglio by night, for panoramas over the Forum and the Palatine, or the top of the Spanish Steps, for a view over the Centro Storico to St Peter's – one Shelley and Keats doubtless swooned over.
Arts and culture Wherever you wander, Rome's importance to Western civilisation is inscribed in stone: the Colosseum, the Forum, St Peter's and the Vatican, the Sistine Chapel, and the Pantheon – the most perfectly preserved ancient building in the city. Its dramatic interior is richly decorated in a multitude of marbles, all beneath a massive masonry dome. If you want to visit the Vatican, plan carefully: queues can be horrific and if you're only here for a few days, your time might be better spent elsewhere: Galleria Doria Pamphilj (www.doriapamphilj.it) is a palazzo groaning with 15th- to 18th-century treasures; Villa Borghese boasts spectacular grounds and a magnificent art collection (www.galleriaborghese.it). Rome's cake-layers of history are illustrated near the Colosseum by the Basilica di San Clemente (www.basilicasanclemente.com), a 12th-century church built on top of a 4th-century Christian basilica, founded on an older pagan temple.
Activities Attend a wine-tasting class at the prestigious International Wine Academy (06 699 0878), adjacent to Il Palazzetto hotel (www.mrandmrssmith.com) just off Piazza Spagna. Row, row, row your boat gently across the lake at Villa Borghese (http://en.villaborghese.it). Saddle up and ride along the catacomb-lined Appian Way with private guiding company Nerone (www.nerone.cc). If swordplay in sandals lights your fire, train as a gladiator with Gruppo Storico Romano (www.gsr-roma.com). Prefer less bloodthirsty spectator sports? There's an air of the Colosseum about the Stadio Olimpico, home to Rome's two soccer teams: AS Roma and Lazio. Weekend game seats between September and May cost from €20; book tickets at www.ticketliquidator.com or at the Orbis ticket agency (06 474 4776) in Piazza dell' Esquilino; you'll need ID.

Perfect picnic With so many trattorie to try, picnicking won't be top of your to-do list; that said, there are few pleasures as great as licking a hazelnut gelato while you stroll the sunny side of the streets. Try Giolitti (06 699 1423) at 40 via Uffici del Vicario; or Il Gelato di San Crispino (06 679 3924), near the Trevi fountain at 42 via della Panetteria.
Daytripper Bypass the beaches and join the locals as they head for the cool waters of Lake Bracciano (www.lakebracciano.com), a picturesque reservoir just outside Rome.
Walks A stroll at sunset in the lush Pincio Gardens, above Piazza del Popolo, is a pleasantly romantic way to wind down (and cool down) after a day's sightseeing.
Shopping Via Condotti, starting at the foot of the Spanish Steps, is Rome's most prominent shopping street; Via Frattina runs parallel, along the same big-label lines. Via del Corso focuses on younger styles. If you prefer edgy and unusual, poke about near Piazza del Popolo; Via Sistina is good for small, stylish outlets. On Via Nazionale, you'll find leather stores and a handful of boutiques. In Trastevere, the open-air Porta Portese fleamarket (every Sunday from 5am till about 2pm) is the largest in Europe.
Something for nothing An audience with the Pope is free (www.vatican.va). Or test the world's oldest lie detector in the portico of Santa Maria in Cosmedin, where you can play at being Hepburn and Peck in *Roman Holiday*. No fibbing, though: if you lie while your hand is in the carved-marble Bocca della Verità ('mouth of truth'), it will be bitten off.
Don't go home without taking a morning stroll round the lively farmers' market in Campo de' Fiori by Piazza Navona.

ROMANTICALLY ROME

Think of Rome and you'll probably picture Italy's gilded youth zipping around astride hornet-like mopeds. Do as Fellini's dashing journalist Marcello did and scoot the sights aboard a vintage Vespa or polished Piaggio with Happy Rent (www.happyrent.com). Hire one and wobble wherever your wheels take you, or let Happy drivers ferry you on a city tour. If bikes just ain't your thing, you can also rent cute-as-a-button mini-motors, including Smart cars and Fiat 500s.

DIARY

March/April On Good Friday, a torch-lit procession from the Colosseum up Monte Palatino re-enacts the stations of the cross. **May** Primo Maggio (www.primomaggio.com) in Piazza San Giovanni welcomes spring with a big free gig. **June–July** Around Sound, a month of nightly jazz at La Palma Club (www.lapalmaclub.it). On 29 June, the feast day of Rome's patron saints shuts the city down. **September** Photography festival FotoGrafia (www.fotografiafestival.it). La Notte Bianca (www.lanottebianca.it) keeps you up all night with music, drama and dance. Big-hitting culture at the RomaEuropa Festival (www.romaeuropa.net). **October** Celluloid is celebrated at the Rome Film Fest (www.romacinemafest.org). **November** Roma Jazz Festival (www.romajazzfestival.it) brings bebop, swing and all things snazzy to the Eternal City.

Portrait Suites

STYLE Eternal City fashion house
SETTING Spanish Steps shopping streets
DESTINATION Rome

'On the way up to our room, we climb a staircase lined with shoe-themed photographs and sketches, and smouldering pictures of old-Hollywood glamour girls'

'I 'll talk to the big man and see what he can do,' says Andrea, our concierge. We were discussing the weather, so I'm a little confused. Having just flown from grey London to Rome – to stay in the Eternal City's Portrait Suites, a sleek townhouse hotel owned by iconic shoe-design family Ferragamo – we are disappointed to discover the forecast for the next few days isn't good. I visualise bruise-coloured clouds hanging ominously over piazzas and palazzos, and can't help but wish for a little divine intervention, too.

Situated above the Salvatore Ferragamo men's store, Portrait Suites occupies an elegant building just minutes from the Spanish Steps and the fashion thoroughfares of vias Condotti, Borgognona and Frattina. We couldn't be closer to the action. Indeed, Mr Smith and I are even given a Salvatore Ferragamo lookbook to flick through while Andrea makes our dinner reservations. Only in Italy...

The dedication to style continues inside. On the way to our room, we climb a staircase lined with shoe-themed photographs and sketches, and smouldering portraits of old-Hollywood glamour girls. Our simple-but-luxurious room is equally chic. It has beautiful black wood walls, complemented by a grey colour scheme that allows the occasional bright pop of lime green in unexpected places such as the curtain lining. And there's a lovely window seat overlooking the beautiful yellow Hermès store on the other side of Via Condotti – it's the ideal place to curl up with an early morning espresso or late-evening prosecco.

Mr Smith and I spend a delightful couple of hours lounging on the enormous emperor-size bed and watching the massive flatscreen TV. Mr Smith particularly enjoys opening and closing the cupboards in the in-room kitchen but, alas, refuses to rise to my challenge to whip us up a quick gnocchi alla Romana. It's so peaceful. Though we can hear hints of the bustle on via Condotti below, all that changing-room swishing and credit-card swiping at street level seems a long way away.

We finally rouse ourselves to shower and get dressed for the evening – me in a navy 3.1 Phillip Lim sweater and

jeans, and Mr Smith in a shirt and white linen trousers – and head out to begin our own Roman holiday. Inspired by a photograph of a stunning pair of heels on the wall, I decide to wear my new six-inch Louboutins. But, oh, how unforgiving cobblestone streets can be to stiletto-clad feet. Despite the fact I'm clinging onto Mr Smith's arm, the stones on the Via della Pace nearly claim my dignity a few times. I eventually persuade him to set me down outside a nearby trattoria, where we indulge in delicious artichoke antipasti, wonderful pasta with bacon, pecorino and more artichokes, and the kind of tiramisu Mr Smith has been searching for his entire life.

After a refreshing sleep, Mr Smith and I spend the following morning wandering around the gardens of the Villa Borghese, one of the city's finest art galleries. They're beautiful. We make our way along wooded avenues to sit beside fountains and ornate Renaissance statues, and watch with concern as an elderly couple, seated beside a running track, shear off their dog's hair with evident relish. Is this an attempt to make him more aerodynamic? Afterwards, fully aware we're a big romantic cliché, we hire a boat and row out to the middle of a tranquil, terrapin-filled lake. It's turtle bliss.

We return to Portrait Suites and climb to the roof terrace. It's one of the hotel's biggest draws. On one side we can see the Villa Medici and the Spanish Steps; on the other, the domes of the city's churches are ascending heavenwards. More charming than any of these, though, are the tiny rooftop gardens the citizens of Rome have cultivated amid the pinnacles. The sun is setting, and the heady mix of yellows, browns and oranges, bathed in that heavy evening light, is just breathtaking. 'We need to start taking more mini-breaks,' says Mr Smith as he reclines in a deckchair. I couldn't agree more.

The next morning, we finally make it inside Villa Borghese, where both Mr Smith and I are stunned into uncharacteristic silence by the sheer dynamism of Bernini's four exquisite sculptures. Afterwards, we head to Piazza Navona for a final ice-cream. We sit on a bench and savour our last hours. But, for now, the skies are blue and the sun warms my upturned face, its heat seeping down into my body. The big man has definitely come through for us.

Reviewed by Bee Shaffer

'Though we can hear hints of bustle on
Via Condotti, it all seems a long way away'

NEED TO KNOW

Rooms 14, including six suites.

Rates In low season, €380–€1,600; in high season, €480–€2,000, including Continental breakfast; excludes 10 per cent VAT.

Check-out Noon, though later check-out is available on request. Earliest check-in, 2pm.

Facilities DVD library, free WiFi throughout. In rooms, flatscreen TV, DVD/CD player, iPod dock, kitchenette.

Children Under-threes stay free, and extra beds can be provided for older children (check rates when booking). Babysitters are available with 48 hours' notice, and charge €20 an hour.

Also Portrait Suites is within walking distance of almost everything you'd want to see in Rome, but the hotel can call for a chauffeured car if you're too lazy for legwork. Pets are welcome – as long as they weigh less than 10kg.

IN THE KNOW

Our favourite rooms Deluxe Studio 53 gets our vote, with its large marble bathroom and a balcony that's ideal for breakfast with a view. The Penthouse Trinità dei Monti occupies the hotel's top two floors and has an L-shaped terrace overlooking the famous church, as well as a shower-sauna in the bathroom. Superior Studio 11 has a lovely view over via Bocca di Leone.

Hotel bar Cushioned wooden furniture, lanterns and potted shrubs line the roof terrace, which also boasts an open fire for warming you up in winter. There's a fully stocked honesty bar. For €20 a day, you can have unlimited access to the stash.

Hotel restaurant There's no restaurant at Portrait Suites, but a generous breakfast platter of cereals, pastries, eggs and yoghurt is served every morning on the rooftop terrace.

Top table Perch on the edge of the rooftop terrace with a glass of prosecco and look out over the skyline as the sun sets.

Room service Drinks and a short snack menu are available in rooms between 7am and 1am.

Dress code Palazzo pants and platform shoes.

Local knowledge If all roads lead to Rome, then all catwalks lead to Via Condotti: as well as Ferragamo on the hotel's ground floor, you'll find a bevy of boutiques, including Bulgari, Valentino and Laura Biagiotti there. Swap high fashion for high culture at the Keats-Shelley House (06 678 4235), part museum, part monument to the Romantic poets who all but colonised the area in the 18th century. You'll find it at the foot of the Spanish Steps on the Piazza di Spagna.

LOCAL EATING AND DRINKING

Portrait Suites nestles in a hotbed of excellent places to boost your shopping stamina. Two streets away on Via Borgognona, **Nino** (06 679 5676) has been feeding the glitterati classic Italian dishes with a Tuscan accent for decades. Over in Piazza Augusto Imperatore, **Gusto** (06 322 6273) is justly famed for its pizzas, but in truth it's a culinary polymath, with a restaurant, wine bar, cheese shop and kitchenware store, all boasting beautiful interiors. **Il Brillo Parlante** (06 324 3334) on Via della Fontanella is the perfect low-key lunch stop, with a well-stocked little wine bar upstairs. **Porto di Ripetta** (06 361 2376), on Via di Ripetta, specialises in innovative seafood dishes – the swordfish roulades are not to be missed.

GET A ROOM!

To book this hotel, go to www.mrandmrssmith.com or ring our expert travel team on 1 800 464 2040. Activate your free membership online (see page 4) to qualify for the exclusive Smith card offer shown below when you book with us.

 SMITH CARD OFFER A gift from the luxurious Lungarno Details bath and beauty range, and a bottle of wine.

Portrait Suites 23 Via Bocca di Leone, 00187 Rome (www.mrandmrssmith.com/portrait-suites)

SORRENTO

COASTLINE Pastel-painted Amalfi
COAST LIFE Sailors and sirens

The Ancients believed that mariners were lured to the islands and towering cliffs of the Amalfi Coast by the songs of the Sirens, mythical maritime temptresses who gave their name to the seductive town of Sorrento. The orange and lemon groves, ancient vineyards and perfect climate of the Campania region prove no less irresistible today. Even the sumptuous villas that clamber up the vertiginous mountainsides in pastel ranks of peach, pink and primrose seem to be jostling to get the perfect view of the Bay of Naples and the brooding volcano of Vesuvius. Cruise across to Capri or along the coast to Positano and you'll feel very much the Fifties starlet (or swell) as you hop off boats and hit the boutiques. With an elegant palazzo or piazza at every turn, the clifftop town of Sorrento bewitches all comers, and its tiny beaches and family-run restaurants are deservedly bustling in summer. All this, and sunshine, too...

GETTING THERE

Planes Naples' Capodichino airport (www.gesac.it), around 40 miles from Sorrento, is the most convenient entry point for the Campania region, with regular international flights.
Trains Naples has three main rail stations: Mergellina, Campi Flegrei, and Napoli Centrale on Piazza Garibaldi, which is linked to Sorrento by the twice-hourly Circumvesuviana train; see www.vesuviana.it for details.
Automobiles It's worth renting a car to be able to explore Campania's countryside, but traffic can be bumper to bumper on the coastal road in summer. If you're brave, you might fancy getting a moped for scooting along the streets.
Boats There are regular hydrofoils from Naples to Sorrento; they take about 35 minutes (and are therefore a faster option than the Circumvesuviana) and leave from Molo Beverello harbour, off Piazza Municipio.

LOCAL KNOWLEDGE

Taxis Expensive, but most sights in Sorrento are walkable anyway; if you need a ride, taxis line up at ranks outside stations and on squares. Alternatively, ring 081 878 2204.
Currency Euro (€).
Dialling codes Italy: 39. Sorrento: 081. (Don't drop the zero from the area code when dialling from abroad.)
Tipping culture Although restaurant bills usually include a service charge, an additional 10 per cent tip is customary.
Siesta and fiesta Increasingly, there is a trend towards more flexible hours. Roughly: Monday to Sunday, 9am–1pm and 5pm–10pm; in low season, some shops close on Saturday afternoons and Monday mornings. Evenings start late here; people are often only leaving for dinner at 10pm.
Do go/don't go High summer can see temperatures soar to nearly 40ºC and the traffic become unbearable, but if you avoid August you'll be spoilt for sunshine and have a bit more elbow room. The winter wind can be brisk.
Packing tips Binoculars, for speedboat spotting. Leave room for some handmade leather sandals from Amedeo Canfora (081 837 0487; www.canfora.com) in Capri.
Recommended reads *The Last Days of Pompeii* by Edgar Bulwer-Lytton peers into the lives of the city's ill-fated inhabitants; *The Talented Mr Ripley* by Patricia Highsmith follows the Italian exploits of a cunning sociopath; *The Volcano Lover: A Romance* by Susan Sontag explores a historic love triangle in 18th-century Naples.
Cuisine Fish and crustaceans are the starlets of the

Sorrentine kitchen – no doubt lured onto dry land by the siren call of sharing a dish with one of Campania's mainstay ingredients: sweet extra-virgin olive oil, plump tomatoes, fior di latte cow's-milk mozzarella (which, in Sorrento, is plaited) and robust herbs. Specialities include a rich lobster dish cooked with tomatoes, unctuous octopus casserole and sautéed shrimp. Pick up some sweetly strong limoncello liqueur, infused with Sorrentine lemon peel, or nocino, made from walnuts and coffee beans.

WORTH GETTING OUT OF BED FOR

Viewpoint There are fantastic coastal views from the Villa Communale park next to the 14th-century church of San Francesco, which also holds regular classical concerts.
Arts and culture The Greeks and Romans respectively left their highly civilised mark on this coastline, in the form of temples, roads and civic architecture. In 79AD, Sorrento had an awesome view of the eruption of Mount Vesuvius and the destruction of Pompeii. It's possible to wander the well-preserved ruins of the doomed city; see www.pompeii sites.org for details. (Wear comfortable shoes – Roman roads are surprisingly ill-suited to sandals.) Most of the best treasures dug out from beneath the ash (as well as finds from Egypt, Ephesus and Herculaneum) are on show at the Museo Archeologico Nazionale di Napoli (081 442 2149), a Battenberg-pink building atop Santa Teresa hill.
Activities Promenade along the marinas and lie on one of the little sundecks, or charter a boat to take you on a jaunt along the Amalfi coast to the pretty town of Positano – try Mediterraneo Charter (081 807 2947; www.mediterraneocharter.it) for bespoke day trips aboard the *Princess*. Take your love of the ocean to a deeper level with D&D Sorrento Diving Center (081 877 4812; www.sorrentodivingcenter.it): there are plenty of excellent local scuba-diving sites to explore. Fiery temperament and a head for heights? Scale the flanks of Mount Vesuvius to peer down into its smoky crater and out across the Bay of Naples (or you can just enjoy its flora and fauna; visit www.parconationaledelvesuvio.it for walking routes). Learn to make pasta at the Sorrento Cooking School (www.sorrentocookingschool.com).
Perfect picnic Take a packed lunch of prosciutto platters or pastries and head out of town: a mile west of Sorrento is the Bagni della Regina Giovanna at Punta del Capo, a landlocked lagoon where the 15th-century Queen Joan II of Naples reputedly bathed. An opening in the cliffs creates a calm natural seawater pool.

Daytripper On the fabulous island of Capri, you can explore dramatic scenery or rub shoulders with the jet-set while you shop in a miniature Milan of boutiques. The hydrofoil takes 20 minutes, but if you hire a speedboat in Sorrento, you can explore coves and secluded beaches – try Nautica Sic Sic (081 807 2283; www.nauticasicsic.com). Inland, Ravello is a charming town near Amalfi, famed for its splendid views and ancient villas (www.ravellotime.it); notable visitors from Boccaccio and Wagner to Virginia Woolf and Gore Vidal have all fallen under its spell.
Walks Hike along the Sentiero degli Dei (Path of the Gods), a spectacularly scenic route along the cliffs of the Amalfi coast; go solo or trek with a guide (www.onthegodspath.com). Alternatively, follow the Via del Capo from the Corso Italia as it winds around the little cape of Sorrento for surround-vision views of the town.
Shopping Via San Cesareo is Sorrento's liveliest shopping street, with lots of browsable boutiques, and it's the place to find regional handicrafts such as ceramics, scented candles, lace and embroidered linens; Pelleteria Lolanda has great leather belts and bags. More shops line Corso Italia. There's also a weekly street market on Tuesdays.
Something for nothing Sneak into one of the wood-inlay workshops and observe the traditional craft of intricate marquetry (tarsia); try Gargiulo Salvatore at 33 Via Fuoro. Don't go home without... some exquisite handmade Amalfi paper: if you hanker for the days when mail meant ink and parchment instead of a 'ping' in your inbox, visit La Scuderia del Duca (089 872 976) on Largo Cesareo Console.

SUITABLY SORRENTO

Massa Lubrense, a gorgeous stretch of coast and country at the tip of the Sorrentine peninsula, is an area of hamlets, lemon groves and unrivalled sea views. The groves are criss-crossed by mule paths and marked footpaths – fantastic for an afternoon of strolling, especially in spring, when the lemon and orange blossom is in bloom.

DIARY

March/April Brass bands parade Sorrento's streets before an incense-waving crowd for Easter. **Late June** The Festa di Sant'Andrea on the 27th sees the statue of Amalfi's patron saint hiked down to the sea, followed by pyrotechnic performances. **Late July** Boats and fireworks in the bay beneath La Minervetta for the Festival of Sant'Anna on the 26th. **July–September** The Sorrento Summer of Music pulls in internationally renowned classical and jazz musicians. **November** Sorrento's International Film Festival, Italy's foremost silver-screen salute (www. sorrentotourism.com). The 30th is Saint Andrea's birthday: cue more statue-toting processions.

La Minervetta

STYLE Quirky nautical
SETTING Neapolitan cliffhanger
DESTINATION Sorrento

'What a view it is: fishing vessels bob
prettily, boats carry day-trippers back
and forth to Capri — and Vesuvius looms
in the background to complete the scene'

So, we're heading for the Amalfi Coast, after a detour to Pompeii, which this Mr Smith (no fan of a crumbling Doric column, me) hopes will be brief. My fellow traveller, however, has other ideas, confessing to a hitherto unrevealed fascination with the Romans.

When we roll up at La Minervetta, all parched and sun-weary, the turquoise-tiled lobby and white walls feel cooling and refreshing. The Fifties villa above Sorrento has a prime clifftop position overlooking the Bay of Naples, that postcard-perfect swathe of the Amalfi Coast immortalised in *The Talented Mr Ripley*. Steadfastly refusing to turn its back on the bay, the hotel has floor-to-ceiling windows in every room, and its three sun terraces (the upper for cocktails, mid-level for chilling and a Jacuzzi pool on the lowest) are perfect platforms for admiring the panoramic view.

And what a view it is: fishing vessels bob prettily, boats carry day-trippers back and forth to Capri – and you've only got Vesuvius in the background to complete the scene. Inside the hotel, the visual impression is of clean contemporary lines. Splashes of navy and red canvas break up the all-over white; freeform eclecticism means European design mags are piled neatly on Indonesian coffee tables; old ships' maps hang alongside flamboyant modern art; and brightly coloured ceramic bowls overflow with lemons. The overall effect is cosy, comfortable and welcoming – stylish, but never styled.

At sundown, we head to the upper terrace, order a Negroni each, and relax on stripy canvas steamer chairs. Our reverie is briefly interrupted by the faint and very distant sound of raised voices from the harbour below. We strain to hear, and can just about make out that a heated debate seems to have broken out between two fishermen in a single wooden boat. A flame-haired temptress literally wades into the fray to sort them out; eventually, the two hotheads are pulled apart, and retreat to nurse their bruised machismo. We half expect someone to pass the hat round, but this is no show – just a display of Neapolitan fuse-blowing.

It's all peace and harmony in our world and, suitably clad for a summer night, we trip 300 steps down to the harbour for dinner at Delfino, where the Med laps mesmerically beneath our boardwalk table. The staff speaka da kinda Eenglish you'd think confined to amateur dramatics, but the fresh fish, tricolore salad and jugs of rosato they deliver are authentic, down to the last drizzle of locally pressed extra-virgin. We skip pudding and join the *passeggiata* round the town square, seeking our new passion: lemon granita. It's the ideal street food: refreshing, tasty and low-cal. (Just as well, since over the course of the weekend, we try it from every outlet going.) We can reliably recommend you don't bother with anything from a machine or a gelateria; for the best, visit one of

'We head to the upper terrace, order a Negroni each and relax on stripy canvas steamer chairs'

153

the street vendors, who'll shave off a cupful of fragrant crystals from a barrel set over ice. Lemon's the only option worth considering. No point messing with a true classic, after all.

The soft tolling of church bells provides our wake-up call on Saturday. Time for buckets of cappuccino and platefuls of fresh fruit on the terrace with all the other Mr and Mrs Smiths: Swedish architects, French designers and, um, us. We decide to grab an early hydrofoil and head for the island of Capri to sate our upmarket-shopping appetites at MaxMara, Gucci, Prada, Tod's et al.

That evening, we dine at Il Buco, which wears its Michelin star proudly on its sleeve. We're lucky to land one of the sought-after tables outside, and lap up the amuse-bouches, obedient service and culinary twists with everything. The chef's signature seems to be a scoop of sorbet. There's a spoonful of iced balsamic with the cuttlefish starter, and a scoop of delicious prosecco sorbet to cut through the lemon and almond soufflé.

Stuffed to the gills, we talk about exploring the town. We're certainly tempted, but there's something that draws us back to La Minervetta. We settle down with a limoncello nightcap or two and leave the blinds up. It's hard to beat a room with a view of the starlit Bay of Naples and Italy's best granita shack just around the corner.

Reviewed by Neil McLennan

NEED TO KNOW

Rooms 12, including one junior suite.

Rates €180–€400, including hot breakfast and taxes.

Check-out 11.30am, but flexible; check-in, 2pm.

Facilities Oversized outdoor hydro-massage tub (open 1 May to 15 October), sundeck with wooden loungers, plenty of books. In rooms, flatscreen TV with Sky, WiFi, minibar, Crabtree & Evelyn bathroom products, hairdryer, laptop-sized safe.

Children Under-14s can share parents' rooms, with baby cots provided at no extra charge, and additional beds costing €50 a night. Babysitting can be arranged (€10 an hour).

Also There's plenty of free on-site parking, which is handy if you've rented a car.

IN THE KNOW

Our favourite rooms Every room is sea-facing, with fantastic views: some have floor-to-ceiling windows, some have balconies. Rooms 7 and 8, 11 and 12 are adjoining pairs, ideal for families (all the rooms are sound-proofed, too). The junior suite has two balconies and a large walk-in hydro massage shower – no bath, though.

Hotel bar Guests can take drinks anywhere they like; La Minervetta feels more like a private home than a hotel, and every guest soon locates their favourite spot.

Hotel restaurant No restaurant – breakfast is served buffet-style at the kitchen table, with hot eggs and bacon cooked to order. The hotel's dramatic cliff-clinging location means getting to a restaurant in the fishing village below involves a steep climb down the stone stairs; however, there are plenty of restaurants in town, an easy 10-minute walk away.

Top table On the terrace with a splendid view across the Bay of Naples.

Room service Bar snacks are available 24 hours a day, and there's a mini-fridge in your room for drinks.

Dress code Laid-back summer cool.

Local knowledge If you're catching a boat to one of the islands, La Minervetta can pre-book you a parking space in the underground carpark at Sorrento's main port – which is usually full by 9am.

LOCAL EATING AND DRINKING

Delfino on the Marina Grande (081 878 2038), just down the steps from the hotel, is the place for a relaxed waterside lunch of wonderfully fresh fish and seafood. For a more formal lunch, try next-door at **Taverna Azzurra** (081 877 2510). Michelin-starred **Il Buco** on Il Rampa Marina Piccola (081 878 2354) is one of the best restaurants in Sorrento – it's a good idea to reserve one of the tables outside on a warm summer evening. The tasting menu is an excellent choice. Have drinks at **Photo**, a lounge bar-turned-restaurant just off Piazza Tasso (081 877 3686). In summer, its garden is perfect for cocktails or a glass of wine. **Da Gigino** on Via degli Archi (081 878 1927) is the best place for a pizza, and has super spaghetti vongole. La Minervetta can also whisk you to and from the charming family-run restaurant **Da Filippo** (081 877 2448), just outside Sorrento, for a taste of authentic local cooking.

GET A ROOM!

To book this hotel, go to www.mrandmrssmith.com or ring our expert travel team on 1 800 464 2040. Activate your free membership online (see page 4) to qualify for the exclusive Smith card offer shown below when you book with us.

 SMITH CARD OFFER A bottle of prosecco.

La Minervetta 25 Via Capo, 80067 Sorrento, Campania (www.mrandmrssmith.com/la-minervetta)

TUSCANY

When mother Nature was handing out charm, she really piled the goods up high when it came to this above-the-knee patch of Italy. If the slopes dotted with cypress trees and olive groves don't win your heart, the aromas and flavours of the flourishing farmlands will, via your stomach. Perfectly preserved Renaissance treasures in culture-packed ancient cities scream out for attention, while the quieter lure of Maremma, Italy's Wild West, is characterised by beautiful coastline, hot springs and marshes once patrolled by cowboys. Don't let Tuscany's popularity with tourists fool you into thinking you can't get away from it all here – sure, this beloved province will treat you to the gamut of holiday activities, but whether you feel like touring mediaeval hilltop villages, hitting the designer boutiques or flopping on a lounger-for-two for poolside sun-kissed snoozing, Tuscany's allure can be enjoyed at every pace.

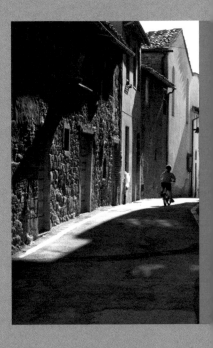

GETTING THERE

Planes Pisa's Galileo Galilei airport (www.pisa-airport.com) is the most convenient regional gateway, but Florence and Rome Fiumicino are options; a two-hour drive from either will get you into southern Tuscany.
Trains Florence acts as a hub for services to other Tuscan cities, including Siena and Pisa (www.trenitalia.com). Grosseto is on the main Rome-Genoa line and has frequent express services.
Automobiles The cities are best explored on foot, but nothing's more fun than driving cross-country with the roof down. Rent classic cars from CLM Viaggi (0577 287415).

LOCAL KNOWLEDGE

Taxis You won't be able to hail one in the hills; your best bet is to ask your hotel to organise pick-ups and transfers.
Currency Euro (€).
Dialling codes Italy: 39. Florence: 055; Grosseto: 0564; Siena: 0577. Don't ditch the '0' when ringing from abroad.
Tipping culture Service charges aren't a huge deal here, so forking out five or 10 per cent is the polite thing to do.
Siesta and fiesta Many shops close between 1pm and 5pm. Restaurants get especially busy from 8pm to 9pm.

Do go/don't go Tuscany can be busy with tourists throughout the summer months, although once you've escaped to your retreat you won't notice. The cities of Florence and Siena in particular are best enjoyed outside the peak summer season.
Packing tips Bring tress-taming headscarves and caps for open-top touring; a designer bikini and some walking shoes will ensure you get the best of coast and country.
Recommended reads Frances Mayes restores a villa and lives the rural dream in *Under the Tuscan Sun*; gothic novel *In Maremma* by Ouida recalls the grittier side of 19th-century romance; John Mortimer's Chiantishire comedy thriller *Summer's Lease*.
Cuisine Peasant fare is at its finest in Tuscany, with fagioli-filled tasty soups and stews often the headline acts. Supporting roles are played by beautiful green cold-pressed olive oil, pecorino cheese, spinach, truffles, mushrooms and wild boar from Maremma's pine forests. You'll certainly appreciate a hearty meal, to help you soak up the irresistible liquid enticements of Chiantis, Brunellos and Montepulcianos. The sweet-toothed should sample the rainbow of tempting flavours on offer at a gelateria,

or try a slice of Panforte di Siena: a spicy, chewy calorie bomb of almonds, honey, cocoa and candied peel. Head to Nannini's patisserie (0577 236009) in Siena at Conca d'Oro on Via Banchi di Sopra for the best panforte, cantucci and orange-infused riciarelli biscuits.

WORTH GETTING OUT OF BED FOR

Viewpoint Tuscany has enough postcard-perfect vistas to fill a book; you'll soon find your own favourite. That said, to the south, there are spectacular views from the ruins of Scarlino Castle, and from Montepulciano's unfinished cathedral.
Arts and culture Great Renaissance treasures gild the entire region – not just Florence. Siena in particular has a wealth of Gothic riches, including the humbug-striped Duomo and its marble pulpit, as well as important works by Donatello (in the baptistery), Duccio (in the Museo dell'Opera del Duomo) and Lorenzetti (in the Palazzo Pubblico). Mediaeval Arezzo boasts Piero della Francesca frescoes; Maremma was once the heartland of the Etruscan civilisation, and their ruins can be seen around Sovana, Sorano and Pitigliano. These beautiful hilltop towns, 20 miles southeast of Grosseto near Saturnia, seem as though they're carved out of the soft volcanic tufa rock. Sovana has some particularly impressive Etruscan tombs.
Activities Soak in geothermal hot springs such as the famous Terme di Saturnia (0564 600111) near Manciano. Spot flocks of flamingos in October at Orbetello lagoon – a popular holiday spot with migratory birds. If you have your own car and want a spectacular ocean drive, try the Via Panoramica on Monte Argentario. There are fabulous walking trails around Monte d'Alma and Poggio Ballone to the north of Castiglione della Pescaia. Maremma provides perfect terrain for horse riding, whilst gaining insight into the traditions of the *butteri* or cowboys; Grosseto-based Equinus (0564 24988; www.cavallomaremmano.it) runs cattle drives in the Alberese park. Visit the Petra winery (0565 845308; www.petrawine.it) for a spot of wine tasting in a spectacular building designed by Mario Botta.
Best beach In the Punta Ala area at the southern end of the Gulf of Follonica, two of the finest beaches are Cala Martina and Cala Violina. Find other sandy beauties around Castiglione della Pescaia, particularly in the Tombolo forest.
Daytripper San Gimignano, Arezzo, Lucca and Pisa are all within easy driving distance of southern Tuscany. Famed for its Leaning Tower, Pisa's other marvels – the cathedral and the baptistery in the beautiful Campo dei Miracoli – are no less spectacular... and a lot more stable. If you like your

architecture unsullied by spandex-clad happy snappers, the ancient village of Volterra is a hands-down winner.
Walks Take a gastronomic tour of Florence's Central Market with charismatic Judy Witts Francini, tasting vintage balsamico and snaffling mouthfuls of cheese before holing up in a traditional trattoria or having a cooking lesson; contact her at Divina Cucina (www.divinacucina.com) for bespoke tasting trips in Chianti and elsewhere in Tuscany.
Shopping Grosseto has some fantastic boutiques, but with all the designer outlets on the outskirts of Florence, it's tempting to head there for cut-price Italian fashion; try the Mall (055 865 7775) on Via Europa in Leccio Reggello. For those who prefer browsing to buying, a local market's the place to head. We love the daily fish market at Castiglione della Pescaia; Siena's Wednesday-morning food market at La Lizza; and, on the third Sunday of every month, the antiques market at the city's Piazza del Mercato.
Something for nothing Siena's Palio race is contested twice a year by the city's 17 *contrade* (town districts), each with their own loyalty-stirring symbol, such as eagle, panther and, um, snail. Enjoy a haphazard tour of the city by trying to find statues of all 17. Or visit stunning Sant'Antimo (www.antimo.it), a 12th-century abbey in Montalcino late in the afternoon; stand outside afterwards, at 7pm (6.30pm on Sundays), and you'll hear the monks singing at vespers.
Don't go home without... visiting the beautiful Poggio Antico winery (0577 848044; www.poggioantico.com) in Montalcino, high in the Brunello range. Have lunch or dinner in its excellent Tuscan restaurant while you're there.

TOTALLY TUSCANY

Wend your way through 'Chiantishire', between Siena and Florence, and comb this territory of vineyards for your own favourite bottles of Italy's legendary wine. Just promise us that you won't include one of the straw-covered variety in your haul. Other options include the wine-growing regions of Montepulciano and Montalcino.

DIARY

April–July The auditory delights of Maggio Musicale Fiorentino (www.maggiofiorentino.com) are a must for lovers of classical music. **May** A historic archery contest takes place in the main piazza of Massa Marittima on the first Sunday after the 20th; the crossbowmen get another go on the second Sunday of August. **July/August** The two Palio dates in Siena see bareback horsemen fight tooth and hoof to win the race round the Campo (www.paliosiena.com). **Early September** Where better to get stuck into a wine fair than at Greve, for the Chianti Classico festival. Head to the Joust of the Saracens in Arezzo for mediaeval mayhem and lance-waving; there's a second event at the end of June (www.portacrucifera.it).

Castello di Vicarello

STYLE Mediaeval castle in the clouds
SETTING Hidden hilltop olive groves
DESTINATION Tuscany

'Ringed by fir trees, the imposing
stone building is set against a
backdrop of lush pastures and hazy
hilltops that's pure Renaissance fresco'

One thing Castello di Vicarello isn't is easy to find. It's been two hours since we left the airport, and Mr Smith and I are still winding through vineyards, rolling hills and ancient villages. We're peering desperately at the map for signs of a 12th-century castle, and it's only by chance that we stumble across a small hand-painted sign. 'Aha,' exclaims Mr Smith. 'We're here.'

The track, however, merely leads to several narrower tracks, and another hour of driving into parts of Tuscany I doubt any other hire car has ever reached. Suddenly, though, just as our two-month-old relationship starts to show its first strains, Mr Smith spots another signpost.

Ringed by fir trees, the imposing stone building is set against a backdrop of lush pastures and hazy hilltops that's pure Renaissance fresco. We walk through an archway and into an ancient courtyard, where we stand silently looking at spikes of grass that poke like green hair from between the cobbles. The warm air carries the scent of rosemary and thyme, and the only sound is the buzz of insects. It's hard to remember which century we're in. It wouldn't have surprised me if someone had appeared from behind one of the urns in full *Gladiator* garb – alas, I have to make do with Mr Smith in his shorts.

Lucia, the manager, spots us, and comes out to say *buon giorno*. Our suite, Vicario, is reached via a stone staircase so thick with mediaeval atmosphere that I can almost visualise Mr Smith tripping ahead of me in a doublet and hose. The first thing I see when I enter our room is a fire that licks and crackles in an enormous stone hearth. The furnishings – wooden tables, huge day bed, wing chair in front of the blaze – are obviously inspired by the owners' years in Bali, and our oak bed continues the Brobdingnagian theme. I am six foot and Mr Smith six foot two, and we can both comfortably make starfish shapes in it.

Both windows in the suite's living area frame views like perfectly composed landscape paintings, and the light they're letting in is getting pinker by the second. When I re-enter the main room after taking a bath, the only illumination comes from the fire and flickering candles that Mr Smith has thoughtfully lit. He knows how to garner brownie points, that man.

Two glasses of wine later, we descend the staircase for dinner with fuzzy heads. We start by asking the attentive Sri Lankan concierge, Damit, for gin and tonics, and he plonks a whole bottle of Gordon's in front of us. Oh dear. Soon we're sniggering like schoolchildren as we think up more inventive ways to misuse our friendly attendant's name: 'Damit, that's a lovely G&T.' 'What time's dinner, Damit?'

Castello di Vicarello is not a place you'd come if you wanted to lose weight. We sit at a table big enough to take a castleful of knights – as well as the peasants from the next village – to enjoy the seasonal Tuscan ingredients, most of which come from the estate. Long before dishes are set down, we smell wild-mushroom bruschetta and fresh ricotta and spinach ravioli being prepared. It's

sturdy stuff. By the time two giant slabs of beef are placed in front of us, we're relying on the castle's two grateful dogs to help us clear our plates.

The next morning, as I prepare coffee, I look out of the window to see thick mist filling the valley below, making us an island in a white, gently swelling sea. It's beautiful. I sip my drink by the ledge, while Mr Smith, who's poking around in the fireplace, lets his cup cool on the mantelpiece. It takes until 11am to get him downstairs for breakfast.

I don't want to spend the next few hours watching Mr Smith burn everything in the log pile, so I lure him to Montalcino, a nearby hilltop town renowned for its wine. Its streets make for delightful strolling territory, and we work up an appetite

'In the morning, as I prepare coffee, I look out of the window to see thick mist filling the valley, making us an island in a white, gently swelling sea'

for lunch. In the cave-like Enoteca la Fortezza di Montalcino, we order a pig-sized plate of charcuterie and begin merrily washing it down with a carafe of Brunello.

'Hang on,' says Mr Smith suddenly. 'Someone's got to drive back.' We decide to settle things with a game of rock-paper-scissors. As I move to smother Mr Smith's fist of stone with my palm of paper, the Italian family on the next table, enjoying one of those leisurely meals at which six generations are in attendance, look utterly bemused.

I'm glad Castello di Vicarello is hard to find. If I had my way, no one would know about it. And, though it may be too early for us to talk about marriage – Mr Smith nearly chokes on his breakfast when I jokingly suggest we come back here to tie the knot – we have definitely decided on one thing. We're going to buy a dog and name it after our concierge. Damit, it would be great if he were as good at bringing us *aperitivos* as his Vicarello namesake.

Reviewed by Amanda Lamb

NEED TO KNOW
Rooms Six suites.
Rates €409–€1,000, including breakfast. Excludes 10 per cent tax.
Check-out Noon, but flexible, subject to availability.
Facilities Spa, gardens, library. In rooms, minibar. Some suites have open fireplaces, and all but one have kitchenettes.
Children Under-eights stay free and baby cots can be provided; extra beds are €70 a night for children (€90 for adults).
Babysitting can be arranged for around €25 an hour.
Also Cooking classes and wine tasting can be arranged in the hotel's kitchen, and horse riding, hunting and fishing can all be enjoyed nearby. Ingredients for the treatments at the thermal spa, which includes a hammam, are sourced from Castello di Vicarello's gardens.

IN THE KNOW
Our favourite rooms Secluded Suite Chiesina is beautifully decorated, with two floors, two bedrooms and fabulous views of the rolling countryside. The smaller but more romantic Suite Sassi has a private terrace with a full-frontal countryside outlook – one of the best panoramas in Tuscany.
Hotel bar Although there's no bar as such, Castello di Vicarello's courtyard and gardens are replete with nooks in which to secrete yourself with an aperitivo or a glass of the hotel's own vintage red.
Hotel restaurant Aurora, the hotel's owner, cooks up a daily-changing menu of home-grown, home-made Tuscan cuisine, served in the candlelit, flower-filled courtyard in summer and by the fireside in winter.
Top table The round table in the corner by reception overlooks the whole dining area and the gardens – perfect for a romantic tête-à-tête. The owners will also arrange a secret spot in the gardens for you to dine in on request.
Room service Snacks are always available in the kitchen, and you can have food brought to your room from 8am to 9pm.
Dress code Rustic and relaxed: skirts for sprawling in, and shirts all a-billow.
Local knowledge Ask Aurora to pack you a picnic and set out for the Ucellina National Park, 100 eye-opening square kilometres that stretch along the coast from the rocky south to the sandy north. Be prepared to gawp at the beautiful Uccellina mountains.

LOCAL EATING AND DRINKING
Paganico is the nearest village of any notable size, with a couple of restaurants and pizzerias; **I Tre Cantoni** (056 490 5041) on Via della Stazione is a great trattoria. **La Locanda nel Cassero** (056 490 0680) in Civitella Marittima, housed in an old olive press, produces rustic regional dishes with flair. Authentic Tuscan trattoria abound in Pienza, about an hour's drive east. Be sure to book a terrace table at **Latte di Luna** (057 874 8606) on Via San Carlo; it serves pici al ragu (spaghetti in wild boar sauce) worth making pilgrimages for. **Il Rossellino** (057 874 9064) in the Piazza di Spagna is a tiny but elegant couple-run eatery with a great wine selection. Humbler, but no less flavoursome, is the fare at child-friendly **Buca delle Fate** on the Corso Il Rossellino (057 874 8272), where locals come in droves to savour the steaks.

GET A ROOM!
To book this hotel, go to www.mrandmrssmith.com or ring our expert travel team on 1 800 464 2040. Activate your free membership online (see page 4) to qualify for the exclusive Smith card offer shown below when you book with us.

 SMITH CARD OFFER A personalised ceramic gift designed by Aurora, the owner, and free entry to Castello di Vicarello's thermal spa.

Castello di Vicarello Strada di Vicarello, 58044 Poggi del Sasso, Cinigiano (Grosseto), Tuscany
(www.mrandmrssmith.com/castello-di-vicarello)

VENICE

CITYSCAPE Archipelago of alleyways
CITY LIFE Walking on water

It may seem curious in a city that sits out in the sea and is characterised by its glittering waterways, but it's walking you should prepare for when you visit Venice. One of the most beautiful cities on earth, despite throngs of tourists in high season, it's an atmopheric maze in which to lose yourself. With most of its buildings right on the water's edge, La Serenissima hides all the snap-happy sightseers well; drift along the canals by gondola and float back in time as you admire Byzantine, Renaissance and Baroque architecture. Give the film-familiar Piazza San Marco a chance to sink in, then follow the locals off the main drags to the best restaurants, hidden churches and lively markets. With so many palazzi and piazze to discover, this is a place for early nights and misty mornings spent wandering charming, traffic-free alleys: it's the romance capital of the world.

GETTING THERE

Planes From Marco Polo (www.veniceairport.com), take the public ferry, or arrive in style aboard a speedboat (this will set you back around €100 each). From Treviso (www.trevisoairport.com), it's a 25-minute taxi journey (€70); or hop on a ATVO Eurobus for €5; it takes 80 minutes. Trains Padua, Vicenza and Treviso are all within easy reach. You can also travel overnight from London or Paris to Venice on the train; see www.eurostar.com or www.italiarail.com for details. Santa Lucia station is on the Grand Canal, so jump on a water taxi or the Grand Canal water bus. Automobiles You'll have to park your rental car on the mainland and get a train or water taxi into the city centre. Boats Venice's vaporettos provide an inexpensive way to get from A to B (www.actv.it). They all take the same route; the difference is how many stops they make.

LOCAL KNOWLEDGE

Taxis Use water buses (€6.50 a journey; €16 for a 24-hour travelcard); you can hail a water taxi, but they're pricey. Currency Euro (€). Dialling codes Italy: 39. Venice: 041. (Always dial the '0'.) Tipping culture In restaurants, service is generally included; Venetians will just round the bill up a few euros, or leave a handful of coins. If you must, add five to 10 per cent extra. Siesta and fiesta Business hours are standard, with food shops closing in the afternoon and reopening 4pm–8pm. Do go/don't go August is hot, sticky and crowded. Autumn can be lovely; November is quietly fabulous when the city is cloaked in fog. February is great if you're going to a carnival ball, but trying to find a hotel room then is no picnic. Packing tips Wear-'em-all-day shoes; mosquito repellent in summer; bubble wrap for protecting fragile purchases. Recommended reads Tears before bedtime in Thomas Mann's classic *Death in Venice*; macabre goings-on in *The Comfort of Strangers* by Ian McEwan; a gorgeous romp through time in *A History of Venice* by John Julius Norwich. Cuisine Venetians exploit the fruits of the sea to produce oceanic dishes as intriguing as the city itself: risotto nero, stained black with cuttlefish ink; silky marinated sardines

and hearty fish soup. Recipes often include ingredients recalling Venice's merchant days (pine nuts, raisins and pomegranate). Other regional stars include fegato alla Veneziana (calf's liver and onions), radicchio from Treviso, asparagus and fiery grappa from Bassano and, of course, Veneto wines, especially pinot grigio, merlot, valpolicella and sparkling prosecco. Venice also has a version of tapas – cicchetti, little savoury mouthfuls best enjoyed around noon with a thimbleful of wine.

And... Venice comprises 117 islands, 409 bridges and some 150 canals; it's the only city centre in Europe that functions entirely without cars – even the ambulances here are boats.

WORTH GETTING OUT OF BED FOR

Viewpoint Piazza San Marco, aka St Mark's Square, is the heart of the city; get a 360-degree sunset-enhanced panorama from the top of the Campanile di San Marco.

Arts and culture Venice is packed full of churches, museums and galleries, with the famous Accademia (041 522 2247; www.gallerieaccademia.org), Basilica di San Marco and Doges' Palace (041 271 5911; www.museicivicivenezia.it) being top of every tourist's hit list. We love the International Gallery of Modern Art at Ca' Pesaro (041 721 127; San Stae waterbus stop) and the Peggy Guggenheim Collection in Dorsoduro (041 240 5411; www.guggenheim-venice.it).

Activities Cross the lagoon by speedboat, with Consorzio Motoscafi Venezia (www.motoscafivenezia.it), or fly a figure of eight above it in a helicopter (www.heliair.it). See real, everyday Venice on an early morning stroll through the Rialto Fish Market (Tuesday–Saturday mornings). Once a bazaar for treasures from the Orient, it now sells fresh everything-from-the-sea to some of the planet's canniest shoppers. Have a private cooking lesson in an art deco villa on the Lido, or taste wines in a palazzo, with Venice Gourmet (www.venicevenetogourmet.com). Listen to baroque music played on period instruments at the Scuola di San Rocco (041 523 4864; www.musicinvenice. com). Journey into a romantic otherworld on a gondola ride – negotiate your price first, though.

Best beach You can rent cabanas and umbrellas for the day on the private stretches of Venice's beach, the Lido, but they don't come cheap. There are public beaches at either end of the island; rent bikes on Gran Viale and explore, or find quieter, cleaner shores at Sant'Erasmo near Burano.

Daytripper Visit Asolo (www.asolo.it), spectacularly set among the cypress-covered Dolomite hills, or the island of Torcello, the classic place to go for an afternoon of peace when La Serenissima is less than serene. For calm upon calm, spend five minutes sitting in its 11th-century cathedral, Santa Maria Assunta. To get there, take the LN vaporetto line to Burano, then the T to Torchello.

Walks Unplanned meanders and peeking round corners is best in Venice, but if you like treasure hunts, you'll love *The Ruyi – Venice Act* (www.theruyi.com), an interactive tour of the city based on a coded book. SMS the hidden codes you find at each historic location to get the next clue.

Shopping You'll find designer labels around San Marco, and especially on Calle Larga 22 Marzo. Boutiques and gift shops line the streets between Piazza San Marco and the Rialto. Don't buy masks in the tourist area: in Dorsoduro is Ca'Macana on Calle delle Botteghe (041 277 6142), which made the masks for *Eyes Wide Shut*. For something different, buy a *forcole*, the wooden oar-rest from a gondola; Saverio Pastor's workshop is on Fondamenta Soranzo in Dorsoduro (041 522 5699; www.forcole.com). For Murano glass, try to get to the workshops on the island of the same name; the same goes for Burano lace.

Something for nothing Get a taste of what it feels like to be on a gondola for next to nothing: look for the yellow 'Traghetto' signs that lead to the water. It's a (short) shuttle service that costs just 50c. If you want the real thing, the average gondola price is €100 an hour – more if they sing.

Don't go home without... having a *caffè* in Piazza San Marco. The price will set your heart racing faster than a ristretto will, but there's a reason tourists flock here – it's beautiful. Il Caffè Florian (www.caffeflorian.com) is legendary.

VERY VENICE

Think Venice and you'll automatically think theatrical costumes and masked balls. There's no fee for turning up during Carnival time, but you must buy tickets to attend any given party – certainly for the best events. Tragicomica (041 721 102; www.tragicomica.it) on Calle dei Nomboli is one of the best traditional *mascareri* (mask-makers) and costumiers, and also the organisation behind the Mascheranda ball. Venetian-born Antonia Sautter, another highly respected costume designer, organises the opulent Ballo del Doge (www.ballodeldoge.com). Tickets for events are expensive, starting at around €300 and climbing up to about €600 or so for the Ballo del Doge, but if you are going to go to the ball, it's best to go all out.

DIARY

February Venice Carnival for masked-ball mayhem; for details, visit www.carnivalofvenice.com or www.carnevale.venezia.it. **June** The Venice Biennale (www.labiennale.org), an art-world extravaganza held every two years. **July** Fiesta del Redentore: flamboyant fireworks commemorating the end of the 16th-century plague. **September** The Regatta Storica boat race, with magnificent gondolas and gondoliers in full regalia. Venice Film Festival (www.veneziafilmfestival.com) – celebs and celluloid on the sands of the Lido.

Ca Maria Adele

STYLE Baroque elegance
SETTING Canalside charm
DESTINATION Venice

'The thing about Venice is this: all
the clichés are true. It really is that
beautiful; it really is that romantic;
it really does take your breath away'

Murano chandeliers, flock wallpaper and heavy damask fabrics, Ca Maria Adele is absolutely Venetian, but its African wood, polished concrete and laid-back, bohemian atmosphere mean it is also undeniably modern and sexy. It is in the heart of Venice's most tranquil area, the art quarter (the Accademia and the Peggy Guggenheim Collection are both nearby), and the only tourists you are likely to come across are lost ones.

The galleries, jewellery shops and bars nearby all serve locals; forget the hotels of the masses around Piazza San Marco – the Adele is infinitely cooler. So, what I really need to make my bliss complete is a handsome Mr Smith at the other end of the bath. But I don't have one; instead, I have brought along a very platonic Mrs Smith, and 15 years of friendship are enough for her to know she really doesn't want to share a bath with me.

Strangely, as the weekend unfolds, we realise this is not a problem. Our lover becomes Venice, which, at every twist of mediaeval passageway, every turn of canal and every step of flagstone, causes sharp intakes of breath and ripples of pleasure. And there's Nicola, the ravishing owner of the hotel (fantasising about running off with him on a gondola – who, me?), who performs all the necessary duties of a dominant male: hailing water taxis, booking restaurants, bringing us coffee/champagne/heart-melting smiles.

Indeed, the gentlemen of Venice couldn't be more delighted to find two girls wandering their city unsquired, and we ended up on a tour of Venice that you won't find in any guidebook – except, of course, this one. After dinner at Cipriani's (don't bother with Harry's Bar – we found it squalid and boring in comparison; take the private speedboat at the end of the Cipriani jetty to the hotel and have the same bellini there, among oriental gardens and flowering jasmine), our speedboat driver felt unable to let two ladies disappear off into the night on their own.

Instead, he led us through the back streets of the city to Bar Centrale, which must be Venice's only hip and happening cocktail joint. They make a mean mojito, framed by blue lighting and brushed concrete and steel, and the DJ plays some surprisingly good tunes. Then our

I'm lying in a Jacuzzi bath, bubbles up to my ears, glass of champagne in hand, gazing out of the window, blinking into the setting Italian sun. Just beneath my window I can hear the canal lapping at the walls of the hotel, as the bells of Santa Maria della Salute chime the hour. I know that there is a man in a striped top, boater and jaunty necktie pushing a gondola along the canal below, because I can hear his pole dip in and out of the water, along with his voice echoing up the walls of the narrow waterway. Really, all that's missing is the ice-cream.

The thing about Venice is this: all the clichés are true. It really is that beautiful; it really is that romantic; it really does take your breath away. And there is nowhere else like it on earth – unless you count the fake one they built in Las Vegas. Hotel-wise, what you want in such an architectural museum of a city is something chic, sophisticated and as far from the madding crowds as possible (and the crowds can be quite something, especially in summer). With its huge

escort recommended Piccolo's, a nightclub that throbbed into the early hours of the morning. It seemed that all Venice's gilded youth were there and, my, weren't the boys handsome? And didn't they dance well? And weren't they persuasive?

Our stumbling into the hotel at 5am didn't seem to worry Nicola (although Mrs Smith was convinced he looked jealous), and the big double bed with 300-threadcount sheets ensured that, by noon, we both felt much better than we deserved. The

'Ca Maria Adele is absolutely Venetian, but with a laid-back, bohemian atmosphere'

Adele serves breakfast (coffee, pastries, eggs – in a room with floor-to-ceiling windows overlooking the canal), but for serious eating in La Serenissima, you have to get out and about. The Cipriani experience was expensive, but when the food is that good it seems worth it. Much more affordable is Locanda Montin, a legendary artists' and poets' haunt that has a beautiful terrace covered with vines, where delicious antipasti, fish and meat are served. That Lord Byron died fat from Venetian pasta is no wonder when you discover he used to eat at the Montin.

At this point, you must take an espresso in the Piazza San Marco, and gaze at the gold-mosaic façade of the Basilica; and you really must let one of those gondoliers push you about the canals, so you can lie back and gaze up at centuries' worth of architecture. And I tell you this because, if Venice is not your principal lover for the weekend, you are probably going to spend most of it flat on your back on one of the Adele's sumptuous beds, twisting the sheets around each other as the Salute chimes through the hours. And then, I'm afraid, you really would be missing out.

Reviewed by Tiffanie Darke

NEED TO KNOW

Rooms 12.

Rates €300–€675 (plus 10 per cent tax), including breakfast and soft-drink minibar.

Check-out Noon, but later on request. Check-in, 2pm.

Facilities Private landing stage, CD/DVD library, complimentary WiFi. In rooms, plasma-screen TVs, CD/DVD players.

Children Children aged 14 and over are welcome; the apartment suite, with its extra bedroom, is the one to go for if you're bringing your teenager.

Also The hotel organises tailored tours around the city. You can also choose from a boat or gondola ride across to the Grand Canal to view the Royal Palace.

IN THE KNOW

Our favourite rooms We loved the themed rooms, in particular the Sala Noire, and the Doge's and Fireside rooms. Room 332 and the Moor's Room have the best views. The third-floor suite also has a good view, and a Jacuzzi.

Hotel bar You can order evening drinks anywhere in the hotel. We suggest the breakfast room or the Moroccan bar on the second floor, or in summer you can have a tipple brought to you on the terrace. After 10.30pm, there's an honesty bar, from which you can obtain prosecco, spirits and a selection of soft drinks.

Hotel restaurant Only breakfast is served. Italian-style afternoon tea is available on the terrace, weather permitting.

Top table Find a spot on the ponyskin sofas in the cosy living room, and take your tea there. You're almost at water level, so the fascinating view of the nearby bridge and church is unlike any you'll see from the upper floors.

Room service Breakfast and drinks are the only options available.

Dress code As romantic as you like. A little excess would be extremely welcome.

Local knowledge The city's not just about gondolas and bellinis. Even though there's high culture to be found each day on almost every street corner, it's worth planning your visit around the Venice Biennale (www.labiennale.org), which takes place every two years. International festivals of art, architecture, cinema, theatre, music and dance mean that, for a couple of months, the city plays hosts to some of the world's finest artists and designers.

LOCAL EATING AND DRINKING

Linea d'Ombra (041 241 1881) on Ponte de l'Umiltà is a great local restaurant on the canal. It is the perfect plot to head to in summer, as it has a lovely terrace with views across to the Giudecca; the ambience is fantastic and the Venetian dishes also surprise. Also near the hotel, **Ai Gondolieri** (041 528 6396), in the Dorsoduro district close to the Guggenheim, is popular with local and visiting carnivores for its meaty Veneto dishes of game and pork, and is famed for its gnocchi and polenta. There's a decent wine list, too. **Cantinone Storico** (041 523 9577) on Fondamenta Bragadin is good for seafood, and has an impressive wine cellar. Definitely try to get a seat by the canal in summer or by the window in winter. Ask the waiter to tell you about the specials – and then trust his recommendations. For a cosy, wine-bottles-along-the-wall kind of osteria, try **Ristorante Cantina Canaletto** (041 521 2661) at Castello 5490.

GET A ROOM!

To book this hotel, go to www.mrandmrssmith.com or ring our expert travel team on 1 800 464 2040. Activate your free membership online (see page 4) to qualify for the exclusive Smith card offer shown below when you book with us.

 SMITH CARD OFFER A bottle of Valpolicella.

Ca Maria Adele 111 Dorsoduro, 30123 Venice (www.mrandmrssmith.com/ca-maria-adele)

MEXICO

MAYAN RIVIERA
Esencia

MEXICO CITY
Condesa DF

PUEBLA
La Purificadora

MAYAN RIVIERA

COASTLINE Coral reefs and jungle ruins
COAST LIFE Sun, sea and salsa

When the conquistadors arrived off Mexico's Yucatan Peninsula in the 16th century, they found an idyllic Caribbean coast of white-sand beaches and warm turquoise waters. What the awe-struck Spanish sailors hadn't expected to find were the mighty temples and sophisticated cities of the Mayan people. Today, beyond the margaritas and maracas of Mexico's holiday-resort playgrounds, the evocative ruins of these temples are not the only lasting testament to Mayan culture: its influence is evident in everything from the fiercely fiery food to the exotic and colourful fiestas – even the limestone landscape, riddled with underground rivers and pitted with sacred pools, exudes an aura of primeval mystery. Stray away from the clubs and bars of Playa del Carmen and Cancún, and you'll discover snowdrift-soft beaches, forest villages and laid-back lifestyle that make for perfect days of shore-side lazing.

GETTING THERE

Planes Cancún International (www.cancun-airport.com) has direct flights to the UK and the US; Miami is only an hour away. A taxi to Playa del Carmen will take around 45 minutes ($60); Tulum is about 90 minutes away ($100).
Trains There are currently no passenger services.
Automobiles It's worth renting a car to explore further afield, although taxis are very inexpensive. Highway 307 provides access to the Mayan Riviera from Cancún.
Boats There are ferries almost hourly from Playa del Carmen to Cozumel; the trip takes 55 minutes – buy tickets at the ferry pier. If you want to rent a boat, walk along Playa del Carmen beach and talk to one of the boat owners.

Do go/don't go August and Christmas are peak times; spring and late September generally provide the best combination of good weather and crowd-free beaches. Rainy seasons are April to July and October to January.
Packing tips Insect repellent for the Mayan ruins inland; brimmed hats and sun cream for beaches and boats.
Recommended reads *The Lost Chronicles of the Mayan Kings* by David Drew traces the history of the peninsula; *Beyond the Mexique Bay* is Aldous Huxley's Caribbean travelogue; Charles Portis' humorous novel *Gringos* glances askance at the Yucatan through expat eyes.
Cuisine Chillies are vital in Yucatecan cooking. They range

LOCAL KNOWLEDGE

Taxis Hail them in the street in Playa del Carmen for shorter journeys, or get your hotel to call for one. Establish a price before setting off: few cabs have meters, and you won't be able to dispute the fare once you've arrived.
Currency The Mexican Peso (ME$). The US dollar is also widely accepted.
Dialling codes Mexico: 52. Cancún: 998; Playa/Tulum: 984.
Tipping culture Wages are low here, and most workers survive on their tips; 10–15 per cent is the norm, but taxi drivers don't usually expect a tip.
Siesta and fiesta Shops open early and close at around 9pm, taking a mid-afternoon siesta. Banks often close at 1pm, but you can change money at a *casa de cambio*.

from mildly piquant to eye-wateringly ferocious but, fortunately, they are often served separately, so you can choose your own level of volcanicity; jalapeños are considered 'mild'. Marinades of lime juice and herbs such as coriander are popular, especially with seafood. Even the beer is spiced – order *una michelada* and your pint will be laced with Tabasco, lime, salt, soy and Maggi. Calm things down with velvety guacamole and some maize tortillas. In hotels and resorts, Modern Meso-American menus prevail.

WORTH GETTING OUT OF BED FOR

Viewpoint The views from Tulum are exceptional; you cannot climb the site's tallest structure, El Castillo – the great temple-pyramid – but the vistas from the bluff it stands on, or from the top of the nearby Temple of the God of the Wind, are just as impressive. Take a picnic and linger.

Arts and culture The only cultural diversion likely to be able to compete with paddling in Caribbean lagoons or sipping margaritas in a hammock is a tour of the Mayan ruins. Often reclaimed from the jungle, these ancient sites are scattered throughout the Yucatan region. Aside from Tulum, Cobá and Chichén Itzá are the most famous, boasting sophisticated temple-pyramids, sacred ball courts, palaces, astrological observation platforms and sacrificial altars (including those used for human sacrifice). Arm yourself with site maps, hats and waterproofs if you want to avoid wandering aimlessly in the heat and/or rain.

Activities Show off your buoyancy control over the reefs, or snorkel among whale sharks, with Tank-Ha Dive Center (984 873 0302) in Playa del Carmen. Follow Cousteau to the coral cay island of Cozumel, for world-class diving and snorkelling on Palancar Reef. The cenotes of the Yucatan offer amazing cavern dives, particularly around Cobá; for details, see www.playamayanews.com or www.grancenote.com. If you don't fancy beach activities such as paragliding, windsurfing or fishing, get your motor running and head out on the highway, with Harley Adventures (984 106 0500) in Playa del Carmen. Swap bikes for birdies at Playacar Golf Club (984 873 0624), a stunning par-72 18-holer sweeping through lush Mayan greenery; the jungle is considered a 'lateral hazard'.

Best beach The whole coast is fringed with Caribbean beauties; but Tulum beach is one of the most striking, spreading out south of the main archaeological site. There's another flour-soft stretch of beach loveliness at Xpu-Ha.

Daytripper Chichén Itzá is the Yucatan's finest archaeological treasure. Avoid the coach trips unless you want to see the site in the blistering mid-afternoon heat with thousands of other people: arrive very early or stay a little later – then you can play Indiana Jones in peace. The centrepiece is the 25-metre-high Pyramid of Kukulcán (aka El Castillo), which is also an astoundingly complex calendar: there are 365 steps and 18 terraces to represent the 365 days and 18 'months' of the Mayan year.

Walks Stroll the two-mile length of Xpu-Ha Beach and enjoy soothing sea views and sand-softened feet while you pick which of the private houses lining the shore you'd like to buy. Sip a sundowner at a beach café on your way back.

Shopping For a bit of light retail entertainment, Playa del Carmen has the best selection of shops, although they are decidedly aimed at tourists. Don't expect the Via Condotti, but pedestrianised Fifth Avenue (Quinto Avenida) has international brands and small Mexican boutiques that are worth checking out. If you have somewhere back home to hang it, a hammock is a suitably Yucatecan souvenir.

Something for nothing If you visit Chichén Itzá during spring or autumn equinox, the angle of the sun creates the illusion of a giant snake writhing down Kukulcán temple; another example of Mayan ingenuity and astronomical prowess. If you visit one of the tourist restaurants in Playa, you are almost guaranteed to witness the slightly less magical sight of a roving mariachi band at some point.

Don't go home without... coming over all Latino in one of Playa del Carmen's riotous clubs; Mambo Café (984 803 2656) on Calle 6, between Fifth and 10th Avenues, has live Caribbean and Cuban music from 10pm till late.

MAGICALLY MAYAN RIVIERA

Take a dip in one of the region's cenotes – the water-filled pools connected by a network of limestone caverns and rivers that were revered by the Maya as the entrance to the underworld. Dzitnup Cenote just outside Valladolid is one of the best places, but Dos Ojos, within the Hidden Worlds theme park (www.hiddenworlds.com), is closer to the coast.

DIARY

February Día de la Candelaria – the Candlemas festival – on the second is celebrated all over Mexico with candlelit processions. Carnaval (www.carnavalcancun.com) takes place in the run-up to Ash Wednesday, and has grown in recent years to become a major event in Cozumel and Cancún. **October** The fascinating Day of the Dead festival spans the three days from 31 October to 2 November, and combines pre-Columbian ancestor worship with elements of Halloween. **November** The annual Riviera Maya Jazz Festival (www.rivieramaya jazzfestival.com) in late November brings acts great and small together on the coast.

Esencia

STYLE Less-is-more luxe
SETTING Tropical Caribbean seaside
DESTINATION Mayan Riviera

'The beauty of Esencia is the mandate to do absolutely nothing other than wander a few feet to the next station of luxury'

I rarely drink hard liquor, but we are in Mexico after all, and Mr Smith assures me it would be impolite not to at least test the local tequila. We sit under a hot sun overlooking the sparkling blue ocean and are served two, and then two more, of the most exquisite margaritas, salted. Guacamole and fried chips keep arriving unbidden. As two children splash – but not too loudly – in the water in front of us, we agree we've made an excellent choice.

And then Uma emerges, ruddy and fresh from a facial. Exchanging knowing glances, we simultaneously cite, in whispers, our favourite magazine feature from *US Weekly* – 'Stars! They're just like us!' – which publishes photos of celebrities engaged in mundane activities such as drinking lattes at Starbucks. Today we decide that, in fact, we are just like them.

Before the silliness can continue, our usher appears to tell us our room is ready. We stumble across the lawn to a white stucco villa a short distance away, and are led into a sprawling suite.

Sobriety sets in. This is our dream loft, not a resort hotel room. Up a short flight of stairs, the heavy wooden door opens up onto a split-level room decorated sparsely, all in white. A large sitting area leads out onto a patio with an ocean view. On the upper level, a large bed sits in front of a flatscreen television, with an iPod nano plugged into the surround-sound system. A Spanish music medley compiled by the hotel plays at the just-right romantic level. Before collapsing onto the bed, we inspect further. On each level is a bathroom, one featuring a wood-panelled shower, the other with a walk-in closet and a large bath. Our fridge is full of local beer, juice and water – all complimentary.

'Could you live here now?' I tease. As we are to repeatedly discover over the next two days, the beauty of Esencia is the mandate to do absolutely nothing other than wander a few feet to the next station of luxury – perhaps stopping to admire a small iguana on the way to the bar, or lazing in our private hammock, or staring blankly at the ocean before sloping off to a massage. Although we were informed at check-in about the available activities, including private

Spotting Uma Thurman on the villa veranda helped validate our decision to visit Esencia. We were still pale new arrivals at that point. Only a short time earlier, a hotel taxi had picked us up from Cancún airport and driven us a quick hour south toward the resort, turning down a two-lane road off the highway towards the water. Upon entry, a 'butler' assigned to us made quick work of signing the paperwork before taking us on a tour of the manicured, green grounds, dotted with palm trees. The estate until recently served as the private holiday home of an Italian duchess. I quickly entered into fantasies of owning our own family compound.

'Maybe we should see our room before we buy the place,' sensible Mr Smith cheerfully suggests. But first: noon cocktail hour by the pool.

scuba-diving lessons and daily morning yoga lessons, nothing in the atmosphere (or the room brochure) urges excessive exertion. This dedication to relaxation has even rubbed off on the staff member who shows us the WiFi-equipped common room overlooking the pool. 'Please don't do too much work,' he implores us.

We head to dinner at the early hour of 7pm – something of a tactical mistake, as we find ourselves surrounded by young families with children in high chairs. Still, a tasting from the extensive wine list and ceviche menu quickly puts the family atmosphere at some remove. The next night, at a much later hour, the dimly lit dining area has a more grown-up feel. And yet the open seating encourages interaction among the guests. One couple from San Francisco, having heard us say we had previously been to the Tides Riviera Maya resort down the road, don't hesitate to introduce themselves and ask for a comparison, which leads to a spontaneous, alcohol-fuelled forum on destination weddings that keeps us laughing well into the night.

By day, we do what we do best, examining every feature of the spa and taking advantage of as many extras as we can justify spending money on. Set apart in its own bungalow, the spa welcomes us even when we don't have appointments set, to use both the steam room (with a rosemary aroma) and the outdoor plunge pools. My best moment comes when Claudia, a wiry, tattooed Mexican woman, leads me to a private room for a massage, where for 80 glorious minutes she stretches and kneads muscles I never knew existed. Afterwards, she sits me down in a low wooden chair surrounded by candles to serve me fresh fruit and sweet tea. When I enquire about sitting in the Jacuzzi, a therapist leads me to a private, heated outdoor pool, where I sit and read, sans swimming suit, for more than an hour.

'I'm so happy and relaxed, I just can't believe it,' we overhear a lithe blonde woman at the next patio table say to her Mr Smith on our final afternoon, before they tumble onto the lawn for a bout of tickling. She'd better believe it. After just a couple of days at Esencia, my muscles are as loose as our daily schedule, and my stress levels are down to those of a cat basking in a pool of sunlight. If I'm feeling like a Hollywood star, the mind boggles at what blissful emotions must be flitting through Uma's mind.

Reviewed by Anne Kornblut

'The dedication to relaxation has rubbed off on the staff member who shows us the WiFi room overlooking the pool. "Please don't do too much work," he implores'

NEED TO KNOW

Rooms 29 in total, including 17 suites and two cottages.

Rates $525–$2,800, including breakfast; rates exclude 10 per cent service and 12 per cent tax.

Check-out Noon, but flexible, depending on room availability. Earliest check-in, 3pm.

Facilities Two swimming pools with sun loungers, plus a private stretch of white-sand beach; organic spa with Jacuzzis, steam room, beachside temazcal and phytotherapy treatments; DVD/CD library and iPod loan; chef's tables; complimentary yoga; scuba instructors. In rooms, DVD/CD player, plasma-screen TV, iPod dock, internet access, minibar.

Children Welcome; the resort has multi-lingual nannies and babysitting can be arranged at $25 an hour. High chairs and baby cots are provided. An additional third bed costs $150 a night; $75 for under-12s.

Also Dogs weighing 10 pounds or less are allowed, but owners are responsible for their food. Smoking is permitted; non-smoking rooms are also available.

IN THE KNOW

Our favourite rooms The Deluxe Ocean View suites have 360-degree views. The private two-storey, two-bedroom cottages set in the gardens are enormous and wonderful for family holidays: they even have their own full-sized swimming pool, multimedia room, bar and chef. The Rosa suite in the Casa Grande was the master bedroom when the Duchess of Ferrari owned the property, so the entire hacienda can be viewed from its enormous terrace.

Hotel bar Sip drinks in the chill-out lounge in the main house, by the pool or on the beach up till 11pm. Try one of the tequila-based creations; we love the mezcal and pineapple-packed Esencia Carbeña. The minibar in your room has complimentary beer, too.

Hotel restaurant Meso-American cuisine made with fresh local produce is the focus at Esencia's rustic but elegant restaurant Sal y Fuego (meaning 'salt and fire'), with seafood a particular speciality. The restaurant is open 7am–11pm.

Top table For lunch, go for a beachside table with a sea view; for dinner, one of the tables overlooking the cenote, an underground freshwater pool that's romantically illuminated by night.

Room service Round the clock: hot food is on the menu until 11pm; after the kitchen closes, cold snacks are still available.

Dress code Informal and relaxed; a little dressier in the evening, if you feel like it.

Local knowledge Bikinis are a must-pack, but a swimsuit is probably more practical if you want to try the snorkelling or scuba-diving on offer from Esencia's shores. Bring some suitable shoes if you plan on following any of the walking trails.

LOCAL EATING AND DRINKING

A little way along the coast from Esencia, the **Tides Riviera Maya** resort (984 877 3000) has a number of options if you've exhausted Esencia's menus. Its gourmet **Azul Restaurant** is set right by the sea, and serves international and Yucatecan cuisine; **The Grill at the Pool** has a more relaxed menu of ceviche and grills. Otherwise, aside from a few shacks along Xpu-Ha beach, there's nothing much outside Playa del Carmen. Award-winning and lively, **Yaxche Maya Cuisine Restaurant** (984 873 2502) serves Yucatecan and Mayan-inspired dishes with a Euro twist; savour regional specialities such as Tsotolbichay (Mayan tamale). **Byblos** (984 803 1790), run by chef Sylvie Goetz, is a fun French restaurant and wine bar.

GET A ROOM!

To book this hotel, go to www.mrandmrssmith.com or ring our expert travel team on 1 800 464 2040. Activate your free membership online (see page 4) to qualify for the exclusive Smith card offer shown below when you book with us.

 SMITH CARD OFFER A complimentary cocktail each, and a free snorkelling trip for two.

Esencia Carretera Cancún Tulum, Pedio Rústico Xpu-Ha Lote 18, Quintana Roo (www.mrandmrssmith.com/esencia)

MEXICO CITY

CITYSCAPE Sleeping giant
CITY LIFE Monuments, mescal and mariachi

Mexico City, erstwhile heart of the vast Aztec empire, once stood in the middle of a lake. These days, the water is gone, replaced instead by a churning sea of humanity: with more than 19 million inhabitants, the city is one of the largest and most dynamic on earth. In the Distrito Federal's vast ruins and astounding museums you'll find the glories of the city's ancient past, but walk its bustling streets and you'll discover a vibrant contemporary arts scene and an amazing creative energy. There's a sun-fuelled buzz in the galleries, fashion-forward style in offbeat boutiques and the swagger of happy-go-lucky mariachi music in the air. Restaurants proudly continue the rich culinary traditions of the country that brought the world chocolate, tortillas and the tomato, and, whether it's the Day of the Dead or just another Saturday night in the city, you'll soon see that no one knows how to party like the Mexicans...

GETTING THERE

Planes Benito Juárez International Airport (www.airports mexico.com) is Mexico's main travel gateway, offering direct flights to New York, Los Angeles, London and other destinations in the US and Caribbean. Make sure you allow plenty of time to get to the airport, as heavy traffic can add upwards of 30 minutes to the journey time. Trains Mexico's metro links the airport with the city cheaply and quickly, but it's usually crowded and can be a bit of a hassle – a taxi is the best option.
Automobiles You can rent a car at the airport, but only the most gifted and patient drivers should consider it, as traffic can be chaotic at best. Arrange airport transfers ahead of your trip for headache-free connections.

LOCAL KNOWLEDGE

Taxis Have your hotel arrange a taxi for you where possible, or call Taximex (5634 9912). If you do flag one down, look for a green or red mark along the bottom of the license-plate that denotes a legit vehicle.
Currency The Mexican peso (ME$).
Dialling codes Mexico: 52. Mexico City: 55.
Tipping culture Tips or *propinas* are a big part of Mexican culture and the norm is 10–15 per cent for restaurant and bar staff. Hotel porters will also expect something.
Siesta and fiesta There are no hard and fast rules: shops are generally open from around 9am–8pm, although impromptu siestas do occur. Lunch is usually 2pm or 3pm, and dinner at about 9pm or 10pm. Bars fill up towards midnight and clubs shortly afterwards.
Do go/don't go June is the rainy season, when there are daily downpours, but it can still be uncomfortably hot and humid between showers. The rest of the year is warm; winter can be the most pleasant time to visit.
Packing tips Dancing shoes and drinking boots. And an umbrella will serve you well come rain or shine: when it's dry, you can use your brolly to stave off the sun's unrelenting rays.
Recommended reads *The Conquest of New Spain* by soldier Bernal Diaz de Castillo is a first-person account of the Spanish capture of Mexico City; Carlos Fuentes' sprawling epic *The Years with Laura Diaz* traces the country's social and political history through the eyes of its titular heroine; Sybille Bedford's witty and diverting travelogue *A Visit to Don Otavio*.

Cuisine Mexican cuisine is founded on corn, the staple ingredient used to make tortillas; these small cornflour pancakes are the Mexican equivalent of bread. A typical Mexico City meal will feature tacos – crunchy corn tortillas usually served with meat, chicken or nopales (prickly-pear stems) – and bottle-loads of delicious chilli sauce. Also worth trying are chiles rellenos (stuffed mild peppers), and frijoles (black beans often cooked with pork). Another classic is tamales (cornmeal, usually stuffed with meat or fish, and steamed inside the staple crop's leafy husks).

WORTH GETTING OUT OF BED FOR

Viewpoint The curvy glass-fronted tower of Torre Mayor (www.torremayor.com.mx) on Paseo de la Reforma is Mexico's tallest building, and boasts extraordinary views across town. Talk your way into Piso 51 (www.piso51.com), a members' club with jaw-dropping cityscape panoramas.

Arts and culture Both the archaeology-based Templo Mayor Museum (www.conaculta.gob.mx/templomayor) and the world-class National Museum of Anthropology (www.mna.inah.gob.mx) in Chapultepec are must-sees. With incredible collections of pre-Hispanic sculpture, weapons, sacrificial objects and gold in each, you'll begin to get an appreciation of the one-time grandeur of the Aztec capital. For a more contemporary, experimental view of Mexico, visit the many independent galleries and exhibition spaces dotted around La Condesa.

Activities Head to Xochimilco in the south of the city and hire one of the trajineras – brightly decorated skiffs, complete with boatman – from which you can explore the pretty canals and the plant nurseries that line them. Go on a Sunday when the whole place fills up with waterborne revellers and mariachi bands. Try to catch a performance by the Ballet Folklórico de Mexico (www.balletamalia.com) at Mexico City's art nouveau opera house, the Palacio de Bellas Artes (www.bellasartes.gob.mx); if you can't get tickets, have a nose around inside anyway – it's a fascinating building.

Perfect picnic Load up with tortillas, chilli and a flask of sangria from one of the traders in the vast Chapultepec Park, where a forest has flourished since Aztec times. Most visitors don't make it much further than busy Section 1, but venture a little further into Section 3 for a more peaceful atmosphere, surrounded by greenery. Once you feel sufficiently nourished, wander around and explore the park's lakes, zoo and palace museums.

Daytripper Arrange a car and a driver at your hotel and make the hour-long journey to Teotihuacan, a vast pyramid complex left by a civilisation that predated the Aztecs by 500 years. Try to go early, before the heat of the day hits, and round things off nicely with a lunch of barbacoa (meat slow-cooked in a pit) or roast lamb in nearby San Juan Teotihuacan.

Walks Starting from the Zócalo, visit the Palacio Nacional, where you'll find Diego Rivera's riveting murals. Then head to Plaza Santo Domingo, where clerks still hammer the keys of antique typewriters in their role as public scribes, before hitting the Palacio de Bellas Artes (www.bellasartes.gob.mx) to check out the museum galleries and more murals by Diego Rivera & Co; you could have a snack at the café after.

Shopping Polanco is the home to Mexico City's big-name boutiques, with the Louis Vuitton/Giorgio Armani ilk available all along Avenida Presidente Masaryk. In La Condesa, you'll find a selection of quirky, home-grown designer outlets, plus great homewares and jewellery. Guadalajara-based designers Julia y Renata (www.juliayrenata.com) have an outpost on Avenida Primavera.

Something for nothing The nightly battle of the mariachi bands in Plaza Garibaldi is as pleasing to the eye as the ear, as dozens of sombrero-toting strummers and tooters compete for the crowd's approval.

Don't go home without… a bottle of tequila: with more than 600 brands of the potent agave spirit produced by over 100 distilleries in Mexico alone, you'll be spoiled for choice. 'Worms' are strictly for tourists.

MARVELLOUSLY MEXICO CITY

From 1956 to 2003, Mexico City had a love affair with the VW Beetle, affectionately known as the *vocho*. Production of the old-style version may have stopped, but there are tens of thousands of the curvy cars still roaming the city streets, most of them now serving as taxis. Look out for the distinctive green and white cabs, as much a symbol of the city as tacos or tequila.

DIARY

January Everyone – farmers, children, ladies who lunch – brings their garishly dressed pets and livestock to the cathedral in the Zócalo to be blessed on the feast day of St Anthony on the 17th. **February/March** The period before Lent brings the jubilant atmosphere of Carnaval to the city, as Mexicans celebrate by dressing up, drinking, dancing, drinking, feasting, playing games and drinking. **Mid-August** Ceremonies and celebrations in the Plaza de las Tres Culturas, on La Reforma and in the Zócalo to commemorate the defeat of the Spanish. **October/November** Day of the Dead kicks off on Halloween and ends on 2 November – shops fill with chocolate skulls and relatives flock to cemeteries to leave colourful offerings for their dear departed.

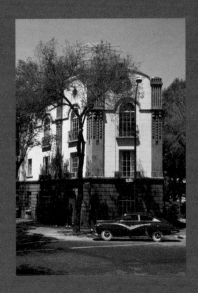

Condesa DF

STYLE Floral Mexi-modern
SETTING Come over to the parkside
DESTINATION Mexico City

'I walk into a light-bathed triangular
courtyard, and look up to see a
Pythagorean vision of sky as blue
as Frida Kahlo's Casa Azul'

I love Mexico City. I love it because it's big and brash, and a little bit mental. And that's the point: if you want peace and quiet, go to Alaska. If it's edge and excitement you're after, the *Distrito Federal* is where it's at. So when I find myself outside an elegant art deco building on a tranquil tree-lined avenue, shortly after arriving at Benito Juárez airport, I feel slightly off-kilter.

As I'm waiting for Señor Smith to fly in from Cancún to join me, I have to drag my luggage into the tiny lobby alone. There to greet me is a huge chocolate labrador, watching imperiously from behind reception with his paws on the counter. Is he making sure I'm dressed appropriately for this chic hotel?

I walk through into a light-bathed, laurel-dotted triangular courtyard, where dressed-down *chilangos* are enjoying a parasol-shaded late lunch. I look up and see a Pythagorean vision of sky as blue as Frida Kahlo's Casa Azul. I'm in the centre of the atrium, and four floors of white walls, constructed from huge rectangular louvred panels, rise up around me. Oblong patterns of light are beamed onto the walls of the corridors behind. It's beautiful *and* geometric. My old maths teacher would be delighted.

This terrace leads onto a series of rooms, filled with mismatched, gently curving, Barbara Hepworth-esque furniture. Bold floral graphics in fresh verdant tones feature heavily, complementing the turquoise walls. Our own room continues the natural theme. Green walls segue into chocolate-coloured wooden floorboards. Huge doors slide closed to separate the bedroom from a pretty lounge, in which sit more flower-emblazoned chairs. I open my window and the sound of birdsong floods in from the palm-filled park across the road.

When Señor Smith arrives, I bounce around the room showing him all our new toys, before realising there are perhaps more important things to focus on after a spell of distance-enforced absence. When we finally make it up to the buzzing rooftop bar, there's a slight chill in the air – but the stylish crowd of young creatives doesn't seem to mind. We ward off the cold by cuddling beneath a blanket, as lounge music and the gentle throb of conversation

provides our soundtrack. Occasionally, we stick out a hand to pick up champagne cocktails or to clamp chopsticks around morsels of Mexican-influenced Japanese cuisine.

We're on Latin time now, so breakfast is still waiting for us when we make it down to the courtyard at 11am the next morning. Another beautiful day beams down into the atrium. With nowhere particular to be, we boutique-hop, gallery-browse and café-idle our way through this genteel, leafy neighbourhood. It's hard to remember we're in Mexico City – this all feels more like a romantic weekend in Paris.

In the afternoon, we brave the hot, frantic and intense city I know. Mr Smith is reluctant to leave our idyll in the suburbs, but I persuade him to come with me to the Zócalo. This bustling square has been the heart of the capital since the time of the Aztecs, and shows no signs of letting up. I drag Mr Smith through tightly packed crowds watching feather-headed dancers spin and whirl to a pounding drumbeat, to the Diego Rivera murals at the

Palacio Nacional. After spending an hour or so admiring the epic frescoes, as chaotic and colourful as the culture from which they came, we head out to brave the burning sun amid the ruins of the Templo Mayor.

By 6pm, though, Mr Smith can bear no more. We jump into a green and white VW Beetle taxi and crawl along traffic-clogged highways, watching people weave between the cars to hawk toys and chewing gum. Stepping out of our cab beside the park, we breathe simultaneous sighs of relief; it's hard to imagine we're still in the same city.

That night, we treat ourselves to dinner in the hotel's El Patio restaurant. Seated at a table in the atrium, we begin with refreshing ginger and champagne cocktails, then I move onto melting black cod in tequila miso while Mr Smith tucks into hearty braised ribs with a roasted apple purée. The food is divine; the service impeccable. We roll out of the hotel with full bellies and head to low-key local bar La Botica, which serves 15 different kinds of mescal, a local tipple caustic enough to strip paint. Bravery buoyed by the cocktails back at Condesa DF, Señor Smith asks for the strongest one they have. Several shots and some chillied peanuts later, he's a little worse for wear.

Next morning, as we sit up in bed with coffee and pastries, we reflect on our weekend. What's not to like about Condesa DF? Nothing. It's a peaceful haven in one of the most frenetic and extreme urban environments on earth; it also happens to be a stylish and fun boutique hotel with world-class food and service. And it has a dog on front-desk duties. I wonder whether – if I tickle his tummy – he'll let us stay for another night.

Reviewed by Mr & Mrs Smith

'I open my bedroom window and the sound of birdsong floods in from the palm-filled park across the road'

NEED TO KNOW

Rooms 40, including 16 suites.

Rates $195–$495, including breakfast; excludes 17 per cent tax.

Check-out Noon, but later check-out may be available on request.

Facilities Spa with pool and hammam, gym, cinema, boutique, library of books, DVDs and CDs, free WiFi and valet parking. In rooms, flatscreen TV, CD/DVD player, pre-loaded iPod sound system, Malin+Goetz toiletries.

Children Discouraged: Condesa DF's neatly pedicured feet are firmly in the couples' camp.

Also Pets are welcome, at no additional cost. Certain areas are designated for smoking.

IN THE KNOW

Our favourite rooms The citywide views from Terrace Suite III.II make it our top choice, but the gorgeous stone-clad wet rooms and huge shower heads in the Balcony and Patio Rooms make them tempting options, too. If you can, go for a room with outside space (Patio Rooms, Terrace Suites, Top Suite): the serene and leafy setting is a rarity in Mexico City – it'd be a shame to miss out.

Hotel bar La Terraza nestles among the treetops, a triangular rooftop lip of dark wooden decking under a canopy of purple-blossomed jacaranda. There's a bar down at patio level, too, and a lounge area with funky flock-fabric chairs.

Hotel restaurant A spa bar serves sushi on the rooftops, but more substantial sustenance is on offer downstairs at El Patio, the popular restaurant that muddles Mexican, European and Asian influences to great effect. Dine alfresco or inside in one of the Fifties-feel chambers adjoining the atrium. Breakfast is served in a tranquil turquoise-themed side room.

Top table Book one of Condesa DF's private dining rooms for uninterrupted intimacy, or ask for one of the tables against the wall with their comfortable cowhide banquettes.

Room service Meals and snacks from the restaurant kitchen are available 24 hours a day.

Dress code It-girl chic and fly-boy cool.

Local knowledge Tequila is just half the story – Mexico's unsung national beverage is mescal, distilled from agave leaves. Close to Condesa DF, La Mezcalería on Campeche is part kitsch bar, part informal museum, with more than 100 bottles of the potent liquor on display. Afterwards, take a walk around pretty and peaceful Parque Mexico in the heart of the district to clear your head.

LOCAL EATING AND DRINKING

Bistro Mosaico (5584 2932) on Michoacán is Mexico City's answer to French fine dining, with a wide-ranging menu that would please the most pernickety Parisian. At the other end of the scale, **El Carifa** (5271 7666) on Altata is an authentic late-night tacquería that does the tastiest tacos in town. Lunch with zest on 'forbidden fruits' at salad, smoothie and sandwich stop **Frutos Prohibidos** (5264 5808), a couple of blocks away from the hotel. The Condesa area is home to some of the city's chicest watering holes: two of the trendiest are Argentinian salsa bar **Pata Negra** (5211 5563) on Tamaulipas, and film-star-owned martini-Mecca **CFNA** (5212 0090), located on Nuevo León.

GET A ROOM!

To book this hotel, go to www.mrandmrssmith.com or ring our expert travel team on 1 800 464 2040. Activate your free membership online (see page 4) to qualify for the exclusive Smith card offer shown below when you book with us.

 SMITH CARD OFFER A cocktail each on arrival, and a bottle of wine.

Condesa DF 102 Avenida Veracruz, Colonia Condesa, Mexico City 06700 (www.mrandmrssmith.com/condesa-df)

PUEBLA

CITYSCAPE Baroque around the block
CITY LIFE Holy mole

Proud, peaceful and undeniably pretty, Puebla sits snugly in the shadow of Popocatépetl, Mexico's feistiest volcano, which burbles out plumes of smoke to wow camera-toting visitors and remind Pueblans of their place in the universe. Thankfully, the steaming giant has left the city well alone since the 1500s, allowing it to thrive architecturally, socially and gastronomically. Slower-paced than its frenetic neighbour Mexico City, Puebla has long been the heart of colonial Mexico. The city's Spanish soul and Catholic roots have left it a trove of architectural treasures, and in the centre you'll find beautiful Baroque buildings, an imposing cathedral and a host of chilli-fuelled kitchens. It's gone by many names over the years – 'City of Tiles' (for its signature ceramics), 'Heroic City of Zaragoza' (after the French-drubbing general) and 'City of Angels' – but to most Mexicans and visitors, it's known as Puebla, meaning, with shrugging simplicity, 'town'.

GETTING THERE

Planes Puebla's airport – Hermanus Serdán – is a tiny affair 40 minutes outside the city, mostly visited by internal flights. International visitors will arrive via Mexico City's much larger airport (www.aicm.com.mx).
Trains There are no rail links to Puebla.
Automobiles The drive from Mexico City to Puebla takes two hours – you can rent a car from Hertz (www.hertz.com), although navigating the wild roads of Mexico City can be daunting to first-timers. Europcar (www.europcar.com) has a branch at Hermanus Serdán Airport in Puebla.

LOCAL KNOWLEDGE

Taxis Puebla's black and white taxis are easy to spot and fine to flag down in the street. The cars aren't metered, so negotiate a price beforehand, and don't be afraid to reject over-inflated fares. It's a small city, so cabs are plentiful – there's a rank beside the bus station if they prove elusive.
Currency Mexican pesos (ME$).
Dialling codes Mexico: 52. Puebla: 222. When dialling within Puebla, you needn't bother with the area code.
Tipping culture In restaurants, 10–15 per cent is standard;

bar staff and porters will expect a few pesos, too. Tips are a big part of Mexican culture, so keep some change handy.
Siesta and fiesta Lunch and dinner are generally late and leisurely (around 2pm–3pm and 9pm–10pm, respectively), meaning that the nightlife doesn't usually kick off until close to midnight. Some places still take an afternoon siesta, but most shops stay open between 11am and 9pm.
Do go/don't go Puebla is warm and sunny most of the year, but the heat can make the June rainy season unpleasantly humid; January and February can be chilly.
Packing tips A rosary will impress the staunchly Catholic populace. Leave room for holiday shopping in your bags.
Recommended reads *The Hummingbird's Daughter* by Luis Alberto Urrea tells the tumultuous tale of the author's great-aunt in a time of revolution; *Like Water for Chocolate* by Laura Esquivel combines love story with recipe book; *Sor Juana Inez de la Cruz: Selected Writings* is a collection of poems by a 17th-century nun now regarded as one of Mexico's finest poets.
Cuisine Puebla's regional cuisine, known as *cocina poblana*, has taken hold throughout the country. The most famous recipe is for mole; not the burrowing mammal,

but a rich, potent sauce of chillis, chocolate, ground nuts, seeds and spices. Between July and September, you should keep an eye (and a mouth) open for chiles en nogada: mild chillis stuffed with fruit and nuts, then drizzled in walnut sauce.

WORTH GETTING OUT OF BED FOR

Viewpoint Drive up to Guadalupe Fort (where the Mexicans famously fought off the French at the Battle of Puebla in 1862), for a spectacular view of the city, the valley below and the snow-capped mountains beyond. **Arts and culture** The church of Santo Domingo on Cinco de Mayo is a wonderful example of Puebla's lavish Baroque architectural style, with an astounding amount of gold leaf and astonishing onyx stonework. Also visit the Museo Regional de la Revolución Mexicana (242 1076) on 6 Oriente, the former house of rebel leader Aquiles Serdán; you can still see the bullet holes left in the wall from his date with destiny. Sited at 2 Sur 708 in the city's historic centre, the Museo Amparo (www. museoamparo.com) is one of the most admired in Mexico, with a fine collection of pre-Columbian and colonial art. **Activities** Puebla became nationally known for its ceramics, and a number of tile factories – producing the region's distinctive blue and white talavera earthenware – still exist. You can catch a permanent exhibition of Pueblan pottery on the Playa de Armas, or go to the Uriarte Taller studio on Poniente (232 1598; www. uriartetalavera.com.mx) to see first-hand how the intricately designed ceramics are made. To make your own dishes (but not in the pottery way), sign up for a three-hour cookery class at antique-filled colonial retreat Mesón Sacristia de la Compañia (232 4513; www.mesones-sacristia.com) and learn to whip up chalupas like a local.
Perfect picnic Stuff a hamper with munchable goodies and make the short trip to Cholula, about 10 miles east of Puebla. It's home to the Great Pyramid of Cholula, the largest structure of its kind in the world (it beats Giza by playing the volume card). Once a sacrificial hot-spot for splatter-happy Aztec god Quetzalcoatl, most of the monument is now a scrub-covered hill crowned by the church of Nuestra Señora de los Remedios, and one of the country's most scenic spots for alfresco eating. **Daytripper** Take the dirt road leading out from Cholula to the Paso de Cortés – the saddle of land between Popocatépetl and Ixtaccíhuatl, Mexico's second and third

largest peaks respectively. The views of the countryside are stunning from here, and you can see Popocatépetl's smoking volcanic top in menacing clarity. You'll find a tasty lunch in one of the restaurants perched on the hillsides. **Walks** On a Sunday, start early and make the three-hour trek up the foggy hills to Cuetzalan, where you'll find a bustling Nahua Indian market underway. Even if you don't buy anything, simply pacing the cobbles and examining the oddball collection of artisan goods – from embroidery and cradles to machetes – will while an afternoon away. You can get the bus back or, if your feet still have it in them, head for the 35-metre waterfall of La Gloria, near Apulco. **Shopping** For local arts and crafts, the pedestrianised streets of El Parian are rife with bargain hawkers and hunters, while the American-style Angelopolis shopping mall has a clutch of high-street designer names. The Callejón de los Sapos (Alley of the Frogs) is lined with antiques shops, and there's a feast-your-eyes fleamarket there on Saturday mornings.
Something for nothing Join the locals in the age-old Mexican tradition of the evening *paseo* and head to the Zócalo at around 6pm. Soak up the relaxed atmosphere as people flood outside to bask in the late-lingering sun; the pretty squares fill with couples and children, all simply taking a stroll.
Don't go home without... a piece of blue and white talavera pottery or something made from the beautiful onyx (travertine) of nearby village, Tecali.

PERFECTLY PUEBLA

Traditional Mexican dress is instantly recognisable: the combination of embroidered white blouse, billowy coloured skirt, shawl and beads is known as *china poblana*. The look is believed to have originated in Puebla when an Asian slave-girl-turned-fashionista refused to adopt local attire and the townswomen began to imitate her distinctive style. Radical.

DIARY

February–March Carnaval: the week leading up to Ash Wednesday is celebrated with brightly costumed, high-kicking abandon. **May** The fifth of the month is a public holiday remembering Mexico's trouncing of the French at the Battle of Puebla, marked by a procession and bombastic re-enactment of the battle. **September** The month begins with processions, fireworks and dances in honour of the Virgen de los Remedios in nearby Cholula. **October** A fiesta in honour of San Francisco de Asís (Francis of Asissi) on the fourth sees the Voladores of Papantia come to Cuetzalan to perform their traditional 'flying' dance, crazily suspended from a 150-foot pole.

La Purificadora

STYLE Industrial revolution
SETTING Colonial old town
DESTINATION Puebla

'Built as a water-bottling factory in
the 1880s, the hotel still exudes a
distinctly 19th-century solidity. It's
a mighty clash between past and present'

203

ecclesiastical-purple cubist-style sofas dominate a lobby with rough granite walls and monolithic reclaimed-wood pillars. It's a mighty clash between past and present.

When we step out of the lift on the third floor, I jump right back in again. Through a glass floor, I can see all the way down to the uneven stone cobbles of the lobby below. Inside our room, it's all sexy dark wood floors and raw-stone walls, and there's a vast inviting bed, a glass wardrobe and an onyx-walled shower big enough for two. We open the huge glass door to the balcony and I instinctively reach for Mr Smith like a damsel in distress: the balcony juts out from the side of the building with no visible support. Mr Smith, knowing I'm scared of heights, is clearly hoping my fear will prove to be an aphrodisiac.

When I finally pluck up the courage for further exploration, we decide to start at the rooftop bar. But, in January, it's just too cold to hang around for long, no matter how warming the spirits on offer. We dip our fingers in the stunning glass-walled swimming pool, admire the glowing onyx pillars and head downstairs, rubbing our hands together.

Despite its smart monochrome decor, the restaurant still feels informal and intimate. I start with squash blossoms stuffed with cheese in a tomato broth, while Mr Smith, ever the risk-taker, opts for thin slices of beef tongue with cactus and lime mayonnaise. We follow this up with regional speciality mole poblano and red snapper cooked in corn leaves. Like the building, the food is a rich mixture of old and new, a modern take on some of Mexico's most classic dishes. Several glasses of local cabernet sauvignon later and we cannot eat another morsel. The guava crème brûlée will just have to wait. We spend the rest of our evening by the fire in the dramatic lobby, watching the city's spires shimmer against the dark night sky.

The remainder of our weekend is divided between our divine bed, braving the cold to swim in the exhibitionist rooftop pool — you're certainly aware of how much food you're eating when you know that everyone on the terrace can see how you look underwater — and exploring Puebla. The old, colonial centre of town is beautiful. There are

La Purificadora, I've decided, is the architectural equivalent of a shot of tequila: momentarily overwhelming, but ultimately makes your weekend go with a bang. Our journey there is equally heady — we get lost within 50 metres of the car-rental office, go past our turn-off for Puebla, cut across five lanes of traffic at a set of lights and have a mini-domestic. I start to question whether Mr Smith and I are really ready to combine romance and adventure to this extent.

We eventually find the hotel. Built as a water-bottling factory in the 1880s, it still exudes a distinctly 19th-century solidity — its exterior is all exposed brickwork and columns. But once we pass through reception, the hotel opens out into a vast cathedral of space, in the midst of which a black volcanic-stone staircase leads to the first floor. A hole in the side of the building frames a church. Water trickles down the staircase and collects in a pool, and two huge fire pits surrounded by

aspects of life here that seem to have changed little with the passing of time; the shoe-shiners and their businessmen clients, the row of shops selling candyfloss-like communion dresses, the stores crammed with religious icons.

Walking through the pretty artists' quarter, I stop to have my fortune read by an old man with a cageful of sparrows. I politely ignore the birdseed he places on the fortune cards to entice little Lupita to divine what lies in store for me – even

'I reach for Mr Smith like a damsel in distress: the balcony juts out with no visible support'

though this seems to have little effect. Finally, he coaxes the tiny bird to pick one out with her beak. I secrete it away for later. After lunch at a low-key restaurant, we admire the beautiful pre-hispanic art at the Amparo museum and peek into baroque churches. Dusk sees us join strolling families in the tree-filled central square, dodging the sellers holding hundreds of brightly coloured balloons in various animal shapes and watching this little, glittering corner of the world go by.

We wind up our weekend and regretfully say goodbye to the wonderful staff and glorious designer bedroom. I never did get used to the glass floors, but they did make the trip down to breakfast feel almost expeditionary. On the way home, feeling brave, we decide to skip the direct highway back to Mexico City and take the winding Paso de Cortes, driving up, along a dirt road, until we pass between two skyline-dominating volcanoes. As we stop to admire the smouldering, snowcapped peak of Popocatépetl, said in local lore to be a warrior holding a burning torch for his lost love, I remember the fortune in my pocket. It tells me that a new sense of romance and adventure will soon enter my life. La Purificadora, whose architecture left me breathless, whose food fired up my tastebuds and whose city was so full of surprises, has given me more than enough of both. My fortune teller, it seems, was uncannily accurate. His little sparrows just don't see very far into the future.

Reviewed by Simone Topolski

NEED TO KNOW

Rooms 26, including three suites.

Rates Midweek, $155–$295; Friday–Sunday, $199–$399, including breakfast but excluding tax at 17 per cent.

Check-out Noon, although later check-out may be arranged on request, subject to availability.

Facilities Swimming pool, spa with two steam rooms and Jacuzzi, gym, library, free WiFi, valet parking ($3 a day). In rooms, plasma TV, iPod dock, Kiehl's toiletries.

Children Leave them at home: La Purificadora is decidedly geared towards grown-ups.

Also Open to the elements, the slender rooftop pool has a glass wall, allowing margarita-sipping bar guests to engage in a spot of voyeurism. Pets are welcome ($40 a night).

IN THE KNOW

Our favourite rooms The balcony-endowed Superior Bedrooms are the cosiest; the views of colonial Puebla are worth paying more for – P and Z have the most impressive outlooks. Suite A at the top of the hotel has a long terrace leading down to a private heated pool, where you can bask with views of the tower of San Francisco church.

Hotel bar Decorated in dark granite and onyx, the smart and sultry rooftop bar inspires Friday-night queues as Puebla's great and good come in search of the perfect cocktail. The signature concoction of mandarin orange, pineapple and curaçao is certainly a contender. The bar closes at midnight during the week; 2am at weekends.

Hotel restaurant The intimate restaurant, in which tables sit between wooden pillars, serves a Modern Mexican menu that breathes new life into classic dishes such as mole and ceviche. There's a DIY element to dining: you can 'build' your own tasting menu by combining meat, fish, sauces and side dishes to suit your palate. It closes at 11pm.

Top table Despite the canteen-style timber tables, restaurant staff ensure seating still feels private – try to sit close to the reclaimed wooden pillars, from where you can see out into the open-air living area and its flaming fire pits.

Room service Mexican meals and snacks are available 24 hours a day.

Dress code Grand designer.

Local knowledge The former convent of Santa Rosa (232 7792), just up the road from the hotel at 14 Poniente, does double duty as a museum of popular art and as the celebrated birthplace of mole poblano. Entry costs $1.

LOCAL EATING AND DRINKING

Although it may seem a trifle perverse to dine on Spanish cuisine in a city that helped put Mexican on the map, **La Conjura** (232 9693) at 9 Oriente has a bold, daily-changing menu that's well worth sampling. The former bodega's seafood is particularly tasty. Lower-key cantina-style **La Guadalupana** (242 4886) at 5 Oriente is the place to come for Pueblan classics on the hoof. For finer and slower local dining, **Fonda la Mexicana** (232 6747) on Avenida 16 Septiembre serves a deliciously fruity mole poblano. **La Boutique** (482 0603) is the city's (deservedly) popular dance club on Final de la Recta.

GET A ROOM!

To book this hotel, go to www.mrandmrssmith.com or ring our expert travel team on 1 800 464 2040. Activate your free membership online (see page 4) to qualify for the exclusive Smith card offer shown below when you book with us.

 SMITH CARD OFFER A complimentary bottle of wine. Mr & Mrs Smith members staying four nights will get 50 per cent off their last night's accommodation (unless it falls on a Friday or Saturday)

La Purificadora 802 Callejón de la 10 Norte, Paseo San Francisco, Barrio el Alto, Puebla 7200 (www.mrandmrssmith.com/la-purificadora)

How to... speak like a native

	MR & MRS SMITH	TAKE ME TO YOUR LEADER	PLEASE CALL OFF YOUR VIOLIN PLAYER	DO YOU KNOW THE WAY TO SAN JOSE?	SHAKEN, NOT STIRRED
FRENCH	Monsieur et Madame Dupont	Portez-moi à votre chef	Dites, s'il vous plaît, au violoniste de quitter le camp	Savez-vous comment arriver à San Jose?	Agité, pas remué
GERMAN	Herr und Frau Schmidt	Bringen sie mich bitte zu ihrem Anführer	Bitte stellen sie dieses Gedudel ab	Kennen sie den weg nach San Jose?	Geschüttelt, nicht gerührt
ITALIAN	Signor e Signora Rossi	Mi porta al suo capo	Gli dica al violinista di andarsene	Conoscete la strada al San Jose?	Agitato, non mescolato
PORTUGUESE	Senhor e Senhora Almeida	Leve-me ao seu chefe	Por favor, pare aquele violinista	O senhor sabe o caminho para San Jose?	Sacudido, não mexido
SPANISH	Señor y Señora Garcia	Lléveme a su líder	Por favor, dígale a su jugador del violín que pare	¿Usted sabe llegar a San Jose?	Sacudarido, no revuelto
THAI	Nai lae Nang Amatayakul	Pa chan pai ha chao nai	Karuna hai kon lain violin yud lain sak tee	Khun saab sentang tee ja pai San Jose mai?	Kha-yao, tae mai khon
TURKISH	Bay ve Bayan Adivar	Mudurunuzle gorusmek istiyorum	Lutfen kemanci calmayi kessin	San Jose'ye nasil gidilir iliyormusunuz?	Sarsildim, ama yikilmadim

GOODNESS, OFFICER, WAS I REALLY DRIVING THAT FAST?	THAT'S NOT AN OFFICIAL HAND SIGNAL	NO, I HAVE NOT STOLEN YOUR BATHROBE	FOLLOW THAT CAR!	I LOVE YOU
Monsieur, est-ce que je conduisais vraiment si vite que ça?	Ca n'est pas un geste de conduire official	Non, je n'ai pas volé votre robe de chambre	Suivez cette voiture-là!	Je t'aime
Mein Gott, bin ich wirklich so schnell gefahren?	Dies ist kein offizielles Handzeichen	Nein, ich habe ihren Morgenmantel nicht gestohlen	Folgen sie diesem Wagen!	Ich liebe dich
Ma ufficiale, andavo davvero a quella velocita?	Questo non è un segnale di mano usato	No, non ho rubato la vostra vestaglia	Segui quella macchina!	Ti amo
Estava indo tão rápido mesmo, senhor?	Isto não parece um sinal oficial	Não, não robei seu ropão	Siga aquele carro!	Te amo
¿De verdad, iba tan rápido, agente?	Eso no es una señal con la mano uniforme	No, no he robado su albornoz	¡Siga ese coche!	Te quiero
Auy-tai, khun tam ruad, phom khub reaw yang nan jing rue?	Nan mai chai san yan mue mad-tra-than	Plao na, phom mai dai kamo-ey chud klum aab nam pai	Tam rot khun nun pai!	Chan rak khun
Memur bey, gercekten o kadar hizli mi suruyordum?	Bu resmi bir trafik isareti degildir	Hayir kiy afetinizi ben calmadim	O arabayi takip et, hizli!	Seni seviyorum

Cape Town

SOUTH AFRICA

CAPE TOWN
Alta Bay

CAPE TOWN

COASTLINE Super-spectacular seaboard
COAST LIFE Lived on a grand scale

Atlantic beaches and soaring mountains cradle this thriving metropolis, which clings to the underskirts of Table Mountain. South Africa's oldest city has a cosmopolitan personality and a welcoming spirit that you'll encounter in the many bars and boutiques of Long and Kloof streets, or wandering through the Malay Quarter. The city centre is walkably compact, tucked neatly between Lion's Head and the Docks; bustling Camps Bay is the strip the sun-seekers flock to by day, and where crowds sip sundowners at dusk. Once you've communed with the surf, there's no shortage of excitement on turf, from safari adventures and cloud-scraping climbs to winelands tours. Dining out in Cape Town means world-class seafood, sushi, steaks, curries, haute cuisine and casual grub: with the city's streets mopping up more sunshine than almost anywhere else on Earth, an empty alfresco café table is a joy to behold.

GETTING THERE

Planes Served by Virgin Atlantic, KLM, BA and South African Airways, Cape Town International Airport (www.airports.co.za) is a 30-minute drive from the centre. You might also arrive via Johannesburg, a two-hour flight away.
Trains The main station is on Adderley Street, with departures to South Africa's major cities. A tempting luxury option is the famous Blue Train (www.bluetrain.co.za).
Automobiles Driving can be an adventure. Tip: at roundabouts there are four-way stops, so whoever gets there first, leaves first; minibus taxis have right of way.

LOCAL KNOWLEDGE

Taxis You'll find metered cabs at ranks, or ask your hotel to arrange one. For anything longer than a hop, call Rikki's (0861 745 547; www.rikkis.co.za), which operates a fleet of London-style taxis and airport shuttles.
Currency South African rand (ZAR).
Dialling codes South Africa: 27. Cape Town: (0)21.
Tipping culture It is customary to tip 10–15 per cent for what is usually super-friendly service.
Siesta and fiesta Dining isn't usually a late date, with most restaurants wrapping things up around 11pm. Shops usually close by 5.30pm, and sometimes 1pm on Saturday.
Do go/don't go Cape Town is fantastic year-round, with autumn cooler and less windy (between March and May). Hotels get very busy around New Year and January.
Packing tips In summer (November to February), bring SPF 30 sunblock, but also a sweater for days when the city gets a visit from the brisk 'Cape Doctor' – the southeasterly wind that means you will get to use your surfing gear.
Recommended reads Stray from feelgood beach reads, and try *A Dry White Season* by Andre Brink, or *July's People* by Nadine Gordimer, both great accomplishments from the apartheid era. Post-apartheid novels, which are strong, though not merry, include *Disgrace* by JM Coetzee and *The Heart of Redness* by Zakes Mda.
Cuisine The local freshwater fish and meat are extremely good; warthog may sound weird, but it's the tastiest ham you'll ever eat. The Malay influences on Cape cuisine bring in semi-sweet curries, and you must try authentic bredie (stew) and sosaties (kebab), but what Capetonians really love is a *braai* or barbecue – carnivorous heaven. Biltong aficionados should visit Joubert & Monty's Biltong (021 421 7272) in the Clock Tower Centre for slices of savoury

satisfaction. Head into the Cape Winelands to sample liquid gold and garnet with a meal at one of the vineyard restaurants; book well ahead for lunch at La Petite Ferme (021 880 8167) in Franschhoek; ask for a window table.

WORTH GETTING OUT OF BED FOR

Viewpoint Don't miss getting to the top of Table Mountain (there's a network of more than 500 routes – Platteklip Gorge is the recommended one for hikers). Or at least take the cable car (www.tablemountain.net); just be aware that if the weather changes, you may have to walk back down. Our top tips are to go early in the day to avoid the crowds; and remember to take some water and a light jacket – it gets chilly up there at the top.

Arts and culture You can get into the National Gallery, the South African Museum (www.iziko.org.za) and the acclaimed new Jewish Museum (www.sajewishmuseum. co.za) via the Gardens, a pretty green space near the city centre originally planted by Cape founder Jan van Riebeeck. Artscape Theatre Centre (www.artscape.co.za) is a venue for opera and classical music in City Bowl. Jazz clubs of note include Dizzy's Jazz Café (www.dizzys. co.za) in Camps Bay, and laid-back Kennedy's Cigar Lounge (021 424 1212; www.kennedys.co.za) at 251 Long Street.

Activities Hire a Harley and take to the spectacular coast roads (www.harley-davidson-capetown.com). Adrenalin junkies can get their fix over and over again, with golf, mountain biking and walking, boat and kayak trips, sailing, surfing and windsurfing all on tap. Companies to consult on keeping busy include Cape Rainbow Tours (021 551 5465; www.caperainbow.com); Tigger 2 Charter (021 790 5256; www.tiggertoo.co.za) for *braai* cruises from Hout Bay harbour; and African Shark Eco Charters (021 785 1947; www.ultimate-animals.com) for shark-spotting trips and cage dives.

Best beach Clifton Beach is made up of four coves; the fourth is the most popular in summer. Camps Bay is a long sandy beach with plenty of good cafés and restaurants; or try quiet Llandudno, a far cry from its Welsh namesake. A 15-minute drive from the city, Hout Bay is great for people- and parasurfer-watching. If icy dips set your teeth on edge, you'll find the water on the False Bay side of the peninsula several degrees warmer than on the Atlantic side.

Daytripper Drive through the lush Cape Winelands: the R45 takes you over the Franschhoek Pass, with wow-factor vineyard and mountain views. At Spier (www.spier.co.za), near Stellenbosch, you can sample five wines for a few bucks, eat pan-African fare in Moyo, and stroke one of the furry inhabitants of its Cheetah Outreach Programme.

Walks Table Mountain is there for the taking (the route from Kirstenbosch National Botanical Garden will make you glad you huffed and puffed your way up there), or you can walk along the seafront, four miles from the Sea Point public swimming pool to Mouille Point lighthouse.

Shopping Long Street is lined with enticing galleries and antiques stores. Explore Pan African Market's maze of passages (021 426 4478), and Burr & Muir (021 422 1319) on the corner of Church Street for art deco and nouveau treasures; they'll happily ship your purchases. If Africana and craftworks ring your bell, try Out Of This World, shop 6147 (021 419 3246) at the popular V&A Waterfront harbour complex (www.waterfront.co.za). Or steal Nelson Mandela's style in one of Desré Buirski's hand-painted silk pieces, from Presidential Shirt (021 421 1695) in the Clock Tower Centre. Keep your receipts so you can claim back taxes at the airport before check-in.

Something for nothing Go animal-spotting: African penguins pose on the rocks all year round at Boulders Beach, half an hour south of the city; monkeys might swing by to say hello along the way. From July to November, you'll see Southern Right whales from the cliff paths at the gentrified fishing village of Hermanus, about 90 minutes away.

Don't go home without... drinking sundowners with a view. Head to Capetonian favourite the Lower Deck at Blue Peter (021 554 1956), on Popham Road, Bloubergstrand, and sit on the lawn looking towards Table Mountain.

CAPTIVATINGLY CAPE TOWN

Tackle Lion's Head, at its most romantic during full moon; get there for sunset over the Atlantic and watch Cape Town 'switching on' at dusk. But please take a flashlight: the bickering and bruises in store for the unilluminated are not what you want to remember of the evening. Also visit Robben Island (021 413 4200; www.robben-island.org.za), where Nelson Mandela was held prisoner with other anti-apartheid campaigners. The tours by former inmates are not only fascinating, but also incredibly touching; ticket prices include ferry transfers.

DIARY

February–April Cape Town Festival (www.capetownfestival.co.za) is an arts extravaganza that takes place in the City Bowl and at the Waterfront; the short-film and food offerings are our favourite part of it. **May** The Cape Town Good Food & Wine Show – yum! (www.gourmetsa. com). **September** Cape Town International Comedy Festival (www.comedyfestival.co.za), when sex and politics are definitely not glossed over. The annual Hermanus Whale Festival (www.whalefestival.co.za) celebrates our big marine pals, with music and gourmet offerings. **November–April** Picnic in the prettiest part of town, to the smooth sounds of Kirstenbosch Summer Sunset Concerts (www.nbi.ac.za). **December** Cape Town's New Year's shenanigans.

Alta Bay

STYLE Elegant and unfussy
SETTING Table Mountain tranquillity
DESTINATION Cape Town

'When it came to capturing our particular
hearts, it was the size of the bed that won
us over. Our eyes lit up when we saw the
scale of that baby: a king among kings'

In a city as small as Cape Town, it should have been easy enough to find a boutique hotel situated on the slopes of Table Mountain. At least, so I thought. It looked simple enough on the map – yet there we were, meandering up and down, through the twisting lanes of the area called Higgovale. Through a process of elimination (and an unintentional game of Ding Dong Ditch), we eventually discovered the discreet entrance of Alta Bay hotel.

We were greeted by the widest of smiles, belonging to Lawrence, the hotel's duty manager. I would offer his Xhosa name but I'm embarrassed to admit I couldn't pronounce it. (Note: there are 11 official languages in South Africa, and I am labouring at this one.) He quickly whisked away our bags and escorted us through the gates, behind which lay a perfect private mountain hideaway right in the heart of the city, with a spectacular view towards the bay.

Fresh from getting a bit lost on our way here, we let Lawrence lead the way and give us a tour. The main house is a carefully designed mixture of bleached floorboards, rich fabrics and minimalist sophistication. We succumbed to its sense of warmth and style, helped no end by the South African sunshine and the free communal house bar. Our room, on the upper level, had its own private terrace, looking directly through the trees and wisteria onto Table Bay. Ensconced down in that lush garden, you could almost forget you were in the heart of Cape Town, except that it's laid out beneath you in plain view.

Anyone who has overdosed on cheap chintz and fusty fussiness in ill-chosen hotels over the years would revel in Alta Bay's understated style, its natural palette, soft linens and suede. There is sufficient gadgetry to keep the kind of people who store their *Star Wars* figurines in the original boxes occupied for hours. When it came to capturing our particular hearts, it was the size of the bed that won us over. We're both on the tall side, so our eyes lit up when we saw the scale of that baby: a king among kings, extended in all directions.

Since Alta Bay doesn't offer dining after 8pm, we decided to venture out. I had booked a table at a local favourite

called Haiku. You know the schtick: a see-and-be-seen crowd; state-of-the-art open kitchen; and the star attraction of highly polished Asian fusion cuisine. It hit the spot perfectly.

Having gone for the sophisticated supper option on our first night, we decided, on our second, to stay at Alta Bay and take advantage of the most intimate option. How could we resist, with a triple-whammy on our laps: an alfresco, candlelit, private terrace? The hotel is obviously keen to put you in 'the mood', too: when we returned to our room after sharing a plate of delicious sandwiches and a bottle of fruity Stellenbosch wine, we discovered a suitably sexy soundtrack streaming from the sound system. (Try saying that 10 times after a few glasses of wine.)

As a break from our relaxation, I did manage to persuade Mrs Smith to get close to Table Mountain. The tourist brochures describe this landmark as 'magical and mystical' but, as it reaches 1,086 metres at its highest point, a walk up to the summit just didn't appeal – especially under such warm African sun. I pointed to the cable car and Mrs Smith smirked conspiratorially. Within 10 minutes, having felt my body and my breakfast rotate several times (the cable car's spinning – OK, gently revolving – floor ensures that all passengers get a 360-degree aerial view), we were at the top, which looks like the mountain fortress in *Where Eagles Dare*. The panoramic eyeful put Alta Bay's location on Cape Town's peninsula, between Table Bay, False Bay and Hout Bay, into perfect perspective. At the top, the flat summit is ideal for a leisurely stroll.

Alta Bay made the ideal private sanctuary in which to unwind lazily. The service remained discreet, and what did grab our attention was how remarkable the level of attentiveness – we were made to feel more like privileged house guests than paying hotel customers. Each evening, an anecdote, poem, weather report or piece of personal advice would be offered, based on the smallest of conversations we'd had with staff. Touches such as these leave a lasting impression.

Days were spent gazing sleepily into the distance, barely focusing on the magazines we were 'reading'. The only

noticeable intrusion would come at midday, when the noon cannon erupted – a local tradition harking back to former colonial days – causing me to sit bolt upright every time. It certainly makes an effective alarm clock. How else would we have roused ourselves to leave the poolside and order another freshly squeezed tropical juice?

Reviewed by Mr & Mrs Smith

'We succumbed to Alta Bay's sense of warmth and style, helped no end by the South African sunshine and the free communal bar'

NEED TO KNOW

Rooms Seven.

Rates R1,300–R2,700.

Check-out 11am but flexible, subject to availability.

Facilities Plunge pool, garden, free WiFi, CD/DVD library, laundry service, complimentary access to Virgin Active gyms, yoga, Pilates and spa treatments on request, In rooms, satellite flatscreen TV, CD/DVD player, air-conditioning, Charlotte Rhys toiletries.

Children The hotel is not suitable for younger ones, but children aged 12 or above are welcome. As rooms are for two people only, though, extra beds are not available.

Also No pets. Over the Christmas and New Year period, there is a minimum stay of six nights.

IN THE KNOW

Our favourite rooms All rooms are unique. The Garden Room is particularly private and secluded, and it has a large bathroom. We also love the Bay Room, which offers beautiful sea views framed by pine trees.

Hotel bar There is a sideboard in the dining room full of complimentary drinks – so there's no last orders. All the management ask is that guests are respectful of others staying at Alta Bay.

Hotel restaurant No restaurant. Breakfast is served daily till 11am. It consists, among other things, of freshly baked croissants, fruit salad and a cold buffet. Lunch and dinner can be ordered from the room-service menu.

Top table You can't go wrong with your private patio or terrace.

Room service Eating and drinking is, like everything at Alta Bay, extremely flexible. There's a light menu available between noon and 8pm daily. Food is served in the dining room or on your terrace.

Dress code Dress up or dress down – whatever makes you feel relaxed and comfortable.

Local knowledge Leave the city behind for a day or two, and drive the 30 minutes out to Constantia, where there are more award-winning winemakers than you can shake a corkscrew at. Go for a tasting at the Constantia Uitsig estate (www.constantia-uitsig.com), and get the vineyard to send a case of your favourite vintage back home for you.

LOCAL EATING AND DRINKING

Haiku (021 424 7000) at 33 Church Street (entrance on Burg Street) specialises in wonderful Asian tapas. The chic interior features a bustling open kitchen; two sections are devoted to Chinese cooking and another two to Japanese. **Ginja** (021 426 2368), on Castle Street in Bo-Kaap, is still at the forefront of Cape Town's experimental fusion scene – serving up dishes such as springbok bresaola with corn ice-cream and venison with bitter chocolate – and, as such, is extremely difficult to get into. Just as well, then, that Alta Bay holds a permanent table at the restaurant. Ask your concierge to make you a booking. We also like the upmarket Italian cuisine at **95 Keerom** (021 422 0765), by the High Court on Keerom Street, and **Salt Restaurant & Bar** (021 439 7258), which serves an ever-changing seasonal menu behind floor-to-ceiling windows that offer dramatic views of Bantry Bay.

GET A ROOM!

To book this hotel, go to www.mrandmrssmith.com or ring our expert travel team on 1 800 464 2040. Activate your free membership online (see page 4) to qualify for the exclusive Smith card offer shown below when you book with us.

 SMITH CARD OFFER A complimentary bottle of South African red or white wine.

Alta Bay 12 Invermark Crescent, Higgovale, Cape Town 8001 (www.mrandmrssmith.com/alta-bay)

Barcelona

Seville Province

SPAIN

BARCELONA
Hotel Omm

SEVILLE PROVINCE
Hacienda de San Rafael

BARCELONA

CITYSCAPE Marvellous modernism
CITY LIFE Energetic and colourful

Basking on the sun-kissed shores of the Mediterranean, the Catalan capital is a naturally romantic, lover-friendly city. From the mountains to the beach, wide tree-lined boulevards unravel into pretty parks and shady squares with tiny, happy bars, where a too-hot afternoon is never wasted. Exploring 2,000 years of history here's a breeze: a port since Roman times, Barcelona has flamboyant art deco architecture to rival that of Paris; Gaudí's fantastical façades beckon from every street corner, and the redeveloped beachfront boasts sleek modern buildings. The Spanish city keeps its finger firmly on the pulse, and has always embraced bold design and all things new. Buzzing bars and restaurants in the Gothic Quarter and El Born ensure the city and her visitors party late into the night. No wonder cava is the drink of choice – this is a place with much to celebrate.

GETTING THERE

Planes From Barcelona Airport (www.barcelona-airport. com), taxis will whisk you into town in 15 minutes, for €15–€20. The Aerobus runs every 15 minutes (€3.50).
Trains The 25-minute train journey from airport to centre costs €2.20; trains run every half an hour. Spain also has a reasonably priced national network. Book ahead, as trains can get busy (www.renfe.com). Barcelona's Metro system is efficient – and air-conditioned (www.tmb.net).
Automobiles Driving is fine once you master the one-way system, but finding a parking space is a nightmare. Taxis are cheap, so it's not worth renting a car anyway; and the train is perfect for day trips.

LOCAL KNOWLEDGE

Taxis You can hail a metered, wasp-coloured cab from anywhere on the street, as long as its green light is on.
Currency Euro (€).
Dialling codes Spain: 34. Barcelona: 93.
Tipping culture In restaurants, tip only if the service was good. Catalans leave behind a few small coins in bars. If you really want to tip your driver, give 5–10 per cent max.
Siesta and fiesta Don't go out until after 9pm as all the

restaurants will be dead – and most of the bars don't start jumping until well after 11pm. Many businesses also close for an afternoon snooze between 1pm and 4pm.
Do go/don't go Locals leave August to the tourists, as the city can be too hot to handle – even some museums are closed. Avoid public holidays if you can: they trigger a city exodus that means things tend to be shut.
Packing tips Swimmers – Barcelona has a beach. Stamina – if you want to make the most of Barça's bar scene.
Recommended reads Carlos Ruiz Zafón's 1950s detective novel *The Shadow of the Wind* is the ultimate book-lover's book; art critic Robert Hughes' *Barcelona* casts an eye over the city's cultural wealth; Catalan author Eduardo Mendoza's *City of Marvels* fictionalises the birth of modern Barcelona.
Cuisine Catalan meals are a surf 'n' turf love affair, spotlighting fresh and marinaded seafood, grills and cured meats; modern favourites include mar i muntanya – seaside lobster with slope-dwelling rabbit. Look out for places offering a lunchtime *menú del día* (set menu) for €10–€15. If you're vegetarian, you might have to do a little restaurant research to find exciting meat-free menus, unless you want to spend your weekend eating

olives and manchego cheese (although, washed down with a glass of fino, this is a fine snack). If you have a sweet tooth, visit century-old patisserie Escribà (93 454 7535; www.escriba.es) on Gran Via, where edible skirts, lickable walls and sugar-coated dragons are a speciality. **And…** Tickets for concerts, films and Barça soccer matches can be bought at ServiCaixa ATMs (or book online at www.servicaixa.com and collect tickets from the machine later).

WORTH GETTING OUT OF BED FOR

Viewpoint Our favourite vistas are from Montjuïc and its cable car; and from Mount Tibidabo – take the blue tram to the foot of the hill, then the funicular railway to the summit. If you're feeling extra brave, ride one of the rickety funfair antiques while you're there. Vertigo sufferers might prefer to have drinks on the strikingly surreal rooftop of Casa Milà (93 484 5900), looking across the Eixample district.

Arts and culture Antoni Gaudí left an incredible legacy in Barcelona, from his undulating apartment block La Pedrera (Casa Milà) to his swansong, the Sagrada Família, still under construction. You can queue up to climb the towers, but your time will be more enjoyably spent wandering around. The city pays tribute to other great artists with the Museu Picasso (93 256 3000; www.museupicasso.bcn.es) and Fundació Joan Miró (www.bcn.fjmiro.cat). The Museu d'Art Contemporani de Barcelona (www.macba.es) focuses on 20th-century Catalan artists.

Activities Pose among the statues or row a boat on the lake in Parc de la Ciutadella. Go for a morning jog or practise your sun salutations on Barceloneta beach. Watch the Spanish Grand Prix at the Circuit de Catalunya (www.circuitcat.com). Give your lungs (and thighs) a workout on the steps at Gaudí's Parc Güell. Hit the high notes at the Gran Teatro del Liceu (www.liceubarcelona.com) – one of Europe's great opera houses, and so beautiful that it's worth a visit even if you're not seeing a performance; for details, ring 93 485 9914.

Perfect picnic One of the best food markets is Mercat la Boquería (www.boqueria.info), just off Las Ramblas. Pick up chorizo, jamón ibérico, manchego and membrillo (quince preserve) from Aroma Ibèric (93 317 6887), and some fresh baguettes from Forn del Mercat, then make for Barceloneta, the city's man-made beach. Can't be bothered to break your own bread? Beachfront restaurant Agua (93 225 1272) has perfect sea views on a sunny day.

Daytripper Seasidey Sitges is a 35-minute train ride away; hit the beach in the morning and then spend the afternoon meandering the town's cobbled streets. The artistic community of Cadaques, ancient city of Girona and Dalí's hometown of Figueres are also a train ride away.

Walks Book a bespoke guided walk with Follow the Baldie (www.followthebaldie.com) for a unique perspective on Barcelona. Choose one of his mad-but-brilliant mountain rambles for amazing views and the occasional pitstop to prop up bars in village cafés; or a city walk focusing on art, anarchy, gypsies, boutiques or bodegas, depending on what tickles your fancy. If you prefer to follow your nose, there are trails aplenty up, down and around Montjuïc.

Shopping For designer labels, head for Passeig de Gràcia, a credit-card-eating luxury-brand paradise, or Avenue Diagonal, where you can also pick up high-cool, low-cost bargains in Zara's three-storey lifestyle megastore. You'll find boutiques and quirkier stores in El Born; swing by La Vinya del Senyor on Plaça Santa Maria for a glass of wine before hitting the younger shops in the Barri Gòtic (Gothic Quarter); Carrer Avinyo has a hip mix of dress-selling hairdressers, boutiques that become bars and vintage sneaker specialists. For foodie souvenirs, we love Colmado Quilez (93 215 2356) on Rambla de Catalunya.

Something for nothing At weekends, drummers play and tumblers, um, tumble in Parc de la Ciutadella. Las Ramblas is full of street entertainers (and pickpockets) every day.

Don't go home without… sneaking a peek at Catedral de la Seu (www.catedralbcn.org) in the Barri Gòtic – even church-phobic culture-dodgers will be impressed by its Gothic façade and sun-dappled, goose-enhanced cloisters.

BRILLIANTLY BARCELONA

Barça's bar culture is renowned – tasty snacking morsels partner delicious drinks, and beautiful people linger over conversation and sharing plates. Our favourite tapas bars are: Cal Pep (93 310 7961) on Plaça de les Olles, for traditional cured hams, daily specials and a bustly atmosphere; Cervecería Catalana (93 216 0368) on Carrer de Mallorca; Ciudad Condal (93 318 1997) on Rambla de Catalunya; Flash Flash (93 237 0990) on La Granada del Penedès for its tortillas; and trendy tapas pioneer Santa Maria on Commerç (93 315 1227).

DIARY

Feb/March The pre-Lent Carnival is a big deal here, particularly in Sitges, where there are feather-covered floats and spangly sequins galore (www.bcn.es/carnaval). **March–June** Festival de Guitarra (www.the-project.net): all strummers welcome for this plucking great international guitar fest. **April** The 23rd is La Diada de Sant Jordi, Barcelona's Valentine's Day, when lovers exchange gifts; ladies get roses, gents get books, everyone dances in Plaça Sant Juane. **June** Body-climbing castellers build human towers in Plaça Catalunya and Gracià's streets are decorated during Festa Major de Gràcia. **October–November** Wailing horns and syncopation at the Festival Internacionál de Jazz de Barcelona (www.barcelonajazzfestival.com).

Hotel Omm

STYLE Architect-designed detail
SETTING Art nouveau side street
DESTINATION Barcelona

'Wow. The pinnacle of urban living
must be an elegant rooftop terrace
with a swimming pool, and this was
an immaculate, wood-lined haven'

slabs is tautly pulled back like a sheet of white metal, and repeatedly slashed, creating slits for thin windows and small balconies protected from the full glare of the Mediterranean sun.

We'd packed light, but though the revolving door is big enough for most visitors' accessories, it was a little too small for ours. Then again, not all lovers take a pram with them on a romantic break – let alone its contents. Fortunately one of the adjacent sheets of glass slid back to reveal a sleek minimalist reception area. No sombre oil paintings, so popular in lobbies of swanky hotels across the world. In fact, there aren't any pictures at all. This is Omm's design ethic in a nutshell: the straight lines and plain materials are in themselves the art.

Even with a 16-month-old ankle-biter in tow, we found ourselves treated kindly from the start, and a sweet receptionist took us straight up to our room. Some couples request oysters and champagne on ice waiting for them in their room... We'd ordered a baby cot. It wasn't there yet but soon arrived, and managed to fit into the room's perfectly integrated minimalist wood-and-metal decor. (Something a grabbing-hands-everywhere Master Smith was having a little trouble doing.)

Everything looked crisp but felt comfy, and the walls, bathroom fixtures, sheets and towels were all a pristine white – a particular treat for parents of a toddler. We had an interior room, so our balcony overlooked the internal courtyard; the contrast of the scruffy rears of the buildings opposite and the elegant, modern perfection of the hotel framing them is a sight to behold. And for those who want to revel only in design-conscious bliss, there's a gauze blind, transparent enough for light to penetrate but sufficiently opaque to keep out the imperfections of the outside world.

Resisting the temptation to collapse on the bed for a siesta, we headed up to the pool bar. Wow. The pinnacle of urban living must be an elegant rooftop terrace with a swimming pool, and this was an immaculate, wood-lined haven. Looking out across the jumbled horizon of Barcelona and the gorgeous Mediterranean sky, we ordered two Spanish-strength gin and tonics to sip as

I have to start with a confession. This Mr and Mrs Smith live in Barcelona, so a visit to a boutique hotel on our home turf was going to have to be pretty special to make it a weekend we'd never forget. When I discovered we were to be staying at Hotel Omm, the sister to my favourite restaurant, Acontraluz, I decided it wasn't going to be a problem...

We hopped in the car, waved goodbye to thirtysomething domesticity and made our journey across town. Finding Hotel Omm, just off Paseo de Grácia, the main avenue in the middle of Barcelona's art nouveau grid, isn't hard. In keeping with its neighbours, it's a seven-storey building with a flat front. However, as this is a city touched by the hand of Gaudí (his apartment block La Pedrera is just around the corner), Hotel Omm clearly felt obliged to do something quirky. The façade of small, white rectangular

we soaked up the view. As well as nuns scurrying around the convent across the road, we could see the eccentric swirls of La Pedrera's fantastical roof, one block away. To our left, the spires of Barcelona's most emblematic building, Gaudí's unfinished cathedral La Sagrada Família, were visible in the distance. Armchair sightseers can delight in two checks in their tourist tick boxes without having to leave the comfort of their sunloungers. Perfect.

We could have happily stayed there all day, but we mustered the energy to stumble down to the spa. Spaciomm transports you to an Asian-accented haven. I put on my grey kimono and Camper slippers, and tottered past an indoor plunge pool to a sweet-smelling treatment room. Here the therapist gave my feet a pre-massage scrub in a bowl of rose petals. Whale music intolerants, fear not – Omm's new-agey tunes are suitably soporific. I'm gently ushered to a relaxation lounge where something hot and herbal from the tea room awaits along with a black curved lounger and bean-bag eye mask; in true Omm style, a switch is pressed and the bed begins to rock.

At 9.30pm, we head to the hotel restaurant, which is called, curiously, Moo. It is the creation of the Roca brothers, world-famous for their creative combinations of ingredients

231

and flavours. Their disdain for convention is perhaps most apparent in the spindly chocolate mixed with salt that arrived with the coffee. With every dish a half portion, we could try twice as many things. Each serving comes with a carefully selected wine: another incentive (as if you needed one) to have as many plates as possible. You find yourself ordering not just to sample the mouthwatering French-influenced food, but also for the wine that comes with it: foie gras and figs with a Pedro Ximénez; entrecôte with an Haut Médoc... We may not have left town, but our tastebuds went all over Europe.

Though we only had five floors to ascend to get to our room, the corridors were an experience in themselves. With no natural light, the charcoal-grey carpet and walls are illuminated only by a purplish glow and two phosphorescent white lines that run either side of the floor, the length of the corridor. The runway effect proved fortunate after six different wines over dinner.

Master Smith awoke a little earlier than usual, and our pitch-black room was quickly transformed from a temple of calculated style to the chaos of a child's playpen. We all went for a morning swim on the roof and then down for breakfast in the open-plan bar. Could there be a more wonderful start to the day than the juice of fresh Sicilian oranges, delicious local breads, cheeses and salamis, exotic jams, and sandwiches of cheese and Mediterranean tomatoes that melt in the mouth? Sadly, just as we had eaten our fill, we realised it was time to leave.

We'd had a wonderful break without even leaving our everyday stomping ground. So fabulous was the aesthetic and gastronomic experience that Mrs Smith insists we do it more often. I give in on the strength of the breakfast alone.

Reviewed by Mr & Mrs Smith

NEED TO KNOW

Rooms 91, including four suites.

Rates €235–€805, including VAT. Breakfast, €22.50.

Check-out Noon. Earliest check-in, 2pm.

Facilities Laundry, car-parking services, limousine service, shoe-cleaning service. In rooms, satellite TV, CD players, internet connection.

Children Little ones are welcome at the hotel, and baby cots can be supplied. The restaurant is not suitable for small Smiths; however, a children's menu at the bar caters for them.

Also The Spaciomm spa offers a world of relaxation for those in need of a pummel and rub after a day pounding city streets. Choose between a Turkish hammam, an oriental Tatimi cabin or even a subaquatic massage.

IN THE KNOW

Our favourite rooms We love the huge suites, which offer great views of Paseo de Grácia and beyond. Rooms facing the interior garden have bigger balconies.

Hotel bar There's one minimalist cocktail bar/lounge, and another that focuses on fine wines. Both are open till 3am.

Hotel restaurant Moo serves Catalan haute cuisine; its Michelin-approved triumvirate of chefs (brothers Joan, Josep and Jordi Roca) have two stars. Set at the back of the open-plan ground floor, it looks onto an enclosed bamboo forest.

Top table Ask for a spot in the corner to maximise people-watching opportunities.

Room service 24 hours; the full restaurant menu is available when Moo is open, otherwise you're looking at sandwiches and salads.

Dress code Fashionably formal.

Local knowledge If you want to follow your cocktails in the Hotel Omm bar with a spot of clubbing, there's no need for any of the usual hailing taxis and joining queues nonsense. OmmSession, open from Wednesday to Saturday, is a scene-stealing basement club that often features live entertainment. It is open until 3am; 3.30am on Saturday nights.

LOCAL EATING AND DRINKING

7 Portes (93 319 3033) on Passeig d'Isabel II is Barcelona 's oldest restaurant, and serves an authentic Catalan menu in a formal environment with a pianist from 10.30pm. Fish-lovers should head to traditional **Botafumeiro** (93 218 4230) on Gran de Gracia. **Commerç 24** (93 319 2102) on Carrer Commerç is a fashionable, modern tapas restaurant: perfect for dinner. **Passadis del Pep** (93 310 1021) on Placa del Palau does good seafood – they call the shots on what you eat, which can be fun. **Acontraluz** (93 203 0658) is a bit out of the way, uptown on Milanesat, but it's a cool, contemporary restaurant with a lively atmosphere and great Mediterranean food; ask for a seat in the conservatory. **Cal Pinxo** (93 221 2211), by the Museum of Catalan History on Placa Pau Vila, is another good option by the seafront. Get a table as close to the water as you can, and order fresh razor clams or monkfish in tomato and garlic.

GET A ROOM!

To book this hotel, go to www.mrandmrssmith.com or ring our expert travel team on 1 800 464 2040. Activate your free membership online (see page 4) to qualify for the exclusive Smith card offer shown below when you book with us.

 SMITH CARD OFFER A complimentary glass of Catalan cava each on arrival, plus a chocolate selection created especially for the hotel by world-renowned confectioner Oriol Balaguer.

Hotel Omm 265 Rosselló, 08008 Barcelona (www.mrandmrssmith.com/hotel-omm)

SEVILLE PROVINCE

COUNTRYSIDE White cottages, orange blossom
COUNTRY LIFE Fiesta and flamenco

The sultry Andalucían province of Seville is the very soul of southern Spain: whitewashed villages decked with orange blossom and bougainvillea; long hot afternoons in peaceful plazas; tapas and sherry after an evening stroll; and passionate nights of foot-stamping, skirt-swirling fiesta. Whether your idea of holiday heaven is the slow burn of a summer's day at a tranquil hacienda, or bundling into a car to explore mountains and mediaeval cities, this region is irresistible. From the sleepy heartlands planted with olives and vines rises the full-blooded, pulsing metropolis of Seville, rich in Moorish heritage and filled with cathedrals, ornate palaces and thrilling flamenco clubs. Equally wild and untamed, the pristine beaches of the Costa de la Luz stretch for miles along the coast; and, inland, you can calm your heartbeat in the chestnut woods and sleepy *pueblos blancos* of the sierras.

GETTING THERE

Planes The nearest airports with regular flights are Jerez, in the neighbouring province of Cadiz, and Seville's San Pablo airport. The airport bus takes 20 minutes to the centre of Seville; a taxi should cost around €20.
Trains Super-fast AVE trains will get you from Madrid to Seville in two and a half hours, from €65. The region's local train network (www.renfe.es) is limited and can be slow.
Automobiles If you're staying in Seville itself, a car isn't worth the effort, but is a necessity for the countryside, especially if you want to visit the mountains or coast.

LOCAL KNOWLEDGE

Taxis Cabs are cheap and, in towns, can be hailed in the street. They display a green 'libre' notice or green light at night if they are available.
Currency Euro (€).
Dialling codes Spain: 34. Seville: 95.
Tipping culture In restaurants, 10 per cent is appreciated; otherwise, a couple of euros with drinks or tapas is enough.
Siesta and fiesta On weekdays, banks and shops close from 2pm–5pm, and at 2pm on Saturdays. Evenings start much later in the south, even compared to the rest of Spain: restaurants and bars aren't busy until well after 9pm.
Do go/don't go The Seville region can be stiflingly hot and crowded in high summer. Spring has fine weather and several of the year's most important festivals, while autumn is warm and peaceful. It's sunny even in winter.

Packing tips Jodhpurs and riding boots, for trekking on the beaches, along the Via Verde or in the Grazamelo region. A sunhat, for fending off the heat in high summer.
Recommended reads *Death in the Afternoon* is Ernest Hemingway's paean to bullfighting; Michael Jacobs takes a wry look at village life in *The Factory of Light*; Douglas Carlton Abrams' romantic thriller *The Lost Diary of Don Juan* puts a racy spin on the legendary seducer of Seville.
Cuisine Freshly grilled fish, prawns and squid from the Costa de la Luz are delicious, but salt cod and pork are the ingredients most likely to appear on menus. Gazpacho – a garlicky tomato soup, served ice-cold with croutons

and condiments – is an Andalucían summer staple; in Seville, try salmorejo, gazpacho's thicker, simpler cousin. As well as heat-beating chilled soups, Seville Province is famous for its tapas, particularly in the city: pick at smoked serrano ham, roasted peppers, peppery cheeses and fat, juicy olives. With Sanlúcar and Jerez nearby, this is the heart of Spain's sherry country, too – a dry fino or manzanilla is the perfect accompaniment to tapas.
And... Pop into El Rinconcillo on Calle Gerona in Seville (95 422 3183); this tapas bar has been serving since 1760.

WORTH GETTING OUT OF BED FOR

Viewpoint The 12th-century Giralda – a 97m bell tower – was once the minaret of Seville's main mosque, and offers superb views. Lebrija – a pretty walled town near Las Cabezas de San Juan – overlooks rolling vineyards.

Arts and culture Seville's cathedral is the world's largest Gothic building, with five naves. The Alcázar's mudéjar architecture, fabulous gardens, fountains and ornate rooms bring Granada's Moorish palaces to mind. The Palacio de Lebrija on Calle Cuna (www.palaciodelebrija.com) has an impressive collection of Roman mosaics. Nearby Jerez is famous for its beautiful dancing horses; if you miss the main Thursday show at the Royal Andalusian School of Riding (www.realescuela.org), the morning practice sessions are open to the public, and you might catch the horses being put through their paces on a guided tour.

Activities There are bullfights every Sunday in Seville's Plaza de Toros de la Maestranza, from Easter Sunday to early October (95 422 4577; www.sptkts.com). If you want to learn a few new flamenco-style moves, book lessons at Estudio Flamenco Carmen de Torres (www. flamenco-carmendetorres.com) or Escuela Flamenca Juan Polvillo (www.escuelaflamenca.com). Horse riding, sailing and visits to the province's bull-breeding ranches are easy to organise once you're in the region. If you have your own transport, the mountains of the Parque Natural Sierra de Grazalema are popular for canyoning, birdwatching, climbing, hiking and spelunking; contact Horizon (www.horizonaventura.com) for more details.

Perfect picnic Grab some snacks and head through the *pueblos blancos* of Cádiz province up to the mountain scenery of the Serranía de Ronda and the village of Zahara de la Sierra, for an idyllic picnic in chestnut woods.

Daytripper The Costa de la Luz offers miles of unspoilt beaches; Conil de la Frontera is one of the coast's finest. There are beautiful sandy coves at Los Caños de Meca,

southwest of Vejer de la Frontera, and the beach at Atlanterra, between Vejer and Tarifa, is pristine. Andalucía is sprinkled with pretty white towns and heritage sites: Carmona, Córdoba and Ronda all merit an excursion.

Walks The forest glades of the Sierra Norte park (www. sierranortedesevilla.com) are refreshed by rivers and pools – walk to the waterfalls of Huesna, 2km downriver of San Nicolas, through stands of cork, oak and elm. Well-marked trails of varying length criss-cross the park.

Shopping Seville's pedestrianised Calle Sierpes, near Plaza Nueva, is great for leather goods (and a quick coffee), and the parallel Calle Tetuan is lined with boutiques. There's a good antiques market on Calle Feria on Thursday mornings. Among the equestrian paraphernalia at El Caballo (95 421 8127) on Calle Antonia Díaz are beautifully crafted leather boots, belts and bags to rival luxury-label superbrands, for a fraction of the price. Nearby Sanlúcar and Jerez are the best places to go if you want to buy sherry direct from the bodega, but Seville is a good place to pick up a bottle of treacly oloroso or bone-dry manzanilla; or visit the 200-year-old Hidalgo bodega near Hacienda de San Rafael.

Something for nothing Dozens of operas are set in and around Seville. You can visit all the sites associated with the most famous – Bizet's *Carmen* – including Plaza de España, the tobacco factory and the bullring.

Don't go home without... trying tinto de verano, a refreshing mix of red wine with lemon or orange soda, or, if you're feeling bolder, agua de Sevilla, a potent mix of pineapple juice, champagne, whisky and rum.

SENSATIONALLY SEVILLE PROVINCE

Seville is the home of passionate flamenco. Casa de la Memoria de al-Andalus on Calle Ximénez de Enciso (95 456 0670) has nightly performances. Alternatively, just wander through la Macarena district to find more spontaneous song-and-dance performances at a small backstreet *peña* (bar/club).

DIARY

February–March The International Flamenco Festival (www.flamenco-world.com) in nearby Jerez is a riot of energetic dancing. **March/April** Semana Santa – candlelight, costumes and Catholicism in Seville's historic centre – marks the end of Lent. A few weeks later, Seville's Feria de Abril is one of the greatest spectacles in Spain, with flamenco, street parties, bullfights and equestrian parades (www.smith52.com). **Early May** The Jerez Horse Fair showcases the finest Spanish horsemanship (www.turismojerez.com). **August** Horse races take place on the beach at Sanlúcar on the second and fourth weekends of the month. **September–October** The Bienal de Flamenco (www.bienal-flamenco.org) takes place every two years (including 2008), and is the world's premier flamenco festival. Sanlúcar has a tapas festival along Calzada del Ejército in the second week of October. Visit www.andalucia.org for more event listings.

Hacienda de San Rafael

STYLE Spanish stately home
SETTING Wild southern ranchland
DESTINATION Seville Province

'We pass a tangle of cerise and orange
bougainvillea, and enter a terracotta-paved
courtyard. Butterflies dance around
the flowers and birdsong fills the air'

Smith and I are cruising in eerie silence along the flatlands between Seville and Jerez. She's brought her TomTom (the portable SatNav system that taxi drivers swear by) and, thanks to this telling us where to go, we haven't argued once. It's bliss. We hang a left, down a long dusty path that appears to be going nowhere. The setting is idyllic – you know the scene: rolling fields of sunflowers and cotton, olive trees, waving wheat... And in the warm evening light (the honey-drenched time that film-makers call the magic hour), it's like cruising into a Van Gogh. We swoosh past hedges of pink and white oleander, and the Hacienda de San Rafael smacks into view.

A gleaming-white, *cortijo*-style country house, with foot-thick walls and huge shuttered windows, the Hacienda offers grandeur without a whiff of ostentation. Two sweet-mannered Englishwomen meet us at the doorway, take away our bags and offer lemon iced tea. We follow them through the doorway – and past a tangle of cerise and orange bougainvillea – to a terracotta-paved courtyard. Butterflies dance around the flowers and evening birdsong fills the air. The owners are milling around and pop over for a chat.

The Hacienda has been in the Reid family for a century and a half, and, up until the 1960s, it was a working olive farm. The youngest generation, twentysomething Anthony and Patrick, run the place. They are responsible for its recent stylish makeover, blending the languorous sensuality of Spanish bullfighting country with Europhile sophistication. Mum Kuky is from nearby Jerez, and it was her dream to turn the family farm into a small guesthouse in keeping with the surrounding white villages. Her husband, Tim, worked as a hotelier with Mandarin Oriental before setting up the superbly luxurious Datai hotel in Langkawi, Malaysia. Patrick used to be a project manager at the Groucho Club in London, and Anthony organised swish safaris in Botswana. Between them, this family have all the skills to challenge any top resort – no wonder they got it so right here.

We are escorted into the living room, which contains a mix of upper-crust European and Far Eastern antiques that hints at the family's travels. Hacienda de San Rafael is a trove of fascinating treasures, and most of them have a story behind them – just get Anthony talking about his grandfather, a 'horseman and a gentleman' who won Jerez's annual Horseman of Gold award too many times to keep count of.

We are staying in a casita, a meticulously converted farm building with a thatched roof, away from the main house. It's expensive, but we do get a private terrace and infinity pool in a lovingly tended cottage garden. The main pool is spectacular, with manicured lawn, huge day beds and palm trees for shade – it's just that Mrs Smith and I have developed a taste for privacy.

The family's attention to detail is what distinguishes the Hacienda de San Rafael from so many other retreats. Not only is it stunning, but there are three pools, and a full complement of staff to cater to your every whim, too. The dining experience illustrates this well. Mrs Smith is a vegetarian who likes neither eggs nor mushrooms, so eating out in Spain has previously been a pain in the posterior. There is no problem here though, thanks to head chef Isabel Quinones, who whips up pumpkin and sage risotto, barbecued tofu kebabs and a delicious baked-aubergine concoction.

The food in the communal dining area is a highlight, and with the nearest café a 20-minute cab ride away, lunchtime tapas and lazy alfresco dinners at the hotel work fabulously. In fact, we spent days experiencing no urge to leave the Hacienda and its grounds, until suddenly we decided we really ought to venture out. So we trekked to Seville's mighty 15th-century cathedral, second only in size to St Peter's in Rome, and to the nearby Alcázar palace and gardens – and the tapas bars in between; all well worth leaving our luxury cocoon for. Mrs Smith was so taken by the Mudéjar architecture, stuccoed patios and intricate mosaic that she had to buy an extra memory card for her camera.

For the more energetic holidaymakers, the hotel can arrange pretty much any activity. As keen riders, we were delighted to meet Cuko, a family member with yet more hospitality credentials, who owns a private estate with 12 horses a short drive away. His morning rides through the Andalucían mountains, and picnics in the dappled light of local chestnut forests, are

hard to beat. For those times when you are feeling intrepid, there's much to do in and around the hotel: bustling Seville is a hop away; nearby Jerez is the sherry capital of the world; and Andalucía has a long equestrian and bullfighting history.

Having found this slice of paradise, though, you'd be forgiven for just flopping by the pool and ordering a martini and a massage. Just ask Mrs Smith – she became quite the expert at this by the end of our three-day sojourn. And I can't say I was too bad at following her lead.

Reviewed by Alex Proud

'A gleaming white *cortijo*-style house with foot-thick walls, the Hacienda offers grandeur without a whiff of ostentation'

NEED TO KNOW

Rooms 14, including three casitas.

Rates €240–€514, including Continental breakfast.

Check-out Noon, but this can be flexible. There is a shower room for use by guests after check-out. Check-in, 2pm.

Facilities Boutique, library, art gallery, massage and yoga on request, laundry service. In rooms, TV and CD player (in casitas), free WiFi.

Children Under-12s are only welcome at Hacienda de San Rafael if the hotel is booked in its entirety (though the hotel will occasionally make an exception to this rule).

Also The hotel can organise a picnic for you for €25 a person. There's also a paddle-tennis court and boules set you can borrow to ensure you don't have to spend the entire afternoon sat on a rug.

IN THE KNOW

Our favourite rooms Rooms 7, 9, 10 and 11 have bedrooms in the eaves and bathrooms, as well as verandas to sit out on. The three separate casitas have living rooms and shaded daybeds, and share their own garden and pool.

Hotel bar Luna Bar, with its live music and comfy white cushions to lounge on, is outdoors; the Sunset Bar is adjacent to the pool. Both serve all the wine, cocktails and spirits you could possibly want until 1am.

Hotel restaurant The indoor dining room is used in cooler weather; otherwise, dinner is served outside. The Mediterranean set menu is €55 a person, including wine. The fish kebabs and the creamy blue cheese and spinach soufflé are particularly delicious.

Top table Outside in the gardens.

Room service Take your pick from the same menu as you'll find in the restaurant, available from 8.30am till midnight.

Dress code Relaxed equestrian chic. Shirts open a couple buttons more than strictly necessary.

Local knowledge With so much beautiful rusticity on your doorstep – sierras, atmospheric villages and forests surround Hacienda de San Rafael – why not be inspired by the hotel's equestrian theme, and ride out into the countryside on horseback? Just speak to the owners, and they will organise a full day's 'safari' for you.

LOCAL EATING AND DRINKING

Egaña Oriza (95 422 7211) on Calle San Fernando in Seville is one of the city's finest restaurants, serving Andalucían and Basque cuisine. Up in the mountains, **Mesón el Tabanco** (95 671 6081) in the village of El Bosque does excellent game dishes in a rustic setting. In Jerez, **La Tasca** (95 631 0340) on Calle Paraíso is renowned for its delicious fish and shellfish. The seafood stew is particularly good. **Le Mesa Redonda** (95 634 0069), on Calle Manuel de Quintana, specialises in traditional Andalucían dishes such as balls of fishmeat in a shellfish sauce, monkfish and prawn pasties, and succulent grilled lamb. **Bar Juanito** (95 633 4838) on Pescadería Vieja is one of the best tapas bars in the province, with a choice of more than 50 dishes.

GET A ROOM!

To book this hotel, go to www.mrandmrssmith.com or ring our expert travel team on 1 800 464 2040. Activate your free membership online (see page 4) to qualify for the exclusive Smith card offer shown below when you book with us.

 SMITH CARD OFFER A free picnic, a private bodega visit, half a bottle of manzanilla when staying in a deluxe room and a bottle of house champagne when staying in a casita.

Hacienda de San Rafael Carretera N-IV Km 594, Las Cabezas de San Juan, Seville Province
(www.mrandmrssmith.com/hacienda-de-san-rafael)

Phuket and
Khao Lak

Aleenta Phuket-Phang Nga

PHUKET AND KHAO LAK

COASTLINE Silvery sands, palm-hung hammocks
COAST LIFE Farangs, flip-flops and fishing boats

Dropped like a giant pearl into the azure Andaman Sea, Phuket is a textbook tropical paradise of perfect beaches and rainforest-coated cliffs. The island hangs from the mainland by a bridge that connects it to Phang Nga province and Khao Lak, a sedate sliver of coast where desert-island beaches separate Thailand's top dive spots from waterfall-riddled national parks. Nature-lovers will revel in the region's lush landscapes and biodiversity, but there's more to life here than flora and fauna. The towns and temples offer their own thrills, from the unique Sino-Portuguese architecture of Phuket Town to the hectic tuk tuk-travelled streets of Patong Beach, home to some of Thailand's most dynamic – and infamous – nightlife. Whether you come here for a party, an insight into Buddhist culture, or just the healthy trinity of sand, sun and serenity, you'll find what you're looking for.

GETTING THERE

Planes 20 miles from Phuket Town, Phuket International Airport (www.phuketairportonline.com) is Thailand's busiest after Bangkok, with charter flights connecting to dozens of long-haul destinations.
Trains There's no rail service to Phuket. Buses travel from the Southern Bus Terminal in Thonburi, Bangkok, but the journey is a back-straining 14 hours. It makes far more sense to hop on a one-hour, no-frills flight.
Automobiles Navigating around Phuket by car is manageable with the help of a decent map. Roads can be treacherous though, so don't scrimp on insurance.

LOCAL KNOWLEDGE

Taxis Flagging down cabs in Phuket is relatively easy; fares start at 50 baht. Three-wheeled tuk tuks are everywhere in Patong and Phuket Town – negotiate a round-trip rate if you'd like one to wait for you while you shop or sightsee. Be prepared to pay upwards of 150 baht an hour.
Currency Thai baht (THB).
Dialling codes Thailand: 66. Phuket: (0)76.
Tipping culture A 10 per cent service charge may be added to your bill, but don't assume this will get as far as the staff; additional cash tips are always welcome. For cabs, round the fare up to the nearest 10 or 20 baht.
Siesta and fiesta Phuket's enthusiastic mercantilism means shops open promptly and regularly. Some cafés and restaurants open as early at 8am to serve the breakfast crowd; some bars stay open till the wee hours.
Do go/don't go Phuket is most alive during the sunny season, from November to March. When the monsoon lull hits, expect slower service and irregular opening hours.
Packing tips Beach yoga-wear for seaside stretchers. Sarongs and sandals will be fine for those who don't plan on anything more strenuous than moonlit strolls along the sand; jungle bunnies and mountaineers will want sturdier shoes and insect repellent.
Recommended reads You'll have heard of *The Beach*, Alex Garland's paradise-lost tale; try the *Traveler's Tales Thailand* anthology, Botan's *Letters from Thailand*, or Steve Rosse's short-story collection *Thai Vignettes: Phuket and Beyond*.
Cuisine Succulent seafood from the Andaman Sea characterises Phuket's menus. Dishes are likely to be barbecued, marinated, and garnished with a medley of herbs and spices. Southern Thais like their food spicier

and often add fresh turmeric to curries. Khanom cheen
– rice noodles soaked with fish-flake soup and served
with fresh vegetables and fruits – is a popular breakfast
dish, while the item that crops up on beach-bar menus
the most is pad thai: egg-fried noodles with chicken or
prawns, fish sauce, chillis, spring onions and peanuts.

WORTH GETTING OUT OF BED FOR

Viewpoint The southernmost point of Phuket, Cape
Promthep is the best place to grab an uninterrupted view
of the heavenly Andaman Sea sunset. There's always a
crowd waiting with their Nikons; get there an hour or so
beforehand to commandeer a good spot.

Arts and culture Phuket Town's Sino-Portuguese
architecture is the island's cultural claim to fame; Phuket's
Town Hall, Provincial Court and Nakorn Luang Bank
building are among the most magnificent examples. Along
Thalang Road, you'll find Thalang National Museum
(www.thailandmuseum.com), the island's most important
repository of history and culture. Like much of Thailand,
Phuket is dotted with ornate Buddhist temples. Pay your
respects at Wat Prahong in Thalang, where a huge golden
Buddha is half-buried in the temple floor – supposedly
bestowing a curse on anyone who attempts to dig it up.

Activities Whether you're looking for beachy gallops or
jungle jaunts, horse riding is a great way to explore the
island – try the Phuket Riding Club (www.phuketriding
club.com) in Chalong Bay. If horses just aren't big
enough, follow in the footsteps of Sir David Attenborough
and take an elephant trek in the Chalong highlands at Siam
Safari elephant camp (www.siamsafari.com). Ocean-going
water babes can kayak around Phuket's semi-submerged
caves with Sea Canoe (076 212172). A seaplane tour with
Destination Air (www.destinationair.com) to Krabi or Phi Phi
provides breathtaking bird's-eye views of the Andaman Sea.

Best beach Hand-painted signs mark the trail to Laem
Singh beach on the island's west coast. This sand-stretch
may just be Phuket's most beautiful – blissfully free of
hotels. While it used to be a secret spot for local
residents, these days the word is out: go early to mark
your territory. The best of the three or four restaurants
here is Ali's, which was also the first.

Daytripper Learn to dive at one of the top 10 spots on
the planet: Similan Islands National Marine Park (076
595045). The varied topography makes the diving ideal
both for beginners and experienced divers, and there are
some truly incredible coral formations. For those who
prefer drier pursuits, Similan is also home to a vast array
of bird species, as well as intriguing landlubbers including
flying lemurs, monitor lizards, porcupines and civets.

Walks With a trio of national parks, Khao Lak is a place
to get lost in. Of the three, Khao Lak-Lam Ru is ideal for
jungle ramblers, with a plethora of offbeat fauna such
as giant squirrels, black bears and langurs, as well as a
selection of dramatic waterfalls with swimmable pools.

Shopping Central Festival Phuket (076 291111) and the
Surin Plaza (076 271241) are the only two malls worth
a trawl. For more selective shopping, Lola (076 271618)
stocks the choicest beachwear, while Mandalay (076
270954) turns out a decent range of hats, lacquerware
and ceramics. Eclectic shops abound in Phuket Town.
To feather your nest, fly by 'Bypass Road' (Chalermprakiat
9 Road), home to dozens of furniture and interiors shops,
including Chan's Antique (076 261416), an Aladdin's cave
of bronzes and teak carving.

Something for nothing Phuket's cinematic environs have
entered film history. Head to Phang Nga Bay to catch a
glimpse of the iconic Koh Ping Gan, dubbed 'James Bond
Island', which made a splash with 007 in *The Man with
the Golden Gun*.

Don't go home without... tasting a durian. This large,
spiky-shelled fruit is notorious for its frankly repellent
odour (hence the nickname, 'stinky fruit'). Although less
intrepid stomachs may baulk at the custardy pulp within,
many regard durian flesh as a delicacy and, among Thais,
its aphrodisiac effects are the stuff of legend.

PECULIARLY PHUKET

One of the remarkable things about Phuket is that there's a strong sense of eco-friendly entrepreneurship and opportunistic ingenuity: look out for crafty DIY-versions of everyday items around the island. Chances are you'll see roadside rubbish bins fashioned from old truck tyres, sunloungers built out of leftover piping, and dumbbells shaped from spare concrete slabs.

DIARY

February Toe-tapping rhythm and blues at the Phuket International Blues Rock Festival (www.phuketbluesfestival.com). The Old Phuket Town Festival brings lively traditional music, dance and spicy food to the streets. **Mid-April** Songkran, the Thai new year, is an excuse for an island-wide water fight. Phuket Bike Week (www.phuketbikeweek.com) welcomes Hondas, Harleys and more roaring engines for charity. **July** Yachting on the high seas at Phuket Race Week (www.phuketraceweek.com). **November** Phuket Carnival on Patong Beach (076 222177) offers plenty of kitschy fun and floats to welcome the start of high season.
December The King Cup Regatta is Asia's biggest boat race, held in honour of the King.

Aleenta Phuket-
Phang Nga

STYLE Sleek seaside sugarcubes
SETTING Andaman sunset sands
DESTINATION Phuket and Khao Lak

'Enormous windows allow the sun
to bathe our room in glorious orange
light. Clever planting outside ensures
our modesty is protected. Thank God'

van (the hotel lays on transfers for those who are staying for three nights or more) to our arrival at the resort, where we are greeted with chilled water and cold scented towels, we knew this would be the perfect place for the two of us to unwind and find some peace. A sunglasses-clad and sunblock-lathered Mr Smith is already looking around for the loungers.

First, though, we have to check into our room. We have chosen a beachfront suite – a freestanding villa that comprises one third of what the resort terms its 'residences'. The other two suites weren't occupied, however, so Mr Smith and I have both the private pool and the spacious communal living area, with its comfy daybeds and huge flatscreen TV, entirely to ourselves. We spend the next half an hour poking around our suite – might as well get the hard work out of the way before we do absolutely nothing for the next 48 hours. Two and a half of the four walls are made entirely of glass, and retract fully to provide instant access to a private beach-facing deck at the front and the private pool to the side. Glass is also a feature of the spacious bathroom-cum-dressing room, with enormous windows that allow the sun to bathe the room in glorious orange light. Clever planting outside ensures our modesty is protected at all times. Thank God.

The clean, contemporary style of the room certainly appeals to this Mrs Smith (known to everyone in her office – hopefully with affection – as 'the neat freak'). Despite all the glass and white surfaces, the use of light wood and natural tones keeps the room from feeling too chilly – Aleenta Phuket-Phang Nga definitely avoids the can't-find-the-door-to-the-bathroom brand of minimalism – and beautifully concealed lighting emphasises the balance of the decor. And despite all the out-and-out luxury, there's also absolutely nothing ostentatious, OTT, or 'gold taps' about it all, which certainly sets it apart from plenty of other resorts in this part of the world.

Though there's a turtle sanctuary, national parks and other such adventures an easy drive away, I'm ashamed to admit we didn't leave the resort. Not once. We drank Singha beer and played Jenga (borrowed from the small library) on our deck in the evenings, we lazed by our pool during the day

Dear reader, a warning: this review is not going to be a whirlwind of adventurous escapades or filled with non-stop activity; in fact, the next 800 words or so are going to be about mostly doing nothing. If doing nothing, however, sounds ideal to you, I can recommend no better place to do it in than Aleenta Phuket-Phang Nga.

By itself on a beautiful and completely empty stretch of coastline just north of Phuket, the accent at this brand-new hotel is most definitely on privacy. There's no central pool area, no buffet breakfasts – no need to mingle with anyone other than your very own Mr or Mrs Smith unless you want to. Aleenta has been designed so that, even if the hotel is full, you feel as though it's your own special place.

And a bit of seclusion is what this stressed-out Mr and Mrs Smith were desperately in need of after a particularly long period of holiday- and sunshine-free time in their hectic working lives. From the moment we hop into a smart

and, once it got cool enough in the late afternoon, we wandered up the beach with our feet in the surf. We were spectacularly slothful. The closest we got to 'frenetic' was booking a massage and a yoga lesson in the same phone call.

There aren't really any places close to Aleenta that you can head out to for a meal, but this didn't faze us in the least. The hotel's stylish Other Restaurant offered a small but perfectly formed menu of Thai and international food, prepared

'I'm ashamed to admit we didn't leave the resort. Not once. We lazed and wandered'

beautifully by a French chef who was happy to adapt dishes for my fussy vegetarian Mr Smith. He still talks about the handmade spring rolls he had on two consecutive nights. We lingered over the wine list and chatted to the lovely staff, all happy to practise their English (Aleenta makes a point of hiring local people, and the resort hosts daily language classes).

Hotel workers have the power to turn a good holiday into a great memory, and the people who brought our drinks, turned down our beds and flapped napkins over our knees at Aleenta were unfailingly accommodating and helpful. The resort claims its staff can guess your future needs. They're not wrong. On arrival, I found myself fretting in that very British way – ie, getting worked up but not daring to complain – about the lack of sunbeds beside our pool. A few minutes later, I looked through our window to see that two panels, complete with towels and cushions, on the deck have been ingeniously lifted to create places in which Mr Smith and I can stretch out. Amazing: they'd managed to anticipate our plans for our entire stay...

Reviewed by Mr & Mrs Smith

NEED TO KNOW

Rooms 30, including 15 villas and 15 suites.

Rates THB9,900–THB31,900, including breakfast and a daily yoga lesson; excludes 17 per cent tax and service charge.

Check-out A lazybones-friendly 2pm.

Facilities Pool, spa, yoga pavilion, gym, library of CDs and books, boutique, complimentary WiFi throughout. In rooms, preloaded iPods, fridge, minibar, yoga mat. Villas also have TVs and DVD players.

Children All ages are welcome in the Ocean View Residences and Beachfront Villas, but other villas are for over-12s only. Free baby cots can be provided.

Also Aleenta has set up a Marine Turtle Foundation to protect Thailand's native species. The hotel matches guests' donations of THB40 a day (included in room rates) to its associated turtle sanctuary in Khao Lumpee-Haad Thaimueang National Park, and arranges day trips to see the hatchlings.

IN THE KNOW

Our favourite rooms The Ocean View Loft suites are particularly high scorers, with two floors, double-height ceilings and private sundecks. For the pinnacle of pampering, go for the presidential dimensions of the Spa Villa, which includes a private pool and Jacuzzi, an outdoor lounge and your own spa treatment room. To lay the luxury on even thicker, you can engage the services of a private butler and a personal chef.

Hotel bar Sharing space with the restaurant, the relaxed beach bar is an essential stop-off for an alfresco cocktail, and plays a chilled-out mixture of lounge, jazz, lo-fi and crooner tunes.

Hotel restaurant Spicy Far Eastern fusion at the open-air Beach Lounge; nouvelle French cuisine with a local touch at the newer Chef's Table. Plump for the pandan-wrapped Andaman lobster and balsamic caramel.

Top table Assuming the weather's obliging, request a table on the beach and dine within inches of the ocean.

Room service Meals can be served in your room between 6am and midnight.

Dress code Assured but unfussy – light crisp linens and flowing summer dresses.

Local knowledge Phang Nga Bay is one of southern Thailand's most scenic spots, with cavern-riddled limestone cliffs and sheer-sided rocky islets towering above the glassy waters. Take a canoe over to Koh Panyi to take in the stilted sea-gypsy village that sits on the water, and check out the ancient paintings on the cave walls of Khao Khien, where you can also catch sight of marine iguanas taking to the waves.

LOCAL EATING AND DRINKING

This part of Khao Lak isn't overly endowed with eateries: you're more likely to find roadside shacks serving up authentic (ie, pretty damn spicy) Thai dishes than upmarket bistros. Phuket itself is a different story, however (although it's not that close). Try Sunday brunch at the bright and buzzing **Oriental Spoon** (076 316577) in Surin Beach, or the foodie favourite **Lim's** (076 344834) on Kalim Beach. Brush up on your culinary skills with Aleenta's daily Thai cookery course, starting with a chef-led tour of local vegetable markets and culminating in a sampling of your own finely spiced creations. There are cocktail mixology courses on offer, too.

GET A ROOM!

To book this hotel, go to www.mrandmrssmith.com or ring our expert travel team on 1 800 464 2040. Activate your free membership online (see page 4) to qualify for the exclusive Smith card offer shown below when you book with us.

 SMITH CARD OFFER A 10 per cent reduction on room rates and a 30-minute massage each if staying three nights or more; members staying seven nights or more will also be given a candlelit dinner for two.

Aleenta Phuket-Phang Nga Natai Beach, Phang Nga, Phuket 82140

(www.mrandmrssmith.com/aleenta-phuket-phang-nga)

TURKEY

ISTANBUL
A'jia Hotel

ISTANBUL

CITYSCAPE The Sublime Porte
CITY LIFE East meets West

Straddling Europe and Asia, Istanbul is the historic crossroads between East and West, a city of sky-reaching minarets and sprawling palaces. It may have been founded more than 2,300 years ago, but this city is no slacker when it comes to keeping pace with modern life, looking resolutely to the future. Climbing the hills around the Golden Horn and overlooking the beautiful Bosphorus, Istanbul cradles the wonders of the Ottoman and Byzantine empires, from the breathtaking Topkapi Palace where sultans and their harems redefined the word 'decadence', to the looming Hagia Sophia – part cathedral, part mosque, total spectacle. Today, the indulgent lifestyle once enjoyed only behind closed palace doors is available on every gilded street. Istanbul has some of the coolest bars and clubs – whichever continent you're standing in – as well as fashion-forward shops and delicious cuisine fit for a sultan himself.

GETTING THERE

Planes Istanbul Atatürk (www.ataturkairport.com) is the main international hub, a 30-minute cab ride from the city centre. Sabiha Gökçen airport (www.sgairport.com), 30 miles from the city centre, is popular with short-haul carriers. You can buy a Turkish visa on arrival.
Trains Istanbul has a modern and efficient metro and tram system. The network goes as far as Atatürk airport and, when the traffic's heavy, is as fast as a taxi.
Automobiles Driving is a bad idea; the twisting streets are traffic-clogged and very difficult to navigate – stick to taxis. Express buses link Taksim and Atatürk airport.
Boats The ferries and water taxis can transport you from Europe to Asia, or whisk you from the city centre out to the peaceful Princes Islands (www.ido.com.tr).

LOCAL KNOWLEDGE

Taxis Yellow *taksis* are relatively inexpensive (have small change handy) but may refuse to take you if they can't face the traffic (or speak English). From midnight to 6am, the *gece* or night rate adds 50 per cent to the fare.
Currency New Turkish Lira (YTL). Euros and US dollars are also commonly used.
Dialling codes Turkey: 90. Istanbul: (0)212 or (0)216.
Tipping culture In restaurants, 10 per cent is standard. If service is included, an additional sum is still expected.
Siesta and fiesta Business hours are 8.30am–5.30pm, sometimes with a break for lunch. Restaurants get busy

from 8pm, and clubs continue until well past midnight.
Do go/don't go Istanbul is hot and humid in the summer, while winter may even see heavy snowfalls. Spring and autumn definitely see the city at its best.
Packing tips Bring long skirts or trousers and cover up if you plan on visiting Istanbul's many mosques; a shawl will also help ward off the occasional waterside chill by night.
Recommended reads Rose Macaulay's witty and still-fresh 1950s novel *The Towers of Trebizond*; Turkish author Orhan Pamuk's melancholic memoir, *Istanbul (Memories and the City)*; *Strolling Through Istanbul* by John Freely and Hilary Sumner-Boyd takes a walk through history.

Cuisine Istanbul's most traditional eateries are *meyhane*, tavernas serving tapas-like meze – best moistened with a slug of Turkey's fearsomely strong raki; try to get Tekirdag rather than the more ubiquitous Yeni Raki. Drawing on its plentiful supply of fresh fish, the city has a burgeoning restaurant scene with excellent Asian and Mediterranean fusion menus, and there's plenty to tempt sweet tooths, from pistachio-packed baklava to lokum (Turkish delight).

WORTH GETTING OUT OF BED FOR

Viewpoint There are several panoramic bars and restaurants atop the city's modern high-rise buildings: Mikla (0212 251 4646), 360 (0212 251 1042) and NuTeras (0212 245 6070) are three of the best.

Arts and culture Hagia Sophia (Ayasofya) was the main cathedral of Byzantium for more than a thousand years, and was the greatest mosque in the Ottoman Empire for five centuries. Now a museum, it's still one of the most fabulous buildings in the world. Next-door is the Topkapi Palace with its opulent harem, and across the park is the Blue Mosque. For contemporary culture, visit Istanbul Modern (www.istanbulmodern.org), an art space that symbolises the city's status as a progressive, creative hub.

Activities A boat ride up the Bosphorus between the Asian and European shores lined with *yalis* (summerhouses) is a wonderful experience. Turkish Maritime Lines runs a leisurely cruise all the way to the Black Sea at least once a day from Eminönü. Departure times vary, so ask your hotel to check for you. Alternatively, you can hop on and off the network of commuter ferries that ply the waterway. If you prefer to cruise more independently, the A'jia Hotel has its own private launch, which will chauffeur guests between Europe and Asia in style. Körfez (0216 413 4314), a respected waterfront fish restaurant on the Asian side, also has a private boat to bring you across the Bosphorus.

Perfect picnic Take a ferry up to Anadolu Kavaği: the village is surrounded by wooded hills and there are great views from the Byzantine ruins of Yoros castle, which once controlled the Black Sea approaches.

Daytripper The Princes Islands in the Sea of Marmara to the south of Istanbul make a wonderful retreat from the city, particularly in summer. Büyükada, with its horse-drawn carriages, is particularly charming. Ferries depart regularly from Eminönü's Adalar pier, taking 90 minutes.

Walks Get a feel for city life by strolling along the pedestrianised Istiklal Caddesi in the Beyoğlu district – Istanbul's answer to Fifth Avenue, Oxford Street or Las Ramblas – especially on a Saturday evening.

Shopping Great fun, the Grand Bazaar is a covered warren of shops selling carpets, caviar, jewellery, touristy junk and textiles. Brush up on your bargaining skills before you go, and carry a Turkish newspaper under your arm to deter aggressive salesmen. If you can't hack the haggling, head straight to Kurtoğlu (0212 519 4003), where Hasan Selamet sells beautiful patchwork-style kilims made from old and new textiles. Also in the Grand Bazaar, Abdulla Natural Products (0212 522 9078), next-door to Fes Café, sells traditional soaps and cotton towels. The Beyoğlu area is the SoHo of Istanbul: its steep narrow streets are lined with vintage and retro shops; Faik Pasa Yokusu is one of the best roads for rummaging. For designer threads, head to Teçsvikiye Caddesi and Abdi Ipekçi Caddesi, north of Taksim Square. The Kanyon centre (www.kanyon.com.tr) has a branch of Harvey Nichols.

Something for nothing Opposite Hagia Sophia, the Blue Mosque, with its soaring minarets and intricate stonework, is one of the city's main landmarks. Remember to dress modestly, or wrap yourself in one of the sheets provided. If you're feeling confident, go to General Yazgan Street and challenge the locals to a game of backgammon – you won't stand a chance.

Don't go home without... having sundown cocktails at Angelique or House Café (both in Ortakoy): get a seat facing the Mecidiye Mosque in time for sunset and enjoy amazing views while the evening call to prayer blasts from the mosque's minaret-perched loudspeakers.

INCREDIBLY ISTANBUL

Get the cleanest you've been since your mama scrubbed behind your ears with a soak at a steamy, traditional Turkish hammam. Cağaloğlu Hamam near the Grand Bazaar was built almost 300 years ago and is absolutely authentic (www.cagalogluhamami.com.tr); Les Ottomans' Caudalie Vinothérapie Spa on Muallim Naci Caddesi offers a luxurious modern take on the Turkish bath (0212 359 1500). If you're so inclined, you can relax further with a *nargile* (hubbly-bubbly pipe) at the cafés off Tophane Iskelesi near the Nusretiye mosque.

DIARY

April Silver screenings on the Golden Horn for the Istanbul International Film Festival.
May The F1 circus comes to town for the Turkish Grand Prix (www.formula1.com).
June/July The International Istanbul Music Festival is the city's most prestigious cultural event featuring ballet, opera and classical music concerts. Events are often staged in the city's historic landmarks, including the Topkapi palace (www.iksv.org). **July** Istanbul's jazz festival attracts acts from Robert Plant and Robin Gibb to Norah Jones. **November** Istanbul literally comes to a standstill on the 10th for a minute's silence to commemorate the death of Mustafa Kemal Atatürk, the founder of modern Turkey. For more events, go to www.istanbul.com.

A'jia Hotel

STYLE Contemporary Ottoman
SETTING Banks of the Bosphorus
DESTINATION Istanbul

'Our journey across to Europe is short but magical. The ancient skyline hovers against a sultry sunset and then, beside us, a family of dolphins breaks the surface of the water and heads on upstream'

Istanbul taxi drivers don't do street names. Their method of pathfinding is an ancient one: they ask directions. Our driver nods as we ask for the A'jia Hotel, sucks on his cigarette, turns up his music and hits the gas. Istanbul streams past the window, ancient domes and minarets jostling up against shiny new apartment blocks, and carpet-sellers, shoeshine hawkers and sharp-suited businessmen hang off buses and spill into the road. Through the window comes the smell of rosewater, spice and meat smoking on hot grills. And every now and then our driver screeches to a halt to ask directions, and off he goes again, his evil-eye talisman swinging from the rear-view mirror.

Istanbul straddles the magnificent Bosphorus, a body of water that separates Asia and Europe. The city's palaces and mosques stud the skyline on both shores. This is where crusaders marched, Romans orgied and sultans ruled, and its heady mix of modern glamour and ancient exoticism makes it one of the world's most romantic and sensual cities. Well that's what we, in the steamy back of our speeding cab, are hoping.

The A'jia Hotel is one of the new wave of boutique hotels in Istanbul and sits on the Asian shore, half an hour away from the mayhem of the centre. Slowly the crowds and chaos begin to give way to lush green gardens and waterside mansions, and we pull up at a discreet set of iron gates. It's an ex-pasha's mansion right on the Bosphorus, but its grand Ottoman exterior belies a contemporary interior of slick modern design. There's not a kilim or belly dancer's tassel in sight, just chic white-on-white glamour. A vast foyer contains nothing but marble and golden sunlight, and quietly attentive check-in staff. We soon discover that A'jia's policy is to leave you to your own devices, unless of course there's anything at all you might require.

The understated modern luxury continues in the sparse, cool bedroom. A wall of windows makes it feel as though it's floating above the Bosphorus before a distant shimmering shore. Geometrical white armchairs are arranged across rich dark-wood floors, but Mr Smith and

I are most impressed with the centrepiece: an enormous bed with the crispest, coolest sheets of Egyptian cotton.

Almost as big as the room itself, the bathroom is a gorgeous Ottoman chamber of creamy marble and tile, and I can't decide between the enormous shower or the deep rectangular bath. Mr Smith decides for me. He runs me a bath and I slide into it under fragrant Molton Brown foam while he prepares himself a gin and tonic on the balcony. With its platform of wood atop an arrangement of white pebbles, the balcony continues the minimal theme outside, and beyond it there's nothing but the brilliant blue of the water. Clean and damp, and wrapped

in fluffy white cotton, I come out to join him. The afternoon sun pours through floor-to-ceiling windows, bathing the bed in warm light – so we slip in for a sun-warmed siesta before dinner.

Waking ravenous, we head to the hotel's private pier. Wooden deckchairs face the water, and cosy tables for two flutter with white linen in the warm breeze. The restaurant and bar are run by the Istanbul Doors group, which also operates some of the city's most glamorous bars, and the food is stylish Modern European. But we're heading to Europe for dinner, so we step into the A'jia's private boat and the captain starts the engine. It's a short but magical

'The understated luxury continues in the bedroom. A wall of windows makes it feel as though it's floating above the Bosphorus before a distant shimmering shore'

journey. The haunting call to prayer drifts from mosques on both shores; the ancient skyline hovers against a sultry sunset; and then, beside us, a family of dolphins breaks the surface and heads on upstream.

We step out on the European shore and take a taxi to Ortakoy, a gorgeous little waterside area filled with hip bars and cafés. We eat on the water at the House Café, one of a chain of five cosy café bars created by Autobahn, Istanbul's hottest young design agency, then we pop into next-door Angelique, a super-slick summer bar where Turkey's glitterati make their entrance on private boats. One passion-fruit martini and we're ready for bed.

We wake to a golden morning and the sound of water lapping below. Ukrainian ships pass our window on their way to the Black Sea. Outside, Mr Smith dons sunglasses and devours pancakes with peaches. I go for A'jia's elegant take on the traditional Turkish breakfast, a spoiling

selection of cheese, olives, honey, cherry jam, cucumber and freshly baked bread, arranged jewel-like on a tray.

The day brings a whirl of exotic sights – Topkapi Palace, the Blue Mosque and Hagia Sophia, the fragrant Spice Bazaar and the crazy colour of the Grand Bazaar – then a visit to the ancient Cemberlitas Hamami, where naked masseuses with huge soapy breasts scrub and pummel as we lie steaming on the hot marble slab. The half-terrified, half-ecstatic look on Mr Smith's face is worth the trip alone.

As exciting as Istanbul is, pretty soon we're aching to get back to the A'jia. The relentless chaos and colour sets our heads awhirl, and returning to the luxurious simplicity of our romantic Ottoman mansion is deeply soothing. This is not a quiet city, and a day spent trawling the teeming streets can send you a little barmy. A'jia, with its magnificent watery view, is the perfect place to get away from it all, together.

Reviewed by Nellie Blundell

NEED TO KNOW

Rooms 16, including six deluxe suites.

Rates €255–€855, including breakfast; excludes VAT at 18 per cent. There is a 50 per cent discount on wedding anniversaries and birthdays on presentation of ID.

Check-out Noon, but some flexibility; check-in, 2pm.

Facilities Private boat, Thai massages and city tours on request, valet parking. In rooms, air-conditioning, LCD satellite TV, DVD players, minibar, WiFi.

Children Little ones can be accommodated, though the hotel, with its terraces over the waterway, was not designed with them in mind. High chairs are available, as are extra beds (€110 a night).

Also No pets. For a VIP arrival, the hotel can organise a boat ride from Atatürk Airport for around €315 one-way. You'll also be glad to know that non-smoking rooms are available – a bit of a rarity in tobacco-loving Turkey.

IN THE KNOW

Our favourite rooms Ask for a room with a view of the Bosphorus and/or a private balcony. Room 10 is a duplex with a sitting room downstairs and bedroom upstairs, and a bathtub right next to the bed. Room 8 has a huge balcony that gives you the feeling you own the place... and has beautiful views over the water. Room 9 is spacious, with a sitting area and a bathtub beneath a sea-view window.

Hotel bar There's a long white bar on the waterfront terrace, and another bar in the restaurant area inside.

Hotel restaurant A'jia's restaurant serves Mediterranean/Italian food – pasta, risotto and lamb fillets with pistachio – and the best Sunday brunch in town (10am–3pm). Guest chefs make occasional visits.

Top table Number 30, a corner table inside, or any table on the river terrace.

Room service There's a well-chosen list of snacks and hot meals available 24 hours a day.

Dress code Hip and urban – make like a stylish young Turk.

Local knowledge Make sure you, um, find thyme to go to the Spice Bazaar (a short boat ride from the A'jia Hotel, on the European side of the city at the southern end of Galata Bridge). Walk through its alleyways and pick up packets of primary-coloured powders and peppers, guaranteed to bring a taste of the East into your kitchen back home.

LOCAL EATING AND DRINKING

Körfez (0216 413 4314), at Körfez Caddesi 78, is one of the city's best seafood restaurants. Specialities include salt-baked grouper cooked with spices. It's reached from the European side of the Bosphorus by a private launch that departs from the wharf near Rumeli Hisari. **MüzedeChanga** (0212 323 0901) at the Sakip Sabanci Museum is a stylish Mediterranean restaurant with a retro Scandinavian interior of light oak and copper-toned mirrors. Its terrace has wonderful views over the water and all those Black Sea-bound boats. **360 Istanbul** (0212 251 1042), raised up above the city's skyline and offering great views (hence the name), is lots of fun. Huge plates of meze and a long cocktail list have made it one of Istanbul's most fashionable hangouts. We also love the grilled lamb at **Beyti** (0212 663 2990), on Orman Sokak, and **Safran** (0212 368 4444) in Taksim.

GET A ROOM!

To book this hotel, go to www.mrandmrssmith.com or ring our expert travel team on 1 800 464 2040. Activate your free membership online (see page 4) to qualify for the exclusive Smith card offer shown below when you book with us.

 SMITH CARD OFFER Two tickets to the Sakip Sabanci Museum, with boat transfers from the hotel. VIP entrance to A'jia's favourite nightclubs. Two free apple margaritas when you dine at the hotel.

A'jia Hotel 27 Çubuklu Caddesi, Kanlica, Istanbul (www.mrandmrssmith.com/ajia-hotel)

UNITED KINGDOM

THE COTSWOLDS
Barnsley House

EDINBURGH
Tigerlily

LONDON
Baglioni Hotel

THE COTSWOLDS

COUNTRYSIDE Hillsides and honey-coloured hamlets
COUNTRY LIFE Gently does it

More typically English than a bowler-hatted Bertie Wooster whistling Elgar, this chunk of gently undulating and seemingly evergreen countryside is enough to send Anglophile visitors into apoplexy. Britain's largest designated area of natural beauty, the Cotswolds covers an area roughly bounded by Oxford to the east, Cheltenham to the west, Stratford to the north and Bath to the south. Long before the tourist invasion, the Romans left their legacy in towns such as Cirencester, and remains of villas and forts can be seen from Bury Hill to Woodchester. Today, besides sheep, the area is home to some of the country's most scenic towns and villages – all thatched cottages, ducks waddling across village greens and honey-hued churches. Other sensory delights include strolls on the beautiful banks of the River Wye, or following Fosse Way, the arrow-straight Roman road that still pierces through the loveliest landscapes imaginable.

GETTING THERE

Planes If you'd rather bypass London, the closest airports to the Cotswolds are Bristol and Birmingham, both of which have daily flights to New York, as well as good domestic links to cities such as Edinburgh and Glasgow with easyJet (www.easyjet.com) or BMI Baby (www.bmibaby.com).
Trains Direct trains from London Paddington run regularly to Cotswold stations, including Chippenham, Kemble, Kingham, Moreton-in-Marsh, Stroud, Gloucester and Cheltenham. Most journeys will only take an hour or two.
Automobiles From London, the Cotswolds is a couple of hours away along the M4 or A40; the nearby M5 offers access from Bristol and Birmingham. It's worth taking a car to the region: the country-lane driving is unparalleled.

LOCAL KNOWLEDGE

Taxis The smaller towns have limited taxi services – book in advance. Hotel staff will know the best local firms.
Currency Pound sterling (£).
Dialling codes UK: 44. Bath: (0)1225; Cirencester: (0)1285.
Tipping culture The standard is 10 or 15 per cent, but beware of inclusive restaurant bills so you don't tip twice.

Siesta and fiesta In bigger towns such as Cheltenham and Bath, it's business as usual, but in sleepy rural hamlets, most shops, restaurants and pretty much everything else bar the pub will be closed on a Sunday.
Do go/don't go In the height of summer – and on UK bank holiday weekends – the Cotswolds' prettiest villages and roads attract daytrippers in droves. Go in spring to catch the countryside at its green and bursting best, or in the deep midwinter for snuggling by cosy log fires.
Packing tips Take a packet of indigestion tablets if you intend to gorge on the region's renowned cheeses; and some decent walking boots and a waterproof jacket will serve you well if you plan to do any exploring on foot.
Recommended reads Laurie Lee's childhood recollections of rural Gloucestershire, *Cider with Rosie* is perhaps the most lyrical literary evocation of the area. In Jerome K Jerome's masterpiece of Victorian wit, the titular *Three Men in a Boat* drift through the Cotswolds on part of their journey. Also try local poet UA Fanthorpe's erudite *Collected Poems*.
Cuisine It would be perverse to come to the Cotswolds and not fill up on delicious Double Gloucester, a whole-milk

cheese first produced in the 1500s. The best is made by octogenarian Diana Smart of Old Ley Court in Churcham, with milk from her herd of Holstein, Brown Swiss and Gloucester cows (www.smartsgloucestercheese.com).

And... Before railway timetables were first drawn up in the mid-19th century, villagers in Stroud set their time by the sun. Being some 90 miles west of the meridian, noon was nine minutes later than in Greenwich. Some locals are still campaigning to bring back 'Stroud Time'.

WORTH GETTING OUT OF BED FOR

Viewpoint Just north of Stow-on-the-Wold, the Broadway Tower is a glorious folly; built like a mock castle and perched 312 metres above sea level, it offers soul-soothing views across the Severn Valley to the Welsh mountains.

Arts and culture The Arts and Crafts design movement began in this area in the 19th century, and its influence is everywhere: Kelmscott Manor (www.kelmscottmanor. co.uk), the house William Morris shared with Dante Gabriel Rossetti, is well worth a visit. There are more Arts and Crafts wonders at Rodmarton Manor (01285 841253) in Cirencester, and Hidcote Manor Garden (01386 438333) near Chipping Campden.

Activities A favourite with Princes Charles, William and Harry, Beaufort Polo Club (www.beaufortpoloclub.co.uk) near Tetbury is one of the finest places in the country to take in a chukka or two. Up the horsepower at Castle Combe (www.castlecombecircuit.co.uk), a racing circuit where you can take a selection of seriously fast cars for a spin – or keep it simple and go go-karting. Fly a plane or microlight with Kemble Flying Club (01285 770077; www.kembleflyingclub.co.uk), near Cirencester. Taking the pace down a notch (or nine), why not bliss out at the fabulous Rococo Garden at Painswick (www. rococogarden.org.uk), which was completely overgrown until the 1970s. Now restored, it's a wonderful place in which to surround yourself with birdsong and bee buzz.

Perfect picnic Bourton-on-the-Water, just a few miles from Stow-on-the-Wold, is an idyllic English village where trees dip their branches into the River Windrush and dragonfiles skim across its surface. Laze the afternoon away on the riverbank with filled baguettes (cheese and pickle, prawn cocktail, lamb and mayo, that kind of thing) from Norah's Pantry (01451 820815).

Daytripper Possibly the most tranquil attraction in the sleepy Cotswolds, the national arboretum at Westonbirt (www.forestry.gov.uk/westonbirt) has one of the world's most spectacular tree collections. You can happily spend a day kicking up leaves and gazing at the neck-crickingly tall redwoods. Take a picnic – and binoculars.

Walks Walking in this neck of the woods is a joy. Pick a section of the 105-mile Cotswold Way. Alternatively, the South Cotswold Ramblers website offers an exhaustive list of tantalising trails in Gloucester and other towns in the region (www.southcotswoldramblers.org.uk).

Shopping Stow-on-the-Wold is the epicentre for antiques – but equally worthwhile is a pokeabout in the dusty shops of Burford, Cirencester, Moreton-in-Marsh and Tetbury. Cotswold markets are invariably rewarding: head for Moreton-in-Marsh on Tuesdays, Tetbury on Wednesdays, and Cirencester on Mondays and Fridays. Foodies can also spend many happy hours in Tetbury's House of Cheese (www.houseofcheese.co.uk), home to a life-affirmingly wonderful selection of fromage, as well as chutneys and pickles; and pick up mouthwatering luxuries at the pre-eminent Daylesford Organic Farm Shop, which also has an excellent café and an indulgent homewares shop (www.daylesfordorganic.com).

Something for nothing Give a little back, and try dry-stone walling. You can volunteer to repair walls or partake in altruistic hedgelaying and tree planting from bases in Cheltenham and Gloucester (www.gvcv.org.uk).

Don't go home without... buying a bottle of easy-drinking English white from the Three Choirs Vineyards in Newent (01531 890223). Team it with Double Gloucester at your next 1970s-themed cheese-and-wine party.

CATEGORICALLY COTSWOLDS

The area's famously photogenic hamlets and villages owe much of their attractiveness to Cotwold stone, a yellow limestone quarried in the region's eponymous hills. The hue changes depending on the source: Northern Cotswold stone is characterised by a rich, honeyed gold; as you approach Bath, the colour is a delicate pale buttermilk.

DIARY

March The Cheltenham Festival horse-racing fixture culminates in the famous Gold Cup (www.cheltenham.co.uk). **May** Cheltenham Jazz Festival (www.cheltenhamfestivals.com) brings in big musical names for goateed men to nod along to. **May/June** Cooper's Hill hosts an annual cheese-rolling competition in which people hurtle down the slope in pursuit of an eight-pound 'squircle' of Double Gloucester – broken bones are apparently not a deterrent. **August** If it's flared nostrils and shimmering fetlocks you're after, head to the Festival of British Eventing at Gatcombe Park (www.gatcombe-horse.co.uk) for daredevil displays of dressage, showjumping and cross-country riding. **September** Find a tuffet to sit on and enjoy the curds and whey at Cheltenham's Great British Cheese Festival and British Cheese Awards (0845 241 2026). Tastings, workshops and cheese tossing! **October** The Cheltenham Festival of Literature is attended by eminent writers such as Maya Angelou and Bret Easton Ellis (www.cheltenhamfestivals.com).

Barnsley House

STYLE Super-stylish manor house
SETTING Gorgeous Gloucestershire gardens
DESTINATION The Cotswolds

'A beguiling collision of the landscaped and
the wild, the grounds of Barnsley House
are the stuff of period-drama fantasy'

I skipper boats, and I live by the sea in Brighton. You'll understand, then, that when I'm not living and breathing the buccaneer's life, I'm probably dreaming about it. So imagine my bewilderment as, roused from my seafaring slumber, I find myself being bundled into a car – and not a boat. No cutlasses or pieces of eight here. Just three large weekend bags, two Ms Smiths, and one very bleary-eyed, hungover would-be pirate. While I'm fighting off the waves of nausea from a bachelor party the night before, Mrs Smith gently reminds me of our mission: to review the luxury hotel Barnsley House in the Cotswolds, with our four-month-old daughter Delilah.

Although many manor houses have an unfortunate tendency to be inland, they have always seriously impressed me, and, pulling up at this 17th-century Gloucestershire skyline-loomer, I'm not disappointed. By the time we've disembarked at the ivy-hugged, hilltop mansion, I've completely recovered my land legs. There's something about the aged Cotswold stone and manicured setting that sends me back to childhood summers at my grandmother's home in Ireland, and it takes the sultry French tones of a Barnsley House staff member to pull me out of my nostalgic reverie. Dispensing with the formality of check-in, she guides us straight to our suite. We're in a split-level Stableyard room. The ground floor consists of a marshmallow-comfy double bed and a sleek, spacious lounge area with windows overlooking the courtyard.

Now is the moment of truth. Mrs Smith is a stylist and has a laser-guided eye for the tiniest design flaws. As she conducts her silent survey, I await the inevitable 'tsk' that greets even the most invisible aesthetic faux pas. But, miraculously, none comes. I sigh with relief, and a smiling Mrs Smith disappears up the wrought-iron staircase into the crow's nest of our suite – a bathroom on a floor all of its own. Running up to join her, I find a glass wall that gives a perfect view of our bedroom below. A roll-top claw-foot bath presides over the space, partnered by a freestanding shower with a frying pan-sized head, a TV set into the wall and a soapstone basin almost a metre in length.

The courtyard below boasts a waterfall surrounded by a medley of meadow flowers: pansies, foxgloves and

heather – but it's the beautiful main gardens that have caught our eye. So, having transferred Delilah from armchair to pushchair, we set off for the formal lawns.

A beguiling collision of the landscaped and the wild, the grounds of Barnsley House are the stuff of period-drama fantasy. Shaded paths weave around hidden statues, curvaceous topiary and bountiful berry bushes. We find ourselves resting in an ivy-draped gazebo, looking out onto a lily-capped carp pond. We can see why horticulturalists from around the world head to this garden of delights (although presumably they don't get presented with delicious apple martinis by a passing barman while they're inspecting the cabbages).

Arriving at seven o'clock on the dot, the hotel's babysitter enables us to enjoy an aperitif before dinner. Sinking into red tulip chairs beside a marble-topped bar, I order monkfish tempura with Barnsley House-grown vegetables. Mrs Smith announces she is not hungry – a claim belied a few minutes later when most of my monkfish has fallen

victim to her scavenging fork. I order another, then follow it with a delectable helping of fresh strawberries, rich cream and crumbly shortbread. Happy, we saunter to our enormous bed (post-nightcap, of course), tuck the snoozing little one between us and sleep the sleep of the fabulously stuffed.

After waking to a leisurely 11am breakfast in bed (muesli, yoghurt, jams and croissants), we're tempted to linger longer in the linens, but we're also determined to squeeze every last drop of grade II-listed glamour from this hotel. We take the path to the spa building – all glass and Cotswold stone – under the shadow of the neighbouring farm. There's a steam room and sauna (as well as bowls of crushed ice on hand for the necessary post-steaming facial cool-down), and a massage menu that's relaxing just to read; but it's the heated outdoor hydrotherapy pool that really gets me excited. Then I realise I've forgotten my swimming shorts (why would I need them this far inland?). Not to worry; the staff seem only mildly alarmed at the sight of a man in his boxers bottle-feeding a baby. Shuffling into the relaxation room, we find ourselves reclining on black-leather loungers and sipping ginger tea, against a backdrop of inimitable Cotswolds countryside spied through floor-to-ceiling glass walls; it's a delicious end to our already perfect day.

It's tempting to skip dinner, but the Village Pub (owners Tim and Rupert's other establishment) has a reputation not to be resisted. Rupert himself recommends the wine to suit our gourmet pub supper, and Richard, the head gardener, regales us with a lesson in veg-growing that reminds me that, sometimes, land does have its advantages over ocean.

We're scheduled to leave Barnsley House tomorrow morning, and normally I'm straining at the moorings to get back to my beloved marina, but I never thought I'd be this reluctant to return to the sea...

Reviewed by Jim McNulty

'The spa has a steam room, sauna and a massage menu that's relaxing just to read'

NEED TO KNOW

Rooms 18, including 11 suites.

Rates £295–£570, including Continental breakfast and a five per cent discretionary hotel-service charge.

Check-out Noon (5pm check-out available on payment of a £75 supplement). Check-in, 3pm.

Facilities Landscaped gardens, tennis court, helipad, holistic spa with hydrotherapy pool, private 30-seat cinema, DVD library. In rooms, plasma-screen TV with surround-sound system, CD/DVD player, iPod dock, free broadband connection, mini-fridge with free water, juice, champagne and chocolates.

Children Extra beds (£45) or baby cots (£20) can be provided. Babysitting costs £10 an hour. Kids' menu available.

Also Minimum two-night stay at weekends. Make sure you book ahead at the restaurant and the Village Pub.

IN THE KNOW

Our favourite rooms Bathrooms are a big draw here, with features such as roll-top baths, twin sinks, walk-through showers and flatscreen TVs. Room 1 has two bathtubs, side by side; Room 2 has a Jacuzzi. Room 8 has a sitting room, and Room 7 has its own conservatory and garden. Stableyard Rooms are attractive duplexes with glamorous wet rooms.

Hotel bar The largely red bar is open until late for guests; champagne cocktails are a speciality.

Hotel restaurant The secret of chef Graham Grafton's super-fresh Modern European dishes is home-grown vegetables, salad leaves and herbs plucked straight from the kitchen garden (when you see zucchini soup and gnocchi with broad beans on the menu, it's easy to tell what's ripe for picking). Breakfast, 7.30am–10.30am (noon for room service).

Top table Table 4, in the bay window overlooking the gardens.

Room service Food is available while the kitchen is open (8am–10pm); they may be able to rustle up snacks out of hours.

Dress code Relaxed but stylish.

Local knowledge Grab a pair of gumboots and a map from reception and explore the countryside; Coln Valley, 10 minutes away by car, is beautiful. Staff can also arrange fantastic activities, from rowing along the Thames with a picnic hamper to side-saddle riding lessons. Chauffeurs can be booked for transfers (including from central London) or private jaunts.

LOCAL EATING AND DRINKING

With polished-wood tables and chairs, crackling fires and exposed beams, **The Village Pub** (01285 740421), across the road from Barnsley House, is not only a wonderful place to nurse a pint or a Pimm's, but it also does fantastic food. **Jesse's Bistro** (01285 641497) in Cirencester is a small, relaxed restaurant with its own cheese shop, serving fresh fish and meat roasted in a wood-burning oven. You'll find it in a stableyard behind the highly regarded butcher's, Jesse Smiths. Just outside Cirencester in Ewen, the 16th-century **Wild Duck Inn** (01285 770310) is a step-back-in-time treat, with oak panelling, an enormous fireplace and ancestral oil paintings hanging on the walls. There's real ale on tap and a killer wine list, but the big draw is the canopied courtyard with an ancient apple tree at its, ahem, core. On Tetbury's Cirencester Road in a converted jail, **Trouble House Inn** (01666 502206) has earned a Michelin star for exceptional country-pub grub, such as rabbit and tarragon pie. Another good dining option is **The Bell at Sapperton** (01285 760298) near Cirencester, where most of the ingredients for its gastropub menu are locally sourced.

GET A ROOM!

To book this hotel, go to www.mrandmrssmith.com or ring our expert travel team on 1 800 464 2040. Activate your free membership online (see page 4) to qualify for the exclusive Smith card offer shown below when you book with us.

 SMITH CARD OFFER A Barnsley House champagne cocktail each – or a glass of champagne in the Village Pub across the road – on each night of your stay.

Barnsley House Barnsley, Cirencester, Gloucestershire GL7 5EE (www.mrandmrssmith.com/barnsley-house)

EDINBURGH

CITYSCAPE Cobbles, crescents and castle views
CITY LIFE Wit, wisdom and wee drams

If Scotland's first city had a front door, it would come with a huge 'Welcome' mat. Whether you're drawn in by the tartan-weaving heritage of the cobbled Royal Mile, the New Town's graciously elegant Georgian façades or the ever-visible Castle, from whichever angle you look at it, Edinburgh is a knockout. But while it may have the highest concentration of listed buildings in the world, this northern capital is not just for looking at: with an international arts calendar and more booksellers per capita than any other British city, its reputation for refinement and culture is richly deserved. Whether you lose yourself in the Old Town *wynds* – the narrow paths between the centuries-old houses – linger over a wee dram in the cosy pubs of Cockburn Street or tuck into the catch of the day at one of up-and-coming Leith's waterfront restaurants, you'll find satisfaction. Guaranteed.

GETTING THERE

Planes Edinburgh International Airport (www.edinburgh airport.com) receives countless daily flights from London, as well as UK and US hubs, and 40+ European airports. The 30-minute taxi ride into town costs about £20.
Trains GNER has fast, frequent trains linking Scotland with London King's Cross, the East Midlands, Yorkshire, the North East of England and Scotland (www.gner.co.uk). ScotRail's overnight sleeper service departs from London Euston seven nights a week (www.firstgroup.com/scotrail).
Automobiles Edinburgh is at the heart of the Scottish motorway network, so is easily accessible by car. It's roughly six and a half hours from London – beyond Newcastle, the route is particularly picturesque.

Do go/don't go How do you cope among huddled masses? During August, Edinburgh Festival-goers swell the population to more than a million; wait until September, when it'll be less packed and still sunny. Intermittently.
Packing tips The weather is reliably unreliable, so carry a sweater, even in the height of summer. A book of Robbie Burns poems offers good poseur value in cafés.
Recommended reads Alexander McCall Smith's *44 Scotland Street* is a witty chronicle of modern life in a local boarding house; Ian Rankin's Inspector Rebus novels are set mostly in 'Auld Reekie'; but Muriel Spark's *The Prime of Miss Jean Brodie* is still the 'crème de la crème'.

LOCAL KNOWLEDGE

Taxis You can hail a black cab from anywhere on the street, or pre-book a minicab through your hotel. Central Radio Taxis (0131 229 2468) is the city's largest operator.
Currency Pound sterling (£).
Dialling codes UK: 44. Edinburgh: (0)131.
Tipping culture Tipping is not expected, but in restaurants, 12.5 per cent is considered fair. Cab drivers don't expect extra, but 10 per cent will get you a smile.
Siesta and fiesta Museums, shops and attractions generally open 9.30am–5pm every day, sometimes extending their hours in summer. Restaurants will be fullest at around 9pm; bars close at midnight or 1am; clubs carry on till 3am.

Cuisine Good haggis – the sheep's-vitals-centric Scottish culinary icon – is a delicacy that visitors simply must try once; the famous MacSweens of Edinburgh (www.macsween.co.uk) even does vegetarian versions. For breakfast, graduate to a plate of Arbroath smokies, strong-flavoured haddock caught off the Angus coast and barrel-smoked; Iain R Spink's are reckoned to be among the finest, but find your own favourites at Edinburgh Farmers' Market, held every Saturday on Castle Terrace. And... Invest in an Edinburgh Pass (www.edinburgh.org/pass), which gets you into more than 30 attractions and allows free bus rides in the city centre, as well as return transfers to the airport. A one-day pass costs £24.

WORTH GETTING OUT OF BED FOR

Viewpoint Head up Calton Hill from the stairs in Waterloo Place and watch the sun setting behind the Castle. For a somewhat wilder vantage point, climb the haunches of Arthur's Seat, an extinct volcano in Holyrood Park.
Arts and culture The Traverse (www.traverse.co.uk) has a great reputation for contemporary theatre. The National Gallery of Scotland (www.nationalgalleries.org) hangs treasures for all tastes, from Titian to Van Gogh to Monet; the Modern Art Galleries do exactly as you'd expect, with work by talents as diverse as Barbara Hepworth and Rachel Whiteread. All aboard – take a tour of the *Royal Yacht Britannia* (www.royalyachtbritannia.co.uk) and you'll get a peek at the Queen's bedroom, as well as her on-board Rolls-Royce.
Activities Play with a bird of prey at Dalhousie (www.falconryscotland.co.uk), a 700-year-old castle seven miles from Edinburgh. By-appointment visitors are taught to handle falcons, hawks, owls and eagles... mind the fingers. Or take to the skies yourself: buzz the city and swoop along the Forth bridges on a thrilling tour with Lothian Helicopters (www.lothianhelicopters.co.uk). Need to burn off some calories after indulging in too much haggis? Cycle 30 miles along the Union Canal towpath from Port Hopetoun to ride the Falkirk Wheel (www.thefalkirkwheel.co.uk), a futuristic rotating boat lift that connects two waterways over a basin drop; you can, of course, drive there.
Perfect picnic Princes Street Gardens offer peerless castle views and is the best place to lay your rug in the city. Follow Edinburgh's cognoscenti and pick up your supplies from deli Valvona & Crolla (0131 556 6066) on Elm Row.
Daytripper Go west along the M8, and you'll reach Glasgow in around an hour. Head east to explore the Lothian coast: Dunbar offers Scotland's best surf; walk along the beach at Musselburgh and top off a great afternoon with a knickerbocker glory from Luca's (0131 665 2237), the high street's historic ice-cream parlour.
Walks Edinburgh is compact and, despite the odd steep gradient, it's just the right size for getting about on foot. Make a day of it by taking the Water of Leith walkway – a public footpath and cycleway. Start at Balerno High School and follow the signs under the Union Canal, all the way (12 miles) to Leith waterfront (www.youredinburgh.info).
Shopping For luxury labels, head for Multrees Walk (www.the-walk.co.uk) on St Andrew's Square, home to Harvey Nichols, Louis Vuitton, Giorgio Armani et al. For vintage finds, second-hand emporium WM Armstrong and Sons (0131 220 5557) on the Grassmarket does a neat line in kilts and cashmere. For iconic wee gifties, cruise the Old Town's specialist shops for Highland dress, traditional quaichs and bags of deliciously crumbly Edinburgh rock.
Something for nothing The city has almost two dozen golf courses, but Bruntsfield Links on Melville Drive is the only 36 short-hole public course that's free, provided you bring your own clubs. If you haven't packed yours, rent some from the nearby Golf Tavern (www.thegolftavern.co.uk).
Don't go home without... acquiring a taste for whisky. If hanging around Old Town pubs hasn't worked, a distillery visit may well do the trick. Check out the entire barley-to-alcohol transformation at Glenkinchie Distillery (01875 342004), home of the Edinburgh Malt in the rolling East Lothian countryside.

EXQUISITELY EDINBURGH

Political devolution in Scotland has provided the capital with its most innovative and controversial modern landmark: Holyrood, the concrete, wood and water-featured parliament building at the foot of the Royal Mile. When the MSPs are in session, you can sit in on a debate for free. That's open government for you (www.scottish.parliament.uk).

DIARY

January Burns Night falls on the 25th, when the populace tucks into haggis, neeps and tatties, toasting the Scottish Bard (www.rabbie-burns.com). **March** Ceilidh Culture Festival (www.ceilidhculture.co.uk) honours Scottish music and song. **April** Science Festival (www.sciencefestival.co.uk) disguises learning with lots of 'ah-haa' moments. **July** Edinburgh Jazz & Blues Festival (www.edinburghjazzfestival.co.uk). **August** The Edinburgh Festival colonises the town, along with the Fringe (comedy, plays aplenty), Book and International Film Festivals (www.edinburgh-festivals.com). **December** The 29th kicks off Edinburgh's legendary four-day New Year's celebrations, better known as Hogmanay (www.edinburghshogmanay.org).

Tigerlily

STYLE Decadent urban dwelling
SETTING Fashionable former finance hub
DESTINATION Edinburgh

'Tigerlily has thrown the rule book out the window, working a bright, modern and luxe theme with mosaic mirror tiles, silver, white and glass. And that's just reception'

The Georgian Suite at Edinburgh's Tigerlily hotel invites guests to 'live like an 18th-century aristocrat'. It's the kind of offer Mr Smith and I just can't refuse, and, since we've come all this way and there's so much indulgence on offer, it'd be rude not to give it our best shot.

We might have known we were in for a treat. As the taxi pulls up outside the Georgian townhouse, the first thing we spot is a smart black-clad bouncer, complete with Madonna-esque earpiece. This could cause guests who hadn't done their homework to wonder if they'd rocked up at a nightclub by mistake. Inside, two beautiful hostesses in slinky black dresses and killer heels are waiting to check us in. We know right away we've stepped inside somewhere special. Forget traditional lobby style: this boutique hotel has thrown the rule book out the window, working a bright, modern and luxe theme with mosaic mirror tiles, silver, white and glass. And that's just reception.

Upstairs, our room has floor-to-ceiling windows running the length of one wall, each swathed in luscious drapings. There's a silky designer sofa for lounging, and an enormous four-poster for bouncing on. Flames flicker cheekily through the artfully arranged pebbles of the ultra-modern fireplace set into one wall, and there's a heavily mirrored, fit-for-Hollywood dressing table, at which I will be lingering even longer than usual.

We discover a laden minibar, and I drool over a tiny tin of Spanish olives, paw some Designers Guild products, and discover an exciting line of sophisticated Scottish cocoa-y treats from Coco of Bruntsfield – as well as a thoughtful selection of spirits, bottled beer and some decent wine. And how could we have missed the bathroom, which could house a family of four? Its shower is big enough to dine in...

Although I sound pretty smitten already, what really gives the room its heavenly hideaway feel is the lighting. As dusk falls, the space becomes bathed in a soft fuchsia glow. The effect is revelatory, like looking out for the first time through a window that's just been cleaned. So we decide not to bother drawing the curtains, wondering: if everyone

else does as we do, what vignettes must have been witnessed by the inhabitants of the dwellings opposite?

Downstairs, it's party night, and Mr Smith and I can't resist joining in. Boldly, we take a table in the middle of Tigerlily's restaurant area, surrounded by a curtain of metal beads, beneath huge chandeliers encased in outsize lampshades. Not that we're taking much notice of the decor when we're in pole people-watching position: Edinburgh's beau monde is parading by in Jimmy Choos and slinky wrap dresses. Even the waiting staff seems fresh from a model casting, which only adds to the enticing aura of film-set glamour. The menu works an Eastern meets local theme, with charred prawns and mango salsa, Aberdeen Angus beef and an Ayrshire pork belly teamed unexpectedly with coconut rice.

For a change of scene, we head for the in-house basement nightclub, Lulu. We're on the guestlist (OK, so it's automatic for residents) and we sashay straight past the waiting queues. With its Swarovski crystal-lined walls,

Lulu is so glamorous that cocktails are the only appropriate drinking choice. Most of those on offer are whisky-based, but they mix the local spirit with a lot more than just soda. My Tigerlily is a long, snapdragon-pink swoosh, and comes garnished with a beautiful flower.

Hours later, Mr Smith offers a balancing arm as I totter up the stunning staircase, unsure whether to focus on the swirly hot-pink carpet at my feet or the revolving disco balls overhead. Despite the party atmosphere of the public areas, our room is a haven: the ideal place to recharge the batteries. With its plasma screens, pre-loaded iPod and atmospheric lighting, we've got all we need to create our own private members' club – with an extremely exclusive guestlist.

However, there is life beyond the hotel's refined façade, and the next morning we head off like good little Edinburgh tourists, destined for the Royal Mile and Arthur's Seat. Unfortunately, Tigerlily's heart-of-the-city location on George Street means the lure of the shops is far too strong, and

our plan starts to unravel. We discover Corniche, where I run my hands enviously over its selection of archive pieces by Thierry Mugler and Jean Paul Gaultier. Then we get distracted on the Royal Mile, too. Before long, we're trudging up the intimidating slopes of Arthur's Seat lugging carrier bags laden with fudge, soap and designer classics.

For lunch, we head back to Tigerlily, where the crowd at this hour is a wonderful mix of Jean Brodie types in their tartan regalia, and ladies who lunch (mainly by pushing a slice of seared tuna round their plate). It's not an unhappy mix though. We've had Georgian façades and disco-ball interiors, tartan and spike heels, shortbread and cocktails. So, if there's a theme to the weekend, it would have to be contrast. And excess. We retire to the Georgian Suite, a land stocked with fine flavours and scents, and, with all the decadent abandon of any self-respecting 18th-century aristocrat, we run a frothy bubble bath, pop open the champagne and turn the iPod up loud. Marie-Antoinette would surely have approved.

Reviewed by Tamara Salman

NEED TO KNOW
Rooms 33, including nine suites.

Rates £195–£245, including breakfast and tax.

Check-out 11am, but flexible on request. Earliest check-in, 2pm.

Facilities CD, DVD and games library, PlayStation Portables, laundry service. In rooms, minibar, plasma-screen TV, fully loaded iPod, free WiFi, umbrella, GHDs, White Company toiletries.

Children Baby cots and babysitters can be provided.

Also Fitness fanatics can get their fix across the road, where Tigerlily guests have access to the Roxburghe Hotel's swimming pool and well-equipped gym. Tigerlily is closed 24–25 December annually.

IN THE KNOW
Our favourite rooms Georgian Suites 1 and 12 are best for making romantic gestures, with four-poster beds, great views, open fires, double sinks, freestanding baths and waterproof remote controls for the bathroom TV.

Hotel bar Rouged up to the hilt and encrusted with crystals, seductive Lulu is the popular bar and club hidden beneath Tigerlily. DJs mix up an interesting blend of Latin, house and electro till 3am, while bartenders mix up interesting blends of the strong stuff.

Hotel restaurant This huge open-plan hangout is gorgeous to look at, and trying to decide whether you fancy British, Mediterranean or Asian cuisine from the extensive menus will necessitate at least one aperitif to keep you going.

Top table The choice of seating is almost as overwhelming as the menu, but you'll soon be feeling territorial about your own cosy breakfast corner or sofa for tea; for dinner, slink into one of the intimate little alcoves.

Room service A selection from the à la carte menu is available 24 hours a day.

Dress code Cool cat by day; glamourpuss by night.

Local knowledge Amble up to Edinburgh Castle – if only to just wander through the surrounding gardens and woodland; ask Tigerlily to arrange a picnic for you. It can also arrange mixology lessons and personal shopping, among other activities.

LOCAL EATING AND DRINKING
For an outstanding brunch with upstanding eco credentials, you can't beat the **Urban Angel** café and deli on Hanover Street (0131 225 6251). On Thistle Street, **Fishers in the City** brings the excellent seafood and fish dishes of its popular Leith outpost to town (0131 225 5109); order Lindisfarne oysters, if they're in season, or one of the Mediterranean-style dishes. Award-winning chef PC Thakur serves up authentic, flavour-packed regional Indian cuisine at the delightful **9 Cellars** restaurant and bar on York Place (0131 557 9899). For an ultra-romantic evening, dinner at **The Witchery by the Castle**'s atmospheric restaurant is second to none (0131 225 5613). Liven things up at one of the many buzzing bars along George Street: ever-vibrant **Candy Bar** (0131 225 9179) is a top cocktail hotspot.

GET A ROOM!
To book this hotel, go to www.mrandmrssmith.com or ring our expert travel team on 1 800 464 2040. Activate your free membership online (see page 4) to qualify for the exclusive Smith card offer shown below when you book with us.

 SMITH CARD OFFER Drinks vouchers for two special 'Smith' signature cocktails, devised by Tigerlily's mixologist, to use on each night of your stay.

Tigerlily 125 George Street, Edinburgh EH2 4JN (www.mrandmrssmith.com/tigerlily)

How to...

play **strip** poker

HOW TO PLAY STRIP POKER (FIVE-CARD DRAW)

Each player should make sure they are suitably well-clad before the game begins; a level playing field is only fair. The dealer shuffles up a complete deck of cards. Each player puts in some money (see poker betting, below), and is dealt five cards, face down. Next, it's a clockwise round of betting. Each player then has the option to discard up to three cards and have them replaced with fresh cards from the top of the pack. There is another round of betting before the hands are revealed; the highest hand (see right) wins the pot and the holder of the lowest hand takes off an item of clothing before the game starts again. The game continues in this fashion until one or all the players are entirely naked, depending on the exact circumstances – and motives – for playing in the first place...

POKER BETTING

The money you wager is put in the centre of the table and is called the pot. You have three choices when the betting gets to you:

Raise – let's say the initial bet is $1: you'd match that, and then add the sum you wish to raise by. Now the other players will either call, raise or fold. The round continues until everybody has called or folded on a bet.

Call – betting enough to match what has been bet since the last time you bet; for example, if you bet $1 and somebody then bets $2, you would owe $1. If you call, you put that $1 into the pot and stay in the hand.

Fold – dropping out of the current hand: you only lose what you have put into the pot up to the point of folding.

And remember: you lose, you strip.

POKER-HAND HIERARCHY

1 Straight flush

Five cards in order (such as 7-8-9-10-jack), all of the same suit. Aces can be high or low. A straight flush including a high ace is called a Royal Flush and is the highest hand.

2 Four of a kind

Four cards of the same rank (four aces or four kings, for example). If two or more hands qualify, the hand with the highest-ranked four wins.

3 Full house

A full house is a three of a kind and a pair – such as king-king-king-2-2. When there are two full houses, the tie is broken by the higher-ranking three of a kind.

4 Flush

A hand in which all the cards are the same suit (such as 5-7-9-jack-queen, all of diamonds). When there are two or more flushes, the flush containing the highest card wins.

5 Straight

Five cards in rank order (ace-2-3-4-5, for example), but not of the same suit. Aces can be high or low. When there are two straights, the highest straight wins. If two straights have the same value, the pot is split.

6 Three of a kind

Three cards of any rank (10-10-10, perhaps), with the remaining cards not a pair. As with the full house, the highest-ranking three of a kind wins.

7 Two pair

Two distinct pairs and a fifth card. The higher-ranking pair wins ties. If both hands have the same high pair, the second pair wins. If both hands have the same pairs, the high card (see below) wins.

8 Pair

One pair, with three other cards. The highest-ranking pair wins. The high card breaks ties.

9 High card

When no player has even a pair, it comes down to who is holding the highest-ranking card. If there is a tie for the high card, the next highest card determines the pot.

LONDON

CITYSCAPE Multidimensional mega-sprawl
CITY LIFE Cosmopolitan, cultured, eccentric

London, baby! The ultimate on-the-river capital. From the refined romance of Kensington and Notting Hill to the trendy belles of Shoreditch and Clerkenwell, heritage beauty here is accessorised with hip style and street smarts. You'll find glorious royal parks and historic squares, monuments galore and museums piled with colonial swag, galleries where art soothes or surprises, and stages attracting theatre's hottest talent. A multi-ethnic English eccentric, this shopper's Valhalla lets you eat and browse your way around the globe: snack on sushi in Soho, try on Savile Row tailoring and buy Italian shoes on Bond Street, or pick out exotic sari silks on Brick Lane – it's all in a day's diversions. And, while architectural icons the Gherkin, the London Eye and Wembley Stadium provide a skyline for the new renaissance, the build-up to the 2012 Olympics provides an endlessly fascinating topic for the city's enthusiastic cabbies...

GETTING THERE

Planes London has several international airports: to the west, Heathrow is on the Piccadilly Line Tube, or 15 minutes from Paddington station on the Heathrow Express (www.heathrowexpress.com). Gatwick, to the south, is 30 minutes from Victoria (www.gatwickexpress.com). Stansted and Luton, to the north, are where most budget carriers land. Trains International trains arrive at St Pancras (www.stpancras.com), which has good links via the Underground, aka the Tube – your travel saviour (www.tfl.gov.uk/tube). Automobiles On weekdays from 7am to 6pm, there's an £8 daily Congestion Charge payable to drive into central London (www.cclondon.com); parking can be costly. Boats There are commuter and leisure boats all along the river: see www.tfl.gov.uk/river for timetables and routes.

LOCAL KNOWLEDGE

Taxis You can hail one of London's trademark black hackney cabs anywhere, or ring Zingo (0870 070 0700) from your cell phone, and the nearest one will find you. Avoid unlicensed minicabs; try Climatecars (020 8968 0440), whose carbon-neutral taxis operate in central London. Currency Pound sterling (£).

Dialling codes UK: 44. London: (0)20.
Tipping culture Many restaurants add a discretionary 12.5 per cent service charge, so be careful not to tip twice. Siesta and fiesta There's always something going on, be it a flower market at dawn or a late-night gallery opening, but banks and a surprising number of shops stick firmly to their nine-to-five habit. Most pubs pull their last pints at 10.45pm; bars and clubs stay open till the wee hours. Do go/don't go London City empties out in August, but tourist sites will still get crowded. Spring and summer can be lovely – even if the weather is reliably unreliable. Packing tips A pocket-sized A–Z guide and Tube map will prevent 'Where am I?' moments.
Recommended reads Martin Amis' *London Fields* follows three characters as nuclear disaster looms; Iain Sinclair circumnavigated the M25 on foot to research *London Orbital*; Peter Ackroyd's epic *London: The Biography* treats the town as a personality.
Cuisine London wins global praise for its authentic multi-cultural fare, from Chinatown's dim sum to Brick Lane's saucy spices and West London's Moroccan tagines... But, hey, even a mega-metropolis can source from its own

garden. At Oliver Rowe's King's Cross restaurant, Konstam at the Prince Albert (020 7833 5040), all the ingredients used in the making of his Northern European menu are grown or produced within the M25. Norbury Blue cheese, Tower Hill honey and Amersham lamb not only lack air miles, they also offer a true taste of London town. And... London moves quickly: by the time you've heard about that hot club, show or under-the-radar boutique, chances are it's, like, so over. Tag along with an Urban Gentry guide, however, and you'll get an up-to-the-minute take on city life; choose a themed tour, or have them tailor an itinerary around your tastes (www.urbangentry.com).

WORTH GETTING OUT OF BED FOR

Viewpoint Book a ride on the London Eye (www.londoneye. com), the South Bank's big wheel, for sight-spotting and vertigo-inducing views of five counties. Then amble over Waterloo Bridge at sunset to reacquaint yourself with the cityscape from the ground. Want to work harder for your views? Climb the spiral steps of St Paul's Cathedral to the Whispering Gallery and then up and out to the Stone and Golden Galleries for magnificent panoramic views of the capital. At King Henry's Mound in Richmond Park, six miles away, there are incredible westward vistas of Berkshire – plus an amazing view back to St Paul's.
Arts and culture London has a wealth of cultural delights to tickle all tastes: Tate Modern and Tate Britain house British and international art collections (www.tate.org.uk). Hoxton's White Cube gallery (www.whitecube.com) is edgier, or, for the experimental and out there, pop in on the art studios and galleries lining Vyner Street in Bethnal Green. Arm yourself with a copy of weekly listings magazine *Time Out* for the latest information about what's on; and visit www.ticketmaster.co.uk to book seats at anything from West End musicals or plays at the Globe Theatre to stand-up comedy, gigs and classical concerts.
Activities Cool off at the Serpentine Lido (www.serpentine lido.com), where you can sling yourself into a deckchair, paddle, or show off your 110-yard crawl. See the city on blades: roll up for the Urban Rites Friday Night Skate (www.thefns.com) and follow the pack through the streets. No skates? That's no excuse: hire some from Slick Willies (020 7225 0004) on Gloucester Road and wheel wherever the wind blows you.
Perfect picnic Huge Hampstead Heath has secret woods, panoramic views and enough grass to spread a rug out and still have room to fling a Frisbee. Fill up your hamper

at the nearby Rosslyn Delicatessen (020 7794 9210). Daytripper Catch the boat from Embankment Pier to Greenwich to see the National Maritime Museum (www. nmm.ac.uk) and the Royal Observatory (www.rog.nmm. ac.uk), where you can, literally, straddle time.
Walks For city strolling, head for the river, then stick with it. Try the towpath from Richmond, Putney or Chiswick for leafy ambling. In town, take in the South Bank from Westminster to Tower Bridge, ticking the reconstructed *Golden Hinde* galleon (www.goldenhinde.org) and City Hall (aka the Leaning Tower of Pizzas) off your to-see list.
Shopping Knightsbridge and Bond Street are the designer-label doyennes, but for something you can't get back home, a market's the place: crowd-pleasing Covent Garden has crafts and collectibles; over east, Spitalfields is best for funky fashion finds; early birds get the best blooms at Columbia Road Flower Market; for organic food-tasting opportunities try Borough Market; and Portobello Road in Notting Hill is a must-go for antiques and vintage fashion.
Something for nothing Entrance to many of London's museums is still free (www.londonnet.co.uk/museums). In summer, pull up a pew on the South Bank: before long, street theatre will start happening all around you.
Don't go home without... taking traditional high tea. Go high luxe at Claridge's (020 7629 8888); high art at the Wallace Collection restaurant (020 7563 9500); or high fashion at the Berkeley (020 7235 6000) – its 'Prêt-à-portea' cakes are modelled on must-have Missoni and Zac Posen designs, and are modishly served on Paul Smith china.

LAUDABLY LONDON

At Hyde Park's Speakers' Corner (www.speakerscorner.net) you are guaranteed the right to free speech. Drag your soapbox along on a Sunday afternoon and get whatever's perplexing you off your chest. You'll be in good company: Karl Marx, William Morris and George Orwell have all spouted their views here over the decades. Be prepared for vigorous heckling, though.

DIARY

March Oxford and Cambridge Boat Race (www.theboatrace.org) from Putney to Mortlake. **April** The London Marathon (www.london-marathon.co.uk): a 26-mile race for fundraisers, athletes and mentalists in diving suits. **May** Chelsea Flower Show (www.rhs.org.uk/chelsea) brings marvellous blooms to SW3. **June** The Wimbledon Championships (www.wimbledon.org) send the capital tennis mad for a fortnight. **July–September** The BBC Proms concerts (www.bbc.co.uk/proms). **August** Notting Hill Carnival, a float-filled, bass-thumping weekend of musical mayhem. **September** Open House Weekend (www.londonopenhouse.org) sees 600 buildings, old and new, open to the public, free of charge. **October** London Film Festival (www.lff.org.uk). **November** On Guy Fawkes' Night, there are fireworks displays in parks all over town; book an eighth-floor table at the Oxo Tower (020 7803 3888) for a premium view of the Lord Mayor's fireworks on the river. London Jazz Festival – nice (www.serious.org.uk).

Baglioni Hotel

STYLE Italian elegance
SETTING Parkside Kensington
DESTINATION London

'Who could blame anyone for wanting
to stay cocooned away in this urban
palazzo? Ultra-modern and super-cool,
it plays out like a scene from an advert
pushing aspiration and success'

of urbane luxury preferred by Rome's beautiful people, or perhaps the image-obsessed Milanese. And now us.

The Baglioni doesn't have the glitzy façade that more insecure five-star establishments grab your attention with; there are no billowing flags or huge neon signs as sported by the neighbouring hotels. Clearly, Baglioni's clientele are in-the-know types, because the Georgian building, although respectable and impeccable, doesn't allude to the over-the-top grandeur that awaits inside. A cascading water feature, stone floors and oversized gold vases spilling enormous white roses create a suitably classy entrée to our new world of carefree indulgence. I feel myself happily slotting into this new lifestyle – at least until the morning, when we'll be asked to hurry along, albeit politely. Back to a life of using the same towels for weeks, and trying not to cry as the kids continue their mission to devalue our home.

It seems fitting, in such polished surroundings, that the staff is also beautiful. Mrs Smith and I are accompanied to our room by one of the perfectly groomed receptionists, via a lift with its own plasma-screen TV. Does this imply that the elevator is going to take an especially long time? Fortunately not, but it's long enough to build some excited anticipation for our VIP suite.

Just east of Kensington High Street, opposite Princess Diana's former home, the Baglioni offers a location as desirable as London has. The room we're given spoils us with the best view imaginable: not over leafy Kensington Gardens, as you might imagine I mean, but across to the Thistle Hotel – the sort of below-par establishment my usual work assignments have me stay in (I must get my manager onto that). I imagine its residents dreaming of one day making it across the road to this decidedly more upmarket address.

My previous knowledge of London boutique hotels doesn't extend much beyond the Park Lane strip where I perform as a comedian – grande dames with an ambience a world away from the intimacy of the Baglioni. Speaking as someone whose only Italian trips have been skiing-oriented, this is clearly a shrine to restrained extravagance – the kind

Purple and gold is the daring colour scheme for the soft furnishings, which extends to the walls – nothing as humdrum as wallpaper at the Baglioni. Outside very secure prisons and police stations, I imagine, this quality of hotel is the only place where padded rooms and bulletproof glass are appropriate. I race to check out the ensuite. It's stunning: marbles, slates and chromes, and a pair of beautiful his 'n' hers copper bowl sinks, with an array of luxurious hair and body products on offer. I react badly. 'Bloody hell! Mrs Smith, check this out! This is too fabulous a place to have people doing what people do in bathrooms,' I shriek. Our escort excuses herself (perhaps twigging we're not the most sophisticated guests ever to have crossed the hotel's threshold) and informs us that our butler will be up shortly to demonstrate the espresso machine. Butler? But of course. I think better of mentioning the fact I'm more of a tea man; it's probably sacrilege to shun coffee at this altar to Italian elegance.

An hour or so into our stay and the dossier of amenities that our suite has to offer has been well and truly tested. Shortly after, a kindly housekeeper calls round to see if she can turn my bed down. I explain that I'm hoping there won't be anything turned down in my bed tonight, thank you. (I put her lack of visible amusement at my reply down to professionalism. She later returns to whip our room back to an immaculate state, and to light candles throughout. Perhaps she didn't think it was a joke, and concluded I need as much help as I can get in the romance department.)

Even though the Natural History Museum and the V&A are a stroll away, we've opted for pure R&R during our South Ken one-night stand. Watching one of the Hollywood classics on offer is just as commendable as viewing any number of Assyrian bas-reliefs and, what with a short trip into Hyde Park for a stroll along the Serpentine, come the evening, we've worked up quite an appetite.

As swanky as the hotel restaurant is, with its central glass bar and sumptuous dining space, all velvet armchairs and black Murano glass chandeliers, the chef of Brunello is facing a challenge. I have in the past been a dedicated fancy-Italian-food-sceptic, perhaps

having experienced lower-rung establishments where the dishes are dressed up with glugs of oil and delivered with dubious accents. Imagine my delight at the starter: a warm mushroom salad with aged balsamic vinegar and shaved parmesan. A lifetime of overcooked ravioli is forgotten in moments. It is so delicious that I consider cancelling my halibut in favour of the same again. As for my appreciation of wine, it extends to knowing that it comes in two colours, but I like an impressive list. (Little comes in at under £30; judging by the gloss of our fellow diners, that isn't usually a problem.) After dinner, we fancy a nightcap and cocktails in one of the many hip hangouts in Knightsbridge, a two-minute cab ride away, have been suggested. But given our exquisite surroundings and the impermanence of this lifestyle, it seems crazy to leave, so we stay in the bar, sipping martinis made with gold.

As tempting as it is to spend a lazy morning taking advantage of acres of comfortable bed, or exploring Kensington Gardens, we have to be up at 7am to catch a flight. We're the first breakfasters of the day. Then it occurs to me: Baglioni residents don't work – they lounge and shop. And the nearby retail temple that is Harvey Nichols is, like them, still sleeping. Who could blame anyone for wanting to stay cocooned away in this urban palazzo? Ultra-modern and super-cool, it plays out like a scene from an advert pushing aspiration and success. I feel tempted to give my fellow residents a congratulatory pat on the back for having made it. I suspect I'm the only one here who even knows there's a hotel chain that shares its name with a prickly Scottish plant.

As we leave the hotel, reality feels harsh, drab, inelegant. We make for the Tube; we're not on expenses anymore. Shut-eye in such a wonderful environment has been an eye-opener. Thanks to the Baglioni, we've had a taste of the high life, and Mrs Smith has loved every minute. She remarks that we should use London more adventurously, and stay in hotels like the Baglioni regularly. I'll have to become funnier, I tell her. 'Yeah right,' she sighs. Note to self: just how many reasonably amusing gags equal another night at the Baglioni? I'd better work on that repertoire.

Reviewed by Dominic Holland

NEED TO KNOW

Rooms 67, with 50 suites, including a Presidential Suite and a Royal Suite (price on request).
Rates £290–£1,900, excluding VAT. Continental breakfast, £25, excluding a 12.5 per cent service charge.
Check-out Noon, though this is flexible, subject to availability; check-in, 2pm.
Facilities Rejuvenation Spa providing Espa treatments, beauty salon and fitness centre, extensive film and music library, WiFi in the lobby, valet parking, bicycles. In rooms, minibar, high-speed internet connection.
Children Embraced – the Baglioni group (like most Italian families) is very child-friendly. Baby cots (free), extra beds (£50) and babysitters (£15 an hour) are all available.
Also Butler service is included. Private dining for up to 60 can be organised, and there's a club downstairs – Boutique 60 – available for hire. A personal shopper can be summoned to your side in a trice.

IN THE KNOW

Our favourite rooms The open-plan Junior Suite 107 has high ceilings, a large walk-in wardrobe, two plasma TVs, a bathtub and walk-in shower. Courtyard Junior Suites are set around a quiet inner patio, with Illy espresso machines, twin TVs and hand-beaten copper sinks from Morocco. Deluxe Junior Suite 405 has a silk-canopied four-poster and a working fireplace.
Hotel bar Marvellous martinis are to be had in the sleek, mirror-lined Brunello Lounge cocktail bar until 1am. Or try a Russian Rose cocktail, frosted with gold dust and laced with vodka. By day, the lounge is a quiet throng of brunchers and tea-takers.
Hotel restaurant Classic Italian dining takes place on plush velvet banquettes in luxe brasserie-style Brunello Restaurant, or on its terrace. Enthusiastic head chef Andrea Vercelli has a fresh take on traditional dishes, and the menu is matched by a super list of Tuscan wines. Last orders, 10.45pm.
Top table To the side of a window overlooking Kensington Gardens, or next to the fireplace.
Room service 24 hours. When the dining room is open, the restaurant menu is available.
Dress code Dripping in designer: Italian labels, preferably.
Local knowledge Bring your jogging kit, jodhpurs or Frisbee, since the beautiful Kensington Gardens and Hyde Park are on your doorstep. You're also ideally located for shopping sprees on Brompton Road, or culture trips to the ridiculously close Royal Albert Hall (www.royalalberthall.com) and V&A museum (www.vam.ac.uk).

LOCAL EATING AND DRINKING

Refuel after a hard day's shopping in the Fifth Floor restaurant of destination department store **Harvey Nichols** (020 7235 5250) in Knightsbridge, where you'll find well-presented Modern British and European dishes. Gourmets will love the daily-changing set menu in the pretty white interior of **Clarke's** (020 7221 9225) at 124 Kensington Church Street. Long-time favourite of London's ladies who lunch, **San Lorenzo** (020 7584 1074) on Beauchamp Place is Italian, cosy and surprisingly low-key. Lovers of Japanese cuisine should put **Zuma** (020 7584 1010) on Raphael Street top of their list; book ahead. **Lonsdale House** (020 7727 4080) on Lonsdale Road in Notting Hill provides a stylish backdrop for elegant tapas-sized dishes and incredible cocktails. **Kensington Roof Gardens** (020 7937 7994) on Kensington High Street boasts a restaurant, a club, and an acre and a half of tropical greenery.

GET A ROOM!

To book this hotel, go to www.mrandmrssmith.com or ring our expert travel team on 1 800 464 2040. Activate your free membership online (see page 4) to qualify for the exclusive Smith card offer shown below when you book with us.

 SMITH CARD OFFER A bottle of red or white wine, and 10 per cent off a treatment each in the Rejuvenation Spa.

Baglioni Hotel 60 Hyde Park Gate, London SW7 5BB (www.mrandmrssmith.com/baglioni-hotel)

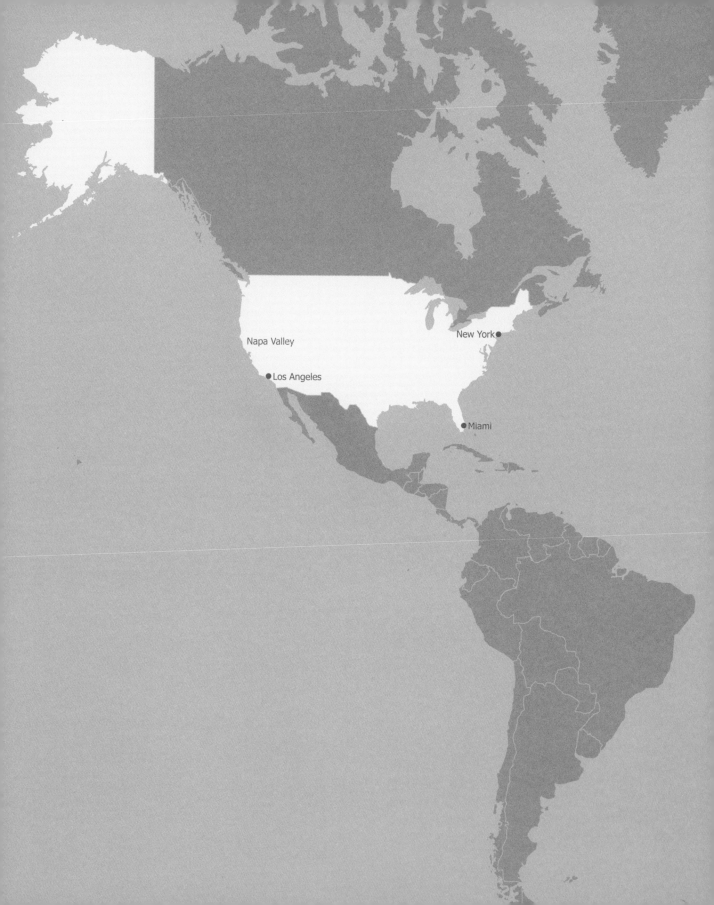

Napa Valley

New York●

●Los Angeles

●Miami

UNITED STATES

LOS ANGELES
Viceroy Santa Monica

MIAMI
The Setai

NAPA VALLEY
Calistoga Ranch

NEW YORK
The Bowery Hotel

LOS ANGELES

LA – a city of silver-screen dreams, where wannabe actors wait tables and budding scriptwriters serve ultra-skinny soy lattes. In this most sun-kissed corner of California, a cross-city drive past A-list addresses and kitsch-glam boardwalks feels like a series of rapid set changes: palm trees and long beaches flank boutique-blessed boulevards; and diner-lined highways transport you via sorbet-coloured mansions to mid-century modern motels. Presided over by the fabled Hollywood Hills, this sprawling megalopolis can be intimidating to the uninitiated, but explore its distinct neighbourhoods and you'll find characterful and cosy slices of Los Angeles life. From Malibu and Bel-Air to WeHo, this is a place where you can write your own storyline – so whether you surf at Venice Beach, stroll Santa Monica's Third Street Promenade or hang out star-style in the fine-dining eateries of Beverly Hills, the way the plot unfolds is up to you…

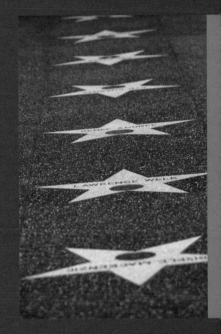

GETTING THERE

Planes LAX international airport (www.lawa.org) is 16 miles from Downtown. Forget public transport: if you don't have a car, take a SuperShuttle minivan (800 258 3826; www.supershuttle.com) or taxi from outside Arrivals. **Trains** Amtrak (www.amtrak.com) connects Los Angeles to other US cities via Union Station on North Alameda Street; Metrolink (www.metrolinktrains.com) serves regional hubs. **Automobiles** Let's cut to the chase: you need one of these to get a real flavour of LA (even if the freeways are hell on wheels). Zoom around like Hollywood starlets in a classic Corvette or Cadillac from Beverly Hills Rent-A-Car (310 337 1400; www.bhrentacar.com). If you care about your carbon footprint, the company also has hybrid vehicles.

LOCAL KNOWLEDGE

Taxis So expensive, you might as well rent a car. You're unlikely to find a taxi rank, so book with one of the large cab firms, such as Yellow Cab Co (877 733 3305). **Currency** US dollar ($). **Dialling codes** US: 1. Downtown: 213; Hollywood: 323; Malibu, Venice, Santa Monica, Beverly Hills: 310. **Tipping culture** Always expected in restaurants, taxis and hair salons: 20 per cent is not unusual, but a little more than double the amount of tax on your bill is about right. Tip a dollar a drink at bars; porters get a dollar a bag. **Siesta and fiesta** Most shops are open till 7pm, although malls often stay open later. Restaurants are normally busiest between 6pm and 9pm. **Do go/don't go** Spring and autumn sees LA is at its best. Days are often warm and sunny, but summer can see a rise in smog levels and sea mist (known as 'June gloom'). **Packing tips** That film script you've been working on (preferably stuffed into a serious It bag). **Recommended reads** LA novels almost invariably feature crime, corruption and sex sirens: classics include *The Big Sleep* by Raymond Chandler; and *The Black Dahlia* or *LA Confidential* by James Ellroy. *My Lucky Star* by Jo Keenan is a farcical, fun-poking, fictional look at Hollywood. **Cuisine** You can get anything and everything in LA, from dim sum in Chinatown to Mexican enchiladas, but in SoCal, it's all about low-cal. This star-struck city is dedicated to fat-free food fads and major-league schmoozing, so don't be surprised if your fellow diners at Ivy are still on a strict raw-food, low-carb 'reverse French' regime that excludes red meat, caffeine and fun. LA is not exactly the greenest of towns, but there are plenty of farmers' markets (particularly in Santa Monica), and wines from the Napa and Sonoma Valleys are justly popular as well as low on air miles.

WORTH GETTING OUT OF BED FOR

Viewpoint Drive up to twisting Mulholland Drive for exhilarating views over the city; the road runs for 50 miles from Hollywood to the Malibu coast. There are also fine views from the Getty Center (www.getty.edu), the art museum in the foothills of the Santa Monica mountains.
Arts and culture After the intellectual heights of the Getty Center, indulge in a something a little more lowbrow: Hollywood Boulevard's Walk of Fame and its 2,000 inlaid stars, honouring industry greats from Orson Welles to Lassie. Keep walking till you hit Grauman's Chinese Theatre (www.manntheatres.com) and its famously footprinted concrete forecourt – book a behind-the-scenes tour on 323 463 9576. The Walt Disney Concert Hall (www.laphil. org) on Grand Avenue in Downtown is home to the LA Philharmonic; it's worth a visit just to see Frank Gehry's fantastic neo-cubist architecture.
Activities Watch the LA Lakers (www.nba.com/lakers) shoot hoops or spend Saturday night at the movies: theatres with unique character include Grauman's Chinese; the Egyptian on Hollywood Boulevard; and the Aero in Santa Monica (www.americancinematheque.com). At ArcLight (www.arclightcinemas.com) on Sunset, you can sip martinis with your movie at its 21+ screenings. Surf dudes and divas can rent boards at ZJ Boarding House (www.zjboarding house.com) on Main Street, Santa Monica; mortals might want to try boogie-boards first, or take a few lessons with Learn to Surf LA (310 663 2479). Watch whales breaching off the coast of Santa Barbara or kayak round the Channel Islands with Condor Cruises (www.condorcruises.com).
Best beach Venice Beach is LA at its weird and wonderful best. Beyond the sand and surf, the Venice boardwalk is a Pacific-view playground for bodybuilders, hippies in bikinis, rollerblading oddballs and chainsaw jugglers. Stroll along the Ocean Front Walk and the Promenade all the way to the fairground rides on Santa Monica Pier.
Daytripper After decades in the doldrums, Palm Springs – and its mid-century modern marvels – is very much back in vogue. Tour the Jetsonian architecture with a Palm Springs Modern Committee map: pick one up from the Visitors Center (760 778 8418; www.palm-springs.org).
Walks With the planet's highest concentration of A-listers,

LA is the home of the star safari. These elusive creatures can be hard to track down but, with luck and patience, you should enjoy a sighting. Guide yourself round their natural habitat with the help of a star map while reflecting on the fact that fabulous wealth rarely guarantees a tasteful home.
Shopping WeHo is the place for retail excess, particularly on Rodeo Drive and Beverly Boulevard, but the less label-conscious will love Robertson Boulevard's boutiques. For cult fashion, seek out the concept store Maxfield (310 274 8800) and vintage wonderlands on Melrose. La Brea Avenue is great for homewares. If you like everything under one enormous roof, go to the Beverly Center (www. beverlycenter.com). The Grove (www.thegrovela.com) is a boutique mall next to the Farmers Market (with butchers and bakers and peanut-butter makers) – worth a peek after you've exhausted the wealth of purchasing possibilities on West Third Street. This is not to be confused with Santa Monica's Third Street Promenade – also good for browsing. Head to boho Abbot Kinney Boulevard in Venice; the best indie stores include Equator Books (310 399 5544), Japanese design emporium Tortoise (310 314 8448), and retro-furniture showroom Surfing Cowboys (310 450 4891).
Something for nothing Almost everywhere in LA has been used as a set: play the Total Recall game (better known as, 'Hey, I bet that diner was in *Pulp Fiction/Pretty Woman*') and settle scores online at www.movielocationsguide.com.
Don't go home without... drinking cocktails at one of LA's see-and-be-seen hangouts. The Standard Downtown's Rooftop Bar boasts stimulating 360-degree cityscape views.

LANGUIDLY LOS ANGELES

Hollywood wannabes aside, beach life – as defined by Beach Boys songs and *Baywatch* babes – epitomises sunny SoCal. The top trio are Venice, Santa Monica and Malibu: the acting elite may jealously guard 'their' sandy patch of celeb suburbia, but Malibu and Zuma beach are perfect for surfing, volleyball, picnics and sunbathing; find surf schools at www.surfline.com.

DIARY

Late February The Academy Awards at the Kodak Theatre on Hollywood Boulevard sends the city into a film frenzy. **March/April** Holy cow! Farm animals and pets are blessed by the city's cardinal at the El Pueblo de Los Angeles Monument on the Saturday before Easter (www.overa-street.com). **Late July** Expect punk music, hot rods and Catholic priests at the Blessing of the Cars – yes, cars (www.blessingofthecars.com). The Honda US Open of Surfing (www.usopenofsurfing.com) kicks off in Orange County. **December** Celebrities, razzmatazz, marching bands and colourful floats can only mean one thing: the Hollywood Christmas Parade.

Viceroy Santa Monica

STYLE Elegant urban beach retreat
SETTING Sunny Ocean Avenue
DESTINATION Los Angeles

'It's so difficult to find the right
space, lighting and mood
suitable for getting red-carpet
ready, but this is the real deal'

can bake a tasty scone – and indulge in the shortbread with lemon curd and waffles with cappuccino-flavoured cream.

We walk out to the poolside area with a fresh round of Mimosas following close behind. Sun-yellow wing-backed chairs are set around an electric-blue pool in front of white cabanas with art deco details. The people-watching isn't so spectacular today – and aside from we three ladies with our red lips and vintage attire, there's just the handsome waitstaff to watch at the water's edge. Miss Smith calls a hot young guy over and asks him to touch up her chipped red nail polish, which he does with panache. Poor chap, though, having to put the 'man' into 'manicure' while three ladies, tipsy on champagne cocktails, watch and giggle.

Afterwards, I check into my ocean-view Empire suite. It's perfect. Each door is painted in a brilliant green, with French hardware in gleaming silver, and there's enough design ideas here to keep me going for life. I adore the damask wallpaper and smoked mirrored walls, the leaf-green chairs with Chinoiserie details, crystal wall sconces and orchids on the white cocktail table. There's ample counter space for my beauty products, oodles of closet room and mirrors everywhere. It's so difficult to find the right space, lighting and mood suitable for getting red-carpet ready, but this is definitely the real deal.

After devoting an hour or so to making myself as glamorous as my surroundings, I head down to dinner in the hotel's acclaimed Whist restaurant. The lighting is cover-shoot impeccable. My friends are all good-looking girls, but in this sexy and subdued atmosphere they look simply ravishing. We immediately make a pact to use this restaurant as a seduction tool in future. I order an exquisitely perfumed lavender martini from the impressive cocktail menu and sit back to watch the stylish, buzzing crowd. What happens next only ever occurs in the chicest of chic restaurants: the waiter brings me a black napkin because I'm wearing a black dress. I'm absolutely devoted to this place – and the starters haven't even arrived yet.

The food is divine – and I know this because I tried a bite from everyone's plate. The seared tuna, lamb ravioli and seafood ceviche are just superb, but it's the bread pudding

Pulling up outside the Viceroy Santa Monica on a sunny afternoon, I am instantly reminded of idyllic childhood summers spent at the Grand Hotel in Michigan. That particular hotel, with its vibrant Hollywood Regency-style mix of baroque and Chinoiserie, has influenced my style choices ever since. Glamour is everything to me, so it's important – no, essential – for my surroundings to reflect that. How wonderful, then, it is to pass the Viceroy's valets and stride into an elegant, colourful foyer filled with vivid kelly green vases, and French-style chairs and chaises. Already, I feel as though I might just be in the most fabulous hotel in Los Angeles.

Accompanying me today are my two best friends – one, alas, now a Miss Smith after a recent break-up – and we head into the dining room for the Viceroy's famous Sunday brunch. We order a round of delicious Mimosas, made with freshly squeezed orange juice, and make for the buffet tables. We eschew the obvious sweet choices – even I

and Earl Grey ice-cream that's perhaps the highlight. I have a second lavender martini, and quite possibly a third. I can't be too sure... Afterwards, when we decide to head to a club downtown, the hotel has a car ready for us in exactly 15 minutes.

It's heaven to slip into my marshmallowy bed at 4am, and I sleep better than I have in ages. When I wake up, there's not even a touch of a hangover. I order up the best plate of huevos rancheros I can recall, and wash it down with a yummy

'The Viceroy combines classic old-Hollywood style with modern chic and sophistication'

311

blueberry smoothie. When I finally make it downstairs around lunchtime, Miss Smith is waiting for me in the bar. We call for two more of the now-legendary lavender martinis.

After an hour or so, we head up to my suite for an in-room massage. I immediately stake my claim on the muscular guy with the ponytail and tribal tattoos. He looks real sensitive, but oh-so strong. Once his palms start working their way up my back, however, I do what any girl in my position would and fall fast asleep. My masseur may well have sat down and read a magazine for an hour, but Miss Smith and I had a good nap and, for us, that's priceless.

As we get dressed, I am struck by how reluctant I am to check out. I've been looking for the refinement, elegance and tradition of those girlhood summers all my life, and the Viceroy combines the same classic old-Hollywood style with modern chic and sophistication. I'll definitely be coming back for a weekend soon. Hopefully with a very lucky Mr Smith in tow.

Reviewed by Dita Von Teese

NEED TO KNOW

Rooms 162, including five suites.

Rates Rooms, $299–$660; suites, $499–$730, including breakfast and daily newspaper.

Check-out Noon, but may be extended on request (subject to availability); earliest check-in, 3pm.

Facilities Two outdoor swimming pools, spa treatments, 24-hour fitness centre, library, laundry/dry-cleaning, valet parking, video check-out facility. In rooms, minibar and beauty bar, WiFi, flatscreen TV, CD/DVD player... all boxes ticked.

Children Rollaway beds can be provided at no extra charge. The concierge team is happy to help you find distractions for your miniature sidekicks, including surfing lessons, family yoga sessions and child-friendly outings.

Also Some smoking rooms are available, otherwise smoking is only permitted in outdoor spaces. Pets are welcome, for a non-refundable fee of $50. Don't worry if you leave your sun protection or skincare behind – you can buy everything here.

IN THE KNOW

Our favourite rooms The Ocean View Viceroy rooms live up to their moniker, with sea vistas that stretch up and down the coast. Viceroy and Grande rooms have private balconies. For oversized bathrooms with enough space for marble wet rooms, vanity tables and cat-swinging, go for a Grande Room or Empire Suite.

Hotel bar The Cameo Bar is one of Santa Monica's hottest hangouts, and is particularly lively from Wednesdays to Saturdays. The martinis are killer; try the Key Lime – ingredients include vanilla vodka, triple sec and Graham crackers. Yes, you read that right. The last vodka-based pick-me-ups are shaken at 1.30am.

Hotel restaurant Whist – a delicious-looking space with plates on walls as well as tables – serves seriously creative Modern American cuisine. We loved the prime Angus ribeye for two, served with garlic-sautéed shrimp, sweet potato fries, asparagus and truffle béarnaise.

Top table The outdoor tables are very romantic, but for maximum privacy, choose one of the banquettes.

Room service The 24-hour menu reflects that of the Whist restaurant (oysters, Kobe beef burgers, parmesan-crusted fries).

Dress code On the smarter side of casual, with the odd jacket thrown in (unless you're by the pool, of course).

Local knowledge The carousels, roller coasters, fun stalls and twinkly lights of the iconic Santa Monica Pier are a siren call to anyone who's still just a big kid at heart. There are regular concerts and plays, usually at sunset and often free.

LOCAL EATING AND DRINKING

For brunch, stroll down to **Cora's Coffee Shoppe** (310 451 9562) at 1802 Ocean Avenue and fill up on healthy omelettes, orange and blueberry pancakes, and bagels. Just next-door, **Capo** (310 394 5550) is a fine Italian with an elegantly low-key vibe, excellent grills and rich lobster risotto. Further down Ocean at 1602, **The Lobster** (310 458 9294) has fabulous views over the beach and Santa Monica Pier, with fittingly fabulous clam chowder to boot. At 2901 Ocean Park Boulevard, **The Counter** (310 399 8383) is a chic modern deli serving up the fattest and juiciest burgers in Santa Monica, so don't wear your favourite T-shirt. In West LA's Fairfax area, **AOC** (323 653 6359) on West Third Street is a great French wine bar; nearby, **The Little Door Restaurant** (323 951 1210) is a tucked-away Mediterranean diamond with four romantic and candlelit rooms. If you're dining there, pop into **El Carmen** (323 852 1552), two doors down, for after-dinner margaritas.

GET A ROOM!

To book this hotel, go to www.mrandmrssmith.com or ring our expert travel team on 1 800 464 2040. Activate your free membership online (see page 4) to qualify for the exclusive Smith card offer shown below when you book with us.

 SMITH CARD OFFER Welcome drinks for two at the Cameo Bar, and a 15 per cent discount on breakfast on each morning of your stay.

Viceroy Santa Monica 1819 Ocean Avenue, Santa Monica, CA 90410 (www.mrandmrssmith.com/viceroy-santa-monica)

MIAMI

CITYSCAPE Art deco decadence
CITY LIFE Miami vices

Miami is a particularly colourful swirl in the great American melting pot; few cities are more diverse and cosmopolitan, and even fewer can boast white-sand beaches and endless days of perfect sunshine, too. The city has a fast-paced rhythm and Latin swagger that owes as much to South America and the Caribbean as Florida. Districts such as Coral Gables, Little Havana and Coconut Grove offer the kind of sultry indulgences their names suggest, but it is South Beach (SoBe) that's the heart of the party scene in a city that takes its hedonism seriously. The wide sweep of sand between the candy-coloured art deco beachfront of Ocean Drive and the Atlantic surf is both Miami's playground and its catwalk. Beyond the bling and bikinis lies a city of stylish restaurants, decadent lounge bars and a burgeoning arts scene, offering irresistible Miami virtues and vices in equal measure.

GETTING THERE

Planes You're more likely to arrive at the busier MIA (Miami International Airport), 12 miles west of Downtown, than FLL (Fort Lauderdale-Hollywood), 30 miles north. A SuperShuttle minivan (305 871 2000) or taxi from MIA costs about $25.
Trains Amtrak (www.amtrak.com) connects Miami to other US cities. Downtown, the efficient Metromover is a free, driverless transit system. The Tri-Rail commuter line runs along the coast to Palm Beach.
Automobiles In the land where the car is king, there really is no substitute unless you're staying rooted in one district. Gotham Dream Cars (www.gothamdreamcars.com) will deliver a shiny Aston Martin or similarly exotic wheels direct to your hotel door, from $695 a day for a BMW M5.

LOCAL KNOWLEDGE

Taxis Taxis are relatively cheap and readily available. Swank it up in a chauffeur-driven vintage Rolls Royce from Vintage Limousines of Coral Gables (305 444 7657).
Currency US dollar ($).
Dialling codes US: 1. Miami: 305.
Tipping culture A must in restaurants; 20 per cent is not unusual. At bars, tip a dollar a drink. To ensure bathroom goodies get stocked up, leave something for housekeeping.
Siesta and fiesta Miami is a serious party town; the lines of hopefuls beyond the velvet ropes at the trendiest clubs will be at their longest just after midnight, so try to get guestlisted by your concierge.
Do go/don't go Peak tourist times are from December to March and the weeks around Carnival in October; book well ahead. There's not really a bad time to go to sunny Florida, unless you can't take the heat.
Packing tips Shades are an essential part of the Miami look; and don't forget your sexiest swimwear. Also bring some insect repellent to ward off the vampire-sized mosquitoes.
Recommended reads *Big Trouble* is former *Miami Herald* columnist Dave Barry's crime-fiction spoof; Joan Didion's *Miami* probes the city's Cuban connections; Elmore Leonard's finely-tuned yarn *Stick* follows ex-con Ernest Stickley as he explores Miami's underworld.
Cuisine In this city, you are what you eat (and drink); ordering a beer rather than a cocktail in one of the many plush bars will not impress. The 'Floribbean' cuisine favoured on the upscale restaurant scene fuses the fresh flavours of Florida's coast with the earthy spices of the

Caribbean, and Miami's Latin influences mean plenty of excellent Cuban food, particularly in Little Havana, where rice and beans and minty mojitos are the order of the day. In season, stone crab is a much-fêted delicacy; the region is also renowned for its citrus fruit and avocados.

WORTH GETTING OUT OF BED FOR

Viewpoint Miami's location between the Everglades and the Atlantic means there are few natural vantage points. Azul restaurant at the waterfront Mandarin Oriental at 500 Brickell Key Drive (305 913 8254) has great views of Biscayne Bay and Downtown (as well as decent food).

Arts and culture The Ancient Spanish Monastery on West Dixie Highway typifies Miami's cultural life: it was imported. Built in Spain in 1141, it was bought by William Randolph Hearst in 1925 and shipped over stone by stone. Little Havana is the centre of the city's Cuban exile community, particularly around Calle Ocho (Southwest Eighth Street) between 11th and 17th Avenues. Design addicts will love North Miami contemporary-art museum Moca (www.mocanomi.org), and browsing the galleries and boutiques in the Miami Design District (www.miamidesigndistrict.net). The Bass Art Museum on Park Avenue (www.bassmuseum.org) is the centre of the South Beach art scene.

Activities Miami is a water-focused playground; charter a yacht (www.waterfantaseas.com); learn to sail one (www.floridayacht.com); or go scuba diving (www.tarpoondivecenter.com). There's also deep-sea sport fishing if you want to satisfy your inner Hemingway; try Blue Waters (305 373 5016) at Bayside Marketplace. If you've had all the sun, sea and sand you can handle, hit the glorious greens at 18-hole Biltmore Golf Course (305 460 5364) – it's a par-71 beauty with a devilishly tricky sixth. Alternatively, watch Shaquille O'Neal shoot hoops for Miami Heat (www.nba.com/heat), or chill out at the Kendall Ice Arena (305 386 8288) – there are live DJs until midnight on Friday and Saturday nights.

Best beach South Beach is *the* beach in Miami. The Lummus Park section between Fifth and 15th Streets is one of the most popular spots with the city's party animals and Riviera wannabes; Third Street beach is where the beautiful young Brazilians strut their stuff.

Daytripper Rent a Harley from Peterson's (www.miamiharley.com), from $100 a day, and cruise the 50 miles down to the start of the Florida Keys, a 130-mile-long island chain connected by the Overseas Highway; swing by Jimmy Buffett's Margaritaville (www.margaritaville.com),

a truly American institution in Key West. Less than an hour west of Miami is the Everglades, a vast area of swamps; go on a private alligator safari by air boat, swamp buggy or helicopter, with Air Boat USA (305 219 1200).

Walks Stroll the two-mile length of SoBe's see-and-be-seen boardwalk along Collins Avenue from 21st to 46th streets.

Shopping Pedestrianised Lincoln Road in South Beach offers big brands as well as sparky boutiques: we love quirky-cool Base (www.baseworld.com) for music, clothes and accessories, and En Avance (305 534 0337) for its edgy pick of designers like Wyeth, Dsquared and Zooey. Collins Avenue offers upmarket merchandise (think Ralph Lauren, Urban Outfitters and Kenneth Cole), while Washington Avenue is grittier, with tattoo parlours and kitsch novelty shops. Vintage treasure trove C.Madeleine's (305 945 770) on Biscayne Boulevard in North Miami Beach is a must for any woman who knows her Halston from her Hermès. The Miracle Mile in Coral Gables (www.shopcoralgables.com) is great for boutique browsing.

Something for nothing On the last Friday night of every month, Viernes Culturales (www.viernesculturales.com) brings free music, dance and art to the streets of Little Havana. Take a yoga mat to Bayfront Park on a Monday, Wednesday or Saturday morning and get bendy with free lessons in the Tina Hills Pavilion (305 358 7550).

Don't go home without... dining at Miami institution Joe's Stone Crab (305 673 0365) at 11 Washington Avenue. Try (what else?) the stone crab claws; if they're not in season, there's plenty of other seafood succulence to savour.

MAGICALLY MIAMI

South Beach is famous for its art deco architecture; in the 1980s, the buildings along Ocean Drive were painted a kaleidoscope of bright colours, adding extra sparkle to Miami's main party district. Drop into the Art Deco Welcome Center (305 672 2014; www.mdlp.org) on Ocean Drive and pick up a guided architectural walking tour of this quintessential Miami district.

DIARY

January Art Miami (www.art-miami.com) brings modern art from around the world. **March** The Miami International Film Festival (www.miamifilmfestival.com). Carnaval Miami (www.carnaval miami.com) turns Little Havana's Calle Ocho into a maelstrom of music and moves. **April** Shiny steeds charge up and down the sand for the Miami Beach Polo World Cup (www.miamipolo.com). **June** Goombay Festival (www.goombayfestivalcoconutgrove.com), a barmy Bahamian blend of rhythm and junkanoos. **September–October** Crazy-cool-colourful Miami Carnival culminates in a massive street parade, but all the events are fun: try the International Caribbean Music Festival (www.crfest.com). **December** Make an exhibition of yourself during Art Basel Miami Beach, when pro partying is as important as spotting the new Picasso (www.artbaselmiamibeach.com).

The Setai

STYLE Deco chic goes East
SETTING Sexy South Beach
DESTINATION Miami

'We soon realise that all-night clubbing is not going to be on the agenda: that would mean spending less time in the understated and luxurious surroundings of the Setai'

On the outside, there is little to distinguish the Setai from the art deco architecture of the other hotels along South Beach. The Miami Design Preservation League heavily polices any work on their exteriors. Originally created as the Jack Dempsey Vanderbilt Hotel in the 1930s, the building has been meticulously brought back to life by architect Jean-Michel Gathy.

Inside is a different story altogether; the Setai's USP is that it brings the style of Asia's best resort hotels to the Florida coast. The Zen-like tranquillity of the interiors created by designer Jaya Ibrahim might be a cliché in Bali, but here in Miami, it offers a welcome contrast to the ubiquitous boutique designs of other hotels in the area.

And – as at the best hotels Asia has to offer – the welcome could not be warmer. Again, this elevates the Setai above the Miami norm; many of South Beach's more fashionable hotels are staffed by out-of-work models and actors with attitudes monstrously greater than their success. A barman at the Delano once grabbed my wrist as I tried to take my drink from the bar because I hadn't given him a big enough tip. That would never happen here.

After a soak in the black granite bath in our palatial bathroom, we hit the sack, although 'sack' seems a somewhat disrespectful term for our Dux bed, which has been specially designed by Swedish scientists to support the body in all the right places for a good night's sleep.

Next morning, rested and refreshed, we wake early and pull back the curtains to be met by the sight of a tropical sunrise over the ocean – a glorious way to start the day. As to how we spend the rest of it, there are options aplenty. But, again, for all the attractions Miami has to offer, we are loath to tear ourselves away from the serenity of the Setai just yet. At the back of the hotel, the landscaped grounds leading down to the beach offer candlelit pergolas, a courtyard and sunken seating areas around calming oases of water and tropical plants. The swimming pools are heated to different temperatures – take your pick from 70-, 80- or 90-degree warmth. As Mrs Smith shuffles off to the spa in her robe, I opt to relax by the pool with a book. My daybed becomes quite literally that: a bed on which I

Who better to greet us after a long-haul flight to Miami than a hotel driver from the Setai bearing a sign with our names on it? Better yet, one who is there to take our bags off the luggage carousel and carry them to the air-conditioned four-wheel-drive Mercedes waiting outside to transfer us to the hotel.

Our driver is full of useful tips on where to go and what to do in Miami, and good job, too: it turns out the clubs that were rocking on our last trip here (for the legendary industry shindig that is the Miami Winter Music Conference) have long since shut down or moved venue. Mansion, Club Deep and Opium Garden have apparently taken over as the top spots in town. In any case, when we reach our hotel, we soon realise that all-night clubbing is not going to be on the agenda this time around. For that would mean spending less time in the beautifully understated and luxurious surroundings of the Setai. And, more specifically, less time in our vast ocean-view suite.

could happily spend all day, working my way through the cocktail menu. But Mrs Smith eventually returns, reporting that the spa is equal to any she has visited in Southeast Asia, and we retire to our room to make plans for the evening.

Having spent all day lounging around, we decide that our original plan to dine at Bed – a hip Supperclub-style restaurant on Washington – will have us snoring into our starters. Our favourite local delicacy of stone crab claws is out of season,

'After a soak, we hit the sack, although "sack" seems a disrespectful term for our bed'

so the legendary Joe's is also off-limits. Instead we decide to go Cuban – after all, you can eat much better Cuban food here than you can in Cuba itself. Yuca (it stands for Young Urban Cuban Americans, which gives you a fair idea of the clientele) on Lincoln Avenue serves Nuevo Latino cuisine of the highest order. We eat rabo encendido, a traditional Cuban dish of oxtail stewed in Rioja and served with cassava mash, and 'South Beach' snapper – a filleted whole fish, stuffed with avocado and jalapeño-infused rice.

After another night of sound sleep, we have enough time before check-out to be shown round one of the apartments in the all-suite residential tower adjacent to the hotel. Inside, it's just as stunning as its neighbour, but with the added advantage of balconies enjoying panoramic views, across the ocean to one side and downtown Miami to the other. Lenny Kravitz has created a recording studio for the Penthouse. When I'm told the price tag, I have to bring Mrs Smith back down to earth. Living like rock stars full-time is well beyond our budget – more's the pity – but a stay at the Setai has certainly allowed us to enjoy the lifestyle for a couple of nights.

Reviewed by Matt Turner

NEED TO KNOW

Rooms 131, including 45 suites.
Rates $1,150–$30,000, excluding tax. Breakfast, from $45.
Check-out Noon, but a late check-out may be available for a charge. Check-in, 3pm.
Facilities Three swimming pools – each one a different temperature – set among tropical gardens leading down to a white-sand beach; spa; boutique. In rooms, plasma TV, DVD/CD system, espresso machine, Acqua di Parma toiletries, Dux beds and rainfall showers. In-room spa treatments are available.
Children Welcome; babysitters can be booked for a maximum of four hours, from $18 an hour.
Also The Oriental spa is outrageously decadent, and offers a full range of beauty and wellbeing treatments. Spa suites with steam showers are available for couples. The Setai is dog-friendly.

IN THE KNOW

Our favourite rooms Every Studio Suite in the Art Deco Building has a massive black granite bath, teak flooring and fine silk drapes – pick one with a courtyard view; the larger suites in the 40-storey residential tower are positively palatial, and have sweeping panoramic views from their private balconies.
Hotel bar The cocktail bar between the lobby and the courtyard seems unbeatable in terms of style and sophistication... until you see the 90-foot beach bar by the pool. The Chili Passion cocktail is pure perfection. The bar closes at 2am.
Hotel restaurant The kitchen produces excellent international cuisine with strong Thai, Chinese and Indian influences. The Restaurant is lined with wine cabinets and offers a wide selection of champagnes and caviar; it closes at 11pm on weekdays, midnight on Fridays and Saturdays. The Grill, serving T-bone steaks and fish, will open in November 2008.
Top table Overlooking the exhibition kitchen if you want to see the Restaurant's crew in action, or in one of the sunken pods around the tranquil swimming pool.
Room service A selection from the Restaurant is available 24 hours a day.
Dress code SoBe sophisticate: couture and shades.
Local knowledge The hotel can arrange private yachts, jets and deep-sea fishing but, if flexing plastic is more your style than flexing muscles, hit the shops. Bal Harbour Shops (www.balharbourshops.com) at the north end of Collins Avenue is an all-inclusive mall with a branch of Saks Fifth Avenue, as well as brands from Banana Republic to Bottega Veneta.

LOCAL EATING AND DRINKING

Nemo (305 532 4550) at 100 Collins Avenue is great for Sunday brunch or a relaxed lunch in the courtyard. **A la Folie** (305 538 4484) at 516 Española Way is a low-key French café and bistro with a fantastic menu and lots of character. **Nobu** (305 695 3100) at the Shore Club is just the other side of Collins Avenue and serves unparalleled Asian cuisine; the rock shrimp tempura is a signature dish. Also at the Shore Club, **Ago** (305 695 3226) is a well-regarded Italian restaurant owned by Robert De Niro; make sure you get a table outside. **Bond St** (305 398 1806) at the Townhouse hotel just across the road prepares excellent sushi and Bloody Marys carefully crafted with sake. **Casa Tua** (305 673 1010) on James Avenue is renowned for its fabulously fine Italian cuisine and is set in a romantic Mediterranean villa.

GET A ROOM!

To book this hotel, go to www.mrandmrssmith.com or ring our expert travel team on 1 800 464 2040. Activate your free membership online (see page 4) to qualify for the exclusive Smith card offer shown below when you book with us.

 SMITH CARD OFFER A complimentary bottle of champagne on arrival. Guests booking a larger suite will also receive lunch for two.

The Setai 2001 Collins Avenue, Miami Beach, Miami, FL 33139 (www.mrandmrssmith.com/the-setai)

NAPA VALLEY

COUNTRYSIDE Californian vineyards
COUNTRY LIFE Wine and dine

If you like driving through lush farmland along sun-dappled roads, eating delicious alfresco meals and nursing giant glasses of wine, then you'll love this neck of the American woods. The rolling hills of the Napa Valley and nearby Sonoma are a magnet for gourmands; the vineyards may not be as extensive and the wineries not as grand as their European counterparts, but what Napa lacks in old-world tradition it makes up for with warmth and informality. Forget about snooty sommeliers brandishing wine lists of terrifying scope: here, tasting is always a pleasure, the restaurants serve impeccable French-inspired cuisine, the climate is balmy and the scenery's beautiful. It's hardly surprising that San Franciscan couples flock here year-round for refined, romantic R&R: after all, there can't be many better ways to spend your sundown than snuggled up on a porch in a fug of cabernet-enhanced contentment...

GETTING THERE

Planes San Francisco International Airport (www.flysfo. com) is a little more than an hour's drive from the southern end of the valley; domestic flights to Oakland (www.flyoakland.com) are often cheaper. Bypass city traffic or fog delays by flying into smaller Sacramento airport (www.sacairports.org), an hour's drive from Napa. Trains Dine fine as you admire the splendid scenery aboard the (touristy but worthwhile) Napa Valley Wine Train (707 253 2111; www.winetrain.com), which runs the length of the valley between Napa and St Helena. Automobiles A fly-drive rental is the most practical option. Although the main roads crawl with traffic during the autumn harvest, this is still great driving country.

LOCAL KNOWLEDGE

Taxis Black Tie Taxi (707 259 1000) operates 24 hours a day and serves the entire Napa Valley area. Keep the number handy, in case you get too tipsy to drive home. Currency US dollar ($).
Dialling codes US: 1. Napa Valley: 707.
Tipping culture Between 15 and 20 per cent is usual for almost every conceivable service; if in doubt, tip.

Siesta and fiesta Weekends are busiest, and late lunchers jam roads out of the most popular towns in the afternoons. Go midweek and you'll have more room to relax.
Do go/don't go The autumn harvest is known as 'the Crush' – which could refer to the tourists it attracts. Summer and mustard season (February to March) are also busy. Go in November or January: the crowds are less madding.
Packing tips Headscarf or cap, unless you want to arrive in your convertible looking windswept and 'interesting'; sunglasses, to dim the dazzling light on those mornings after you've overindulged; corkscrew, for picnicking.
Recommended reads Napa Valley: The Ultimate Winery Guide by Antonia Allegra is exactly that; Robert Louis Stevenson recalls his Napa honeymoon in The Silverado Squatters; James Conaway's Napa: The Story of an American Eden gets under the skin of grape-land society.
Cuisine This is serious gastro territory, with some of the most sophisticated food in the States, much of it organic and locally sourced. There's a strong focus on French cuisine made with top-quality produce. As you'd expect, there's also a big emphasis on Californian wines, too. Learn how to match grape with grain on a wine-pairing

course at the American Center for Wine Food & the Arts, Copia (www.copia.org); or watch expert chefs prepare your meal at the Wine Spectator Greystone Restaurant at the Culinary Institute of America (www.ciachef.edu). The Oxbow Public Market on Napa's First Street is an outstanding under-one-roof foodie stop.

WORTH GETTING OUT OF BED FOR

Viewpoint Feast your eyes at Auberge du Soleil's restaurant (707 967 3111) in Rutherford: the interiors are a bit dated, but sit at a table outside and have lunch with far-yonder vistas. Or ride Sterling Vineyards' sky tram in Calistoga (www.sterlingvineyards.com) for bird's-eye vine views.

Arts and culture The only culture that matters in Wine Country is viniculture: there are almost 300 wineries to choose from, and reservations are often essential. Near Calistoga, Del Dotto (707 256 3332) offers friendly tastings in its 19th-century caves; at Pride Mountain (707 963 4949), the views are a bonus. In Carneros, Artesa (707 224 1668) has a modern aesthetic and a romantic patio; Domaine Carneros by Taittinger (707 257 0101) recalls a French château with a beautiful terrace. Connoisseurs head for Swanson (www.swansonvineyards.com) in the Oakville District; the Altamura winery (www.altamura.com) in Wooden Valley; or Kuleto Estate (www.kuletoestate.com) in St Helena. Antique Tours Limousine Service (707 226 9227) goes the extra mile with tours by knowledgeable guides in a 1940s Packard convertible. Thirsting for art? See a private collection of Northern Californian works in a unique setting at the 217-acre Di Rosa Preserve: Art & Nature (www.diroaspreserve.org) on the Carneros Highway.

Activities There's more to Napa Valley than wine tasting. Drift above the vineyards with Balloons Above the Valley (707 253 2222; www.balloonrides.com); rent a bike and cycle around the valleys, sampling the wines as you go with Getaway Adventures (707 568 3040; www.getaway adventures.com); or enjoy the scenery on horseback (www.triplecreekhorseoutfit.com). Buzz from vineyard to riverbank with Wine Country Helicopters (707 226 8470; www.winecountryhelicopters.com).

Perfect picnic We think you can manage to source some bottled beverages by yourself. But you'll be in need of a caffeine hit after your umpteenth weak filter coffee: stop at Oakville Grocery (707 944 8802) on St Helena Highway for espressos, delicious deli snacks and picnic fixings, then head to Bale Grist Mill or Bothe-Napa Valley State Park.

Daytripper Napa Valley is a day trip from San Francisco. If you fancy something a little more sedate than the bright lights of the Bay Area, head north to the Russian River Valley in Sonoma County. Paddle downstream in a Soar canoe past apple orchards and stands of giant redwoods, stopping for the occasional dip, with Healdsburg-based Russian River Adventures (707 433 5599; www.soar1.com).

Walks If you like hiking, the summit of Mount St Helena offers far-reaching views that stretch up to 200 miles on a good day. The five-mile trail is accessible near Calistoga from Robert Louis Stevenson State Park (www.parks. ca.gov); you'll need sturdy boots and plenty of stamina.

Shopping There are some excellent farmers' markets in Napa Valley during the summer months, selling organic local produce as well as wine. Check out Yountville's on Washington Street (Wednesday afternoons), St Helena's at Crane Park (Friday mornings) and Calistoga's on Lincoln Avenue (Saturday mornings). Lincoln Avenue has various arts and crafts shops, otherwise the downtown area of St Helena has more upscale boutiques.

Something for nothing Combine culture with quaffing at Clos Pegase (www.clospegase.com) in Calistoga, a postmodern temple to art and wine. Free tours of its grounds and winery are given daily at 11.30am and 2pm.

Don't go home without... noticing that not all natural wonders come in bunches: Napa boasts a forest of petrified redwoods (www.petrifiedforest.org); and Calistoga is home to one of only three 'old faithful' geysers in the world. Try a volcanic mud bath while you're in town (www.calistogaspas.com); it's more edifying.

NOTORIOUSLY NAPA VALLEY

Yountville is to Napa Valley what Paris is to France: bursting with culinary excellence. Thomas Keller's thrice-Michelin-starred restaurant the French Laundry (707 944 2380) has a mighty reputation and a waiting list to match. Skip the wait at Keller's informal Yountville bistro, Bouchon (707 944 8037); reserve an alfresco table and fill up on flawless French-flavoured fruits de mer. No room? Buy still-warm bread from Bouchon Bakery (707 944 1565) next-door. Other gastro must-gos include Bistro Jeanty (707 944 0103) for classic French fare from rillettes to cassoulet; and Redd (707 944 2222) for Richard Reddington's seasonal Californian cuisine.

DIARY

January–March Hot stuff is on the agenda at the Mustard Festival (www.mustard festival.org), a celebration of the valley's wine and food, as well as the wild mustard that carpets the vineyards. **July–August** Kino meets vino from the end of July, at the Wine Country Film Festival (www.winecountryfilmfest.com), with evening screenings among the vines. **August** Violins out for Music in the Vineyards (www.napavalleymusic.com) – a string of atmospheric chamber music concerts.

Calistoga Ranch

STYLE Ravishing ranch retreat
SETTING Rugged Californian canyon
DESTINATION Napa Valley

'The resort is understated Cal-luxe,
all low-rise buildings in cedar and
stone, punctuated with modern accents
such as giant cube lampshades'

How, goes the famous Napa Valley joke, do you make a small fortune in wine? Start with a large one. Winemaking is an expensive business, and you have to have serious financial clout if you want to start mucking about with the merlot. Still, if you can't afford your own vineyard, then at least you can experience the Napa Valley lifestyle by staying at Calistoga Ranch. From the moment we arrived, when the cheery valet took the keys of our car to park it on our behalf, to the morning we left, when gorgeous Gloria on reception handed us two bottles of water for our journey home, Mrs Smith and I were made to feel like the most important oenologists in town.

The ranch nestles in a secluded gorge at the north end of Napa Valley, near the spa town of Calistoga. The 157-acre, 46-room resort is understated Cal-luxe, all low-rise buildings in cedar and stone, punctuated with modern accents such as giant cube lampshades in all the public spaces. There's a luxurious spa, the Bathhouse, an outdoor yoga deck with soothing views over the valley's aged oaks, and a dramatic pool overlooked by both a bar and gym. There's also a cosy wine cave for tastings. So, whichever cornerstone of Californian culture you're after – wine or workout – Calistoga caters for you. And it feels more like a hamlet than a hotel. Perhaps because, in addition to the guests, it's occupied by plenty of fractional owners, who've purchased their own generous glug of this fine vintage. As a result, there's a very real sense of being welcomed into a community.

Mrs Smith and I are driven to our accommodation in a dinky electric golf buggy. We've been given a one-bedroom lodge by the creek, which comes with a separate lounge area and bedroom suite connected by a deck. The living room even has its own bar, with a complimentary bottle of the ranch's private-label merlot and a coffeemaker shaped like a rocket. While I'm admiring this, Mrs Smith is making cooing noises in front of the indoor-outdoor fireplace, which promises the enticing option of either snuggling up on a comfy sofa in the lounge or out on the patio next to our personal hot tub. It's a hard life, this wine-making lark.

Our bedroom has glass walls on two sides, allowing us to look at tall pines wafting their branches over the water from the comfort of our bed. But don't worry – there are blinds for those who want a little time to themselves and don't want to be watched, no matter how much fun they're having.

We poke around the bathroom, unwrapping the mudbath soap, and Calistoga Ranch's custom-made eucalyptus and bay laurel toiletries, then lathering them all over our hands. Interest piqued, we head into the discreetly fenced outdoor rainbath shower. Despite the slightly cool temperature of the December air, it's wonderful – like standing beneath a waterfall. What with warm water cascading over our heads, the birds of northern California tweeting away in our ears and the breeze deliciously tickling our wet skin, Mrs Smith and I feel quite the frontiersman and wo more Lewis and Clark than Ernst and Julio Gallo.

That evening, we eat at the Lakehouse restaurant. As its name suggests, it sits on the shores of Calistoga Ranch's private lake, offering the sort of romantic setting that the filmmakers downstate in Hollywood dream about for backdropping their denouements. We knew the restaurant was exclusive – it's only open to guests and those residents who've bought into this paradise – but it's only when we find ourselves seated next to cult singer-songwriter Tom Waits that we realise just how much so.

The food certainly lives up to its environment. Mrs Smith, who has been assured by our waiter that none of the dishes contain her culinary bête noire of cucumber, tucks into scallops with salsify purée and short ribs. My John Dory with leeks and salt cod brandade is exquisite. Every dish on the Modern American menu – zealously seasonal and constructed only from local ingredients – is chosen to complement Calistoga's reassuringly wonderful wine list, and our sommelier makes sure that each mouthful we eat is matched by either a 2003 Chalone Estate

Chardonnay or 2002 Provenance Merlot. We retire to our lodge feeling as fat and drunk as Friar Tuck.

The next morning, keen to experience the area's famed natural beauty (as well as burn off all those calories accrued the night before), we set out on a ramble. The ranch has plenty of its own hiking trails – this is California, after all – and Tiffany, our guide, leads us through woods to a watermill, where local villagers are hosting a 'Pioneer Christmas'. Dressed in historical costume – though, in quaint Calistoga, it's sometimes hard to tell the participants from the onlookers – they buzz about the food and craft stalls, indulging in all manner of 150-year-old activities. Mrs Smith is particularly amused when I am collared by a lace-making lady, and has to rescue me after several uncomfortable minutes of stitching and bobbin-shuffling. We head back to our room, dragging an impulsively bought two-pound bag of stone-ground polenta behind us.

In the afternoon, we do as any good Napa Valley visitors should, and go wine-tasting. Both Sterling and Clos Pegas

wineries are within walking distance of the ranch — well, a short drive, but don't tell anyone — and we spend a pleasant couple of hours running through their delicious range of chardonnays and cabernet sauvignons. That night, after dining at sleek local steak restaurant Press, we return to our lodge, where we sit out on the deck in front of a blazing fire, sipping merlot and gazing up at stars glowing in a grape-black sky. It's beautiful beyond words. Napa Valley is sometimes referred to as the American Eden, and I completely understand why. I'm certainly tempted to stay forever.

Reviewed by Jonathan Lukes

'We head into the discreet outdoor rainbath shower. It's wonderful — like standing beneath a waterfall'

NEED TO KNOW

Rooms 46 lodges.
Rates In low season, $575–$2,650; in high season, $720–$3,500. Breakfast costs about $45 for two.
Check-out Noon; later check-out can be arranged on request, subject to availability.
Facilities Heated outdoor pool, vineyard, gardens, spa, gym, shops, library, free WiFi. In rooms, LCD TV, DVD/CD player, iPod dock, indoor-outdoor fireplace, alfresco shower, free minibar.
Children There's a charge of $100 for each extra person under 18 in rooms; lodge living rooms have pull-out sofa beds.
Also Furry friends are welcome, for a one-off fee of $125, but they must remain on leads at all times. Calistoga Ranch can provide dog beds and food/water bowls. No smoking throughout.

IN THE KNOW

Our favourite rooms All the lodges are freestanding wooden bungalows with outdoor fireplaces. We love the one-bedroom lodges with outdoor Jacuzzis, where you can bubble away under the starlit oak canopy, sipping cocktails from your wet bar.
Hotel bar The cosy patio bar is a relaxed alfresco pleasure – the best place to enjoy a sunset with a glass of fine, fruity meritage. The sommelier corks his bottles at 10pm.
Hotel restaurant The bright, spacious, beamed Lakehouse restaurant creates fresh Californian cuisine, all locally sourced and painstakingly engineered to complement the voluminous wine list.
Top table If you're not lucky enough to wrangle a dinner in the heart-stoppingly romantic chandeliered wine cave, at least grab a table on the Lakehouse terrace so you can overlook the water.
Room service 24 hours. After the Lakehouse kitchens close at 10pm, cold dishes are available through the night.
Dress code Laid-back country chic – open-necked shirts for him, silk scarves for her.
Local knowledge Bring a taste for tannins and a nose for a bouquet – Calistoga Ranch not only has its own vineyard and label, but also has regular visits from vinters to give tastings. Guests who want to get their hands juicy can join in harvesting, pruning and crushing. Calistoga is a natural mineral spring, so its Bathhouse spa on the banks of Lake Lommel offers private therapeutic water treatments, including (appropriately enough), a skin-shimmering Cabernet Wine Bath.

LOCAL EATING AND DRINKING

The Model Bakery (707 963 8192) at 1357 Main Street in St Helena has delicious sandwiches made to order, pizza, salads and soups. At 1347 Main Street, **Market** (707 963 3799) uses seasonal produce to create the dishes on its classic American menu; it's a nice spot for a casual lunch of delicious oysters; the bar here is good, too. Or go Italian at low-key local favourite, **Cook** (707 963 7088), a few doors down on Main Street. At 7399 St Helena Highway, on the way to Calistoga, **Mustards Grill** (707 944 2424) is a Napa Valley institution, with a bustling atmosphere and a French/American bistro menu of tasty burgers, fresh fish and tea-smoked duck. Chef Cindy Pawlcyn's other eaterie, **Cindy's Backstreet Kitchen** (707 963 1200), at 1327 Railroad Avenue, fuses supper-club atmosphere with refined country restaurant (and takeaway). For something entirely grown-up, with Eurasian twists, try **Terra** (707 963 8931) at 1345 Railroad Avenue.

GET A ROOM!

To book this hotel, go to www.mrandmrssmith.com or ring our expert travel team on 1 800 464 2040. Activate your free membership online (see page 4) to qualify for the exclusive Smith card offer shown below when you book with us.

 SMITH CARD OFFER A bottle of Calistoga-label custom-blended wine on arrival, plus either a box of handmade Woodhouse chocolates or a set of locally produced oil and vinegar.

Calistoga Ranch 580 Lommel Road, Calistoga, CA 94515 (www.mrandmrssmith.com/calistoga-ranch)

NEW YORK

CITYSCAPE Bright lights, hip city
CITY LIFE Be a part of it

In this magnificent archipelago city – a frothy blend of caffeine and convenience, with a double shot of culture and commerce – every neighbourhood has its own be-a-part-of-it personality. And NYC is as impatient to surprise you with cutting-edge thrills as it is to provide clichéd big-screen vignettes. Whether you don couture for uptown haute cuisine, or kick back in a downtown diner booth, you'll feel as free to follow the tourist trail as make like the natives. Admire museum masterpieces on the Upper East Side or stumble across street art in the Village; treat yourself to classic tailoring on Fifth Avenue, then forage for quirky one-offs in NoLiTa or SoHo; choose between a Broadway show and an indie flick in TriBeca... or stray from Manhattan altogether for an alternative New York adventure. All this – and more – you can do before dinner. Truly, this city never sleeps; and nor should you.

GETTING THERE

Planes There are three major airports: LaGuardia, Newark in New Jersey and JFK, which is actually the farthest from the city centre. Buses run between Manhattan and JFK and LaGuardia; see www.nyairportservice.com. A cab from JFK will charge a flat rate of $45 plus tolls.
Trains Amtrak (www.amtrak.com) provides long-distance services from Penn Station, which is also the hub for the LIRR (Long Island Rail Road) and NJ Transit.
Automobiles This is definitely not the place to be renting a car: parking is a headache, while the subway and cabs are cheap and easy. If you insist on having wheels, pick a tiny, easy-to-park vehicle and get an E-Z Pass for the tolls.
Boats You can get water taxis (www.nywatertaxi.com), cruise liners and ferries from the west and southern points of Manhattan to New Jersey, Brooklyn and beyond.

LOCAL KNOWLEDGE

Taxis Yellow cabs are abundant (except during rush hour and rain showers), but be warned: drivers aren't always as geographically knowledgeable as you might hope.
Currency US dollar ($).
Dialling codes US: 1. New York City: 212.
Tipping culture New Yorkers pay up to 20 per cent for good service; in Manhattan, double the tax on your bill.
Siesta and fiesta This is the city that never sleeps, and there's always a bar calling out for you to prop it up, so you're more likely to party 24/7 than grab forty winks.

Do go/don't go Winter can be bitter; while Christmas is all jingle bells and fairy lights, you may want to skip the snow in January and February. August is hot, hot, hot, which is why New Yorkers often flee to the Hamptons at weekends.
Packing tips A digicam is a must, and sneakers, too. There ain't much you need that you can't get here at a great price, so bring an empty bag to put your haul in.
Recommended reads Toby Young exposes Manhattanite media-luvvie machinations in *How to Lose Friends and Alienate People*; *The Emperor's Children* by Claire Messud is a more poignant portrayal of NY's social climbers.
Cuisine Every flavour from around the globe is represented

in this cosmopolitan city, but when it comes to homegrown dishes, on-the-hoof is New York's specialty; grab a classic pastrami on rye from Katz's (212 254 2246) or blinis loaded with caviar from Russ & Daughters (212 475 4880), both on East Houston Street. Or sit in and share a pepperoni pie at John's Pizzeria (212 243 1680) on Bleecker Street. And… Embrace your metrosexuality and get a grand grooming. For a shoe-shine, go to Dino's (212 397 4066) at 1806 Broadway; for an old-school wet shave, try Freemans Sporting Club (212 673 3209) on Rivington.

WORTH GETTING OUT OF BED FOR

Viewpoint It's not just the art exhibitions at the Met (www.metmuseum.org) that are worth a look; the views from its roof terrace are also awesome. Head to York Street subway and find the Empire-Fulton Ferry State Park (718 858 4708) on the waterfront, where the Brooklyn and Manhattan bridges merge. The Empire State Building is a bit of a tourist trap, but worth the effort if you time it right: splash out on a queue-jumping ESB Express Pass Ticket and synchronise watches for sunset-kissed city views. Arts and culture MOMA – the Museum of Modern Art (www.moma.org) – occupies a breathtaking six-storey building. For your $20 you'll see pieces by every acclaimed artist, often with more in one room than you'd see at a whole exhibition elsewhere. See what's on at the Guggenheim (www.guggenheim.org), or just enjoy Frank Lloyd Wright's swirling architecture. The Frick Collection (www.frick.org) is worth seeking out for its heritage as much as its contents. Activities Hire a bike in Central Park from the Loeb Boathouse (around 72nd) for $9 an hour. Go ice-skating until March in Central Park, or at the Rockefeller Center (212 332 7654) from October to January. Jump aboard a helicopter at the Downtown Heliport or at West 30th Street at weekends for a 15-minute bird's-eye view of the city; book your ticket for about $130 (www.heliny.com). Perfect picnic Once you have in your mitts a super sub (holding this, with a side of that), you can't beat sitting by the Bethesda Fountain in Central Park. Feeling more intrepid? Catch a ferry from Battery Park to Governors Island – the waterfront stretch treats you to that dramatic Oz-like New York skyline, as well as the Statue of Liberty and Ellis Island. Or venture to Queens and seek out more Manhattan-vista gold care of Socrates Sculpture Park. Daytripper Hot dogs, a boardwalk, fairground rides *and* minor-league baseball: oh yes – catch the Brooklyn Cyclones in action at KeySpan Park on Coney Island

(www.coneyisland.com). Or visit City Island in the Bronx – it's like a little coastal New England town; French-run Le Refuge Inn (718 885 2478) is a darling option for supper. Walks The easy-to-navigate grid of Manhattan is as pedestrian-friendly as city streets get. For a taste of NY life in a leafier frame, the 28-acre Riverside Park on the Hudson is a great alternative to Central Park. Like CP, it has a rink for rollerblade fun or ice-skating, depending on the season. To get you thinking on your feet, Big Onion (www.bigonion.com) organises themed walking tours of historic New York. Shopping Barneys (212 826 8900) on Madison Avenue at 61st is a one-stop fashion shop; the jeans bar at its Co-op section is a must-visit. The glossiest department stores are on Fifth Avenue: Saks, Bergdorf Goodman and Lord & Taylor. If big-scale consumerism brings your inner Naomi Klein out in hives, the Brooklyn Flea in Fort Greene is a retro-retail paradise; or trade in your vintage threads at Williamsburg 'frock exchange' Beacon's Closet (718 486 0816). Snap up limited-editon Nikes at Dave's Quality Meat (212 505 7551) on the Lower East Side; Mr Smiths will also love Odin (212 475 0666) on East 11th Street. Something for nothing Cross Williamsburg Bridge by foot and explore Brooklyn; walk back over the glorious Brooklyn Bridge. Or hop on the free ferry from Battery Park to Staten Island; you'll spy Miss Liberty and it won't cost a cent. Don't go home without… design-savvy gifts from MOMA's shop (www.momastore.org): they give souvenirs a good name. Mugs modelled on the blue-and-white patterned coffee-to-go paper cups are an update on 'I ❤ NY'.

NICELY NEW YORK

Even if you don't have a train to catch, head towards the iconic clock tower of Grand Central Station at 42nd and Park. After a visual taster of the hustle and bustle of a New York minute on the concourse, have an ogle of that ornate ceiling, then head down to the arched cellars of the NY Oyster Bar (212 490 6650; www.oysterbarny.com) for an indulgent crustacean snack.

DIARY

New York just loves a parade. **March** The St Patrick's Day Parade, when thousands flock to Fifth Avenue for the Irish clan march, is held on the 17th. **March/April** If you're bonkers for OTT bonnets and dogs wearing dresses, get involved in the Easter Parade on Easter Sunday. **April–May** The Tribeca Film Festival (www.tribecafilmfestival.org) in Lower Manhattan. **June–August** Free alfresco screenings at the HBO Bryant Park Summer Film Festival (www.bryantpark.org); grab a spot, order sarnies from 'Wichcraft, and guzzle while you gaze. **October** Parade time again! Costumes and music bring the streets alive for the Columbus Day Parade. **November** The Thanksgiving Day Parade takes place on the fourth Thursday of the month. The Rockefeller Center Christmas tree-lighting ceremony is held on the 30th.

The Bowery Hotel

STYLE Retro glamour
SETTING Post-punk East Village
DESTINATION New York

'Opulent Edwardian and art deco
antiques in varying states of tasteful
decay are arranged throughout, atop
fabulously tatty oriental carpets'

trees, is lined with dark, carved wood panels of the type you'd find in an elegantly decrepit English country pile. Opulent Edwardian and art deco antiques in varying states of tasteful decay are arranged throughout atop fabulously tatty oriental carpets. Spanish-style iron lamps that could have doubled as mediaeval torture devices keep the room just shy of total darkness. A massive, hand-painted mural of the Bowery circa 1860 provides additional period cues.

In reality, it was built from scratch – the palm trees are silk, and the panelling was salvaged from old buildings in Philadelphia. But you only know that because I told you.

We find our room as tastefully appointed as the lobby promises. The furnishings are new, but in keeping with the theme; antique-looking Persian carpets, deep green velvet chairs, a white-marble-topped table. The room, a corner King, isn't particularly large, maybe 300 sq ft, but it's Manhattan after all. Like every other space in the hotel, the proportions are what an architect might call 'human'.

The most pleasant surprise is the windows, which are floor-to-ceiling on two sides of the bedroom, and have a direct view of the Empire State Building uptown. For now, at least, the hotel is the highest building in the neighbourhood, affording unfettered views of the action down below. After a night spent in various states of undress, it only occurs to Mrs Smith and I after check-out that the view from the street is equally superb.

Even better than the view is the bathroom. The tub, in particular. With patinated bronze Waterworks fixtures, it is more like a small pool. The woman at the front desk tells us we are among the lucky few to have one, and to make sure we take full advantage...

The hotel's owners, Sean MacPherson and Eric Goode, are celebrated New York nightlife vets responsible for a string of phenomenally successful restaurants and bars throughout the city. Like all world-class hoteliers, they have a unifying aesthetic vision for each of their properties (the Bowery is their second hotel, after the nautical-themed Maritime in Chelsea) and carry it out to the fullest extent possible.

I've lived in New York long enough not to be surprised by the clip at which its neighbourhoods are reinvented. But the transformation of the Bowery – named for the eponymous Manhattan artery stretching from the southern edge of Chinatown up to the East Village – is nothing short of shocking. America's original skid row, for more than two centuries it was a slum of last resort for no-hopers of all stripes; a fetid collection of flophouses for the chronically unlucky and inebriated. Even as neighboring NoLita and the East Village sprouted blocks of fashion boutiques and trendy bars, the Bowery remained a degenerate no man's land, seemingly immune to gentrification. And then the Bowery Hotel opened.

Anyone unfamiliar with its brief history might readily assume it had been here forever – a handsome relic from an age when buildings were made of brick and marble, instead of steel and particleboard. The lobby, sectioned off with vintage leather screens and oversized exotic palm

Although a table at the Waverly Inn, MacPherson and Goode's celeb-packed playpen du jour in the West Village, might be out of the question unless you 'know someone', there's Gemma downstairs if you're in the mood for a casual Hollywood star sighting (one was in the banquette next to ours). The food is classic Northern Italian with little fuss or fanfare, served in a beautiful room designed by Taavo Somer, the brains behind acclaimed taxidermy-and-comfort-food hotspot Freeman's, which is just down the block.

'With its patinated bronze Waterworks features, the bath tub is more like a small pool'

The bar inside the lobby is the most 'done' of all the hotel's public spaces, and is reserved solely for guests. With its zinc bar and high-end boho, *World of Interiors*-ready decor – roe deer heads on carved wooden plaques, high-backed club chairs, a stuffed pit bull – it's the kind of room you'll want to linger in for several rounds. We, however, are in the mood for a movie, and open the guestbook to peruse the DVD directory. We're impressed to find the selection as tightly curated as we suspected it might be. We choose *Sid and Nancy* – listed under 'New York' – and ring the front desk. It's in our hands in four minutes flat. (I timed it.)

In a city as hectic as New York, the need to escape the madding crowd after a long day of pavement pounding is a vital factor in any getaway plan. As it settles into its indisputably chic self, I can only imagine the homey Bowery Hotel is destined for jet-set immortality.

Reviewed by Christopher Tennant

NEED TO KNOW
Rooms 135, including 25 suites.
Rates $525–$1,200; excludes 13.375 per cent tax. Breakfast is chosen from an à la carte menu.
Check-out Noon; later check-out is subject to availability. Check-in, 3pm.
Facilities Gym, DVD library, valet parking, laundry, free WiFi. In rooms, HD plasma TV, DVD/CD player, iPod dock and stereo system, CO Bigelow toiletries.
Children Welcome: high chairs and baby cots are available, and extra beds can be added to larger rooms for $40 a night. The Bowery Hotel works with a nanny service to provide babysitting, from $25 an hour.
Also No smoking (apart from on the fifth floor). Your shoes can be shined and your back can be rubbed – just ask. As a concession to the chihuahua-toting crowd, lightweight pets (weighing 30 pounds or less) are warmly welcomed.

IN THE KNOW
Our favourite rooms The north-facing rooms offer glimpses of the Empire State Building from the comfort of your bed. Number 705, a One-Bedroom Terrace Suite, has a marble-tubbed bathroom that opens directly onto a spacious terrace.
Hotel bar Since its opening, the Lobby Bar has shot to the top of the New York hot list, becoming a favourite destination for A-listers in search of a glam-drenched venue. Antique furniture, art deco wood panelling and a rarefied menu of malts help maintain the sense of old-world cool. Guests can reserve a coveted space.
Hotel restaurant With thatch-covered wine bottles swinging from beamed ceiling, distressed wood tables and a copper-topped bar, Gemma is a picture of Tuscan rusticity. The food, however, is more polished than peasanty, and the Nutella calzone is a particular treat. Breakfast is chosen from an à la carte menu.
Top table Gemma only takes reservations for hotel guests, so sweet-talk your way to a window table for people-watching, or to one of the leather-banquette booths – it's possible to lose hours in them.
Room service A full menu based on Gemma's à la carte offerings is available 24 hours a day.
Dress code Edwardian dandy, backstage with the Ramones.
Local knowledge The Bowery is well placed for culture: the nearby Nuyorican Poets Cafe (212 505 8183) is a great place to catch energetic slam poetry, theatre and alternative film nights, and the architecturally striking contemporary-art hub the New Museum (212 219 1222) has also just opened down the road.

LOCAL EATING AND DRINKING
There's plenty of on-your-doorstep eat treats: make brunch reservations at **Public** (212 343 7011), a huge, loft-like space on Elizabeth Street with a cosmopolitan marvel of a menu. Next-door wine bar **The Monday Room** (212 343 7011) lets you sample a vast variety of vintages with the benefit of a personal wine steward. **Azul** (646 602 2004), an Argentinian bistro at 152 Stanton Street, will sate your appetite for gaucho grills; 17 Prince Street's cosy **Café Habana** (212 625 2001) in NoLita does the same for Cuban cravings – try the divine grilled corn, and wash down with plenty of mojitos. **Freeman's** (212 420 0012) on Chrystie and **Stanton Social** (212 995 0099) on Stanton both offer great menus and people-watching. For dessert, hit **Doughnut Plant** (212 505 3700) on Grand Street and order a 'Tres Leches' – life will never be the same.

GET A ROOM!
To book this hotel, go to www.mrandmrssmith.com or ring our expert travel team on 1 800 464 2040. Activate your free membership online (see page 4) to qualify for the exclusive Smith card offer shown below when you book with us.

 SMITH CARD OFFER A bottle of wine.

The Bowery Hotel 335 The Bowery, New York, NY 10003 (www.mrandmrssmith.com/the-bowery-hotel)

(offers you can't refuse)

 Look out for this Smith card icon at the end of each hotel review

As a BlackSmith member, you're automatically entitled to exclusive added extras: it's our way of saying thank you, and ensuring your stylish stay is as enjoyable as possible. Activate your free membership now (see pages 4–5) to take advantage of the Smith card offers listed below when you book one of these hotels with us. For more information, or to make a reservation, visit www.mrandmrssmith.com or talk to our expert travel team on 1 800 464 2040.

A'jia Hotel Turkey
Two tickets to the Sakip Sabanci Museum, with boat transfers from the hotel. VIP entrance to A'jia's favourite nightclubs. Two free apple margaritas when you dine at the hotel.

Aleenta Phuket-Phang Nga Thailand
A 10 per cent reduction on room rates and a 30-minute massage each if staying three nights or more; members staying seven nights or more will also be given a candlelit dinner for two.

Alta Bay South Africa
A complimentary bottle of South African red or white wine.

Baglioni Hotel United Kingdom
A bottle of red or white wine, and 10 per cent off a treatment each in the Rejuvenation Spa.

Barnsley House United Kingdom
A Barnsley House champagne cocktail each – or a glass of champagne in the Village Pub across the road – on each night of your stay.

Bellinter House Ireland
A Voya seaweed bath for two in the Bathhouse spa; there are two baths, so couples or friends can bathe side by side.

Blancaneaux Lodge Belize
A 30-minute Thai-style massage each.

The Bowery Hotel United States
A bottle of wine.

Ca Maria Adele Italy
A bottle of Valpolicella.

Calistoga Ranch United States
A bottle of Calistoga-label custom-blended wine on arrival, plus either a box of handmade Woodhouse chocolates or a set of locally produced oil and vinegar.

Castello di Vicarello Italy
A personalised ceramic gift designed by Aurora, the owner, and one free session at Castello di Vicarello's thermal spa.

Château de Bagnols France
Wine-tasting at a local vineyard; during the harvest, a bottle of Brouilly – a Beaujolais grand cru – will be offered instead. Those staying two nights or more in a Suite or Apartment receive a free three-course lunch (excluding drinks).

Château les Merles France
A glass of champagne each, a selection of regional amuses-bouches and a bottle of wine from the vineyards of Château les Merles.

Condesa DF Mexico
A cocktail each on arrival, and a bottle of wine.

Esencia Mexico
A complimentary cocktail each, as well as a free snorkelling trip for two.

Gallery Hotel Art Italy
A gift from the luxurious Lungarno Details bath and beauty range, and a bottle of wine.

Hacienda de San Rafael Spain
A free picnic, a private bodega visit, half a bottle of manzanilla when staying in a deluxe room and a bottle of house champagne when staying in a casita.

Hotel Daniel France
Mariage Frères tea served with Ladurée's famous macaroons (when available) or other sweet treats.

Hotel Omm Spain
A complimentary glass of Catalan cava each on arrival, plus a chocolate selection created especially for the hotel by world-renowned confectioner Oriol Balaguer.

Laluna Grenada
A 30-minute massage each and a complimentary bottle of prosecco.

Lux 11 Germany
A bottle of wine from a renowned vineyard. Up to two discounted beauty treatments or massages. VIP entrance to the hotel's favourite nightclubs and lounges on selected days.

Masseria Torre Coccaro Italy
A one-hour massage each in the spa.

La Minervetta Italy
A bottle of prosecco.

Oustau de Baumanière France
A recipe book by Jean-André Charial, Oustau de Baumanière's Michelin-starred chef-patron.

Portrait Suites Italy
A gift from the luxurious Lungarno Details bath and beauty range, and a bottle of wine.

La Purificadora Mexico
A bottle of wine. Mr & Mrs Smith members staying four nights will get 50 per cent off their last night's accommodation (unless it falls on a Friday or Saturday).

The Setai United States
A complimentary bottle of champagne on arrival. Guests booking a larger suite will also receive lunch for two.

La Suite Brazil
A bottle of champagne on arrival.

Tigerlily United Kingdom
Drinks vouchers for two special 'Smith' signature cocktails, devised by Tigerlily's mixologist, to use on each night of your stay.

Viceroy Santa Monica United States
Welcome drinks for two at the Cameo Bar, and a 15 per cent discount on breakfast on each morning of your stay.

(useful numbers)

AIRLINES

Domestic and international carriers:

Air France (1 800 237 2747; www.airfrance.com)
AirTran (1 800 247 8726; www.airtran.com)
Alitalia (1 800 223 5730; www.alitalia.com)
American Airlines (1 800 433 7300; www.aa.com).
British Airways (1 800 247 9297; www.ba.com)
Cathay Pacific (1 800 233 2742; www.cathaypacific.com)
Continental Airlines (1 800 231 0856; www.continental.com)
Copa Airlines (1 800 359 2672; www.copaair.com)
Delta Air Lines (1 800 241 4141; www.delta.com)
Etihad (1 888 838 4423; www.etihadairways.com)
Iberia (1 800 772 4642; www.iberia.com)
JetBlue Airways (1 800 538 2583; www.jetblue.com)
Lufthansa (1 800 399 5838; www.lufthansa.com)
Mexicana (1 800 531 7921; www.mexicana.com)
NWA/KLM (1 800 225 2525; www.nwa.com)
South African Airlines (1 800 722 9675; www.flysaa.com)
Southwest Airlines (1 800 435 9792; www.southwest.com)
Spirit (1 800 772 7117; www.spiritair.com)
Taca (1 800 400 8222; www.taca.com)
United Airlines (1 800 538 2929; www.united.com)
US Airways (1 800 428 4322; www.usairways.com)
Virgin Atlantic (1 800 821 5438; www.virgin-atlantic.com)

European low-cost carriers:

Aer Lingus (1 800 474 7424; www.aerlingus.com)
Air Berlin (1 866 266 5588; www.airberlin.com)
BMI Baby (44 (0)870 126 6726; www.bmibaby.com)
easyJet (44 (0)870 600 0000; www.easyjet.com)
Flybe (44 (0)1392 268500; www.flybe.com)
Meridiana/Eurofly (39 0789 52650; www.meridiana.it)
Ryanair (353 1 249 7791; www.ryanair.com)

iFly.com provides a searchable online guide to airports worldwide.
Kayak (www.kayak.com) helps you track down the best flight deals by comparing air fares.

TRAINS

Amtrak (1 800 872 7245; www.amtrak.com) lists schedules and fares on national US routes.
Eurostar (44 (0)1233 617575; www.eurostar.com). Book tickets from London to Paris and beyond.
Rail Europe (1 888 382 7245; www.raileurope.com). A one-stop shop for European rail travel. View timetables and buy tickets for high-speed TGV and local SNCF trains in France, plus find details about rail links into and around Germany, Italy and Spain.

TAXIS AND TRANSFERS

Dav El (1 800 922 0343; www.davel.com). Arrive at your hotel in style, with pre-booked chauffeured limousine transfers in cities across the globe.
Supershuttle (1 800 258 3826; www.supershuttle.com). Shared taxis from airports and harbours to your door – economical, efficient and eco-friendly. Supershuttle operates from LA, New York, Miami, Palm Beach and San Francisco, among other bases.
Traintaxi (www.traintaxi.co.uk) lets you check details of cab firms at railway stations across Britain, or call 0871 750 0303 from anywhere in the UK to be connected straight to a local taxi service.

ECO-TRAVEL AND HELPFUL WEBSITES

Check Me In (www.checkmein.eu) allows you to check-in online as soon as you have tickets, so you don't have to get up at dawn to reserve the best seats.
Climate Care (44 (0)1865 207000; www.climatecare.org) offers advice on reducing your carbon footprint, and can help you offset CO_2 emissions from your flights or car journeys with its carbon calculator.
Greenspotter (www.greenspotter.org) locates ethical businesses near you; find eco-chic beachwear, green gifts and travel gadgets using its online search.
JiWire (www.jiwire.com). Can't live without your laptop? Find WiFi hotspots around the world; this database pinpoints more than 200,000 access points.
SeatGuru (www.seatguru.com) has handy plans of the best seats to book on planes in most airline fleets.
Timeanddate.com gives you international dialling codes and time zones, so you can plan the perfect time to make your call, and punch all the right digits.

TOURIST BOARDS AND ORGANISATIONS

Belize Tourist Board (www.travelbelize.org)
Brazil Tourism Office (www.braziltourism.org)
British Tourist Authority (www.visitbritain.co.uk)
Caribbean Tourism Organisation
(www.caribbeantravel.com)
English Heritage (www.english-heritage.co.uk)
French Tourist Office (www.franceguide.com)
German National Tourist Board
(www.cometogermany.com)
Irish Tourist Board (www.discoverireland.ie)
Italian Government Tourist Board
(www.italiantourism.com)
Mexico Tourism Board (www.visitmexico.com)
The National Trust, UK (www.nationaltrust.org.uk)
South African Tourism (www.southafrica.net)
Spanish Tourism Institute (www.spain.info)
Tourism Authority of Thailand
(www.tourismthailand.org)
Turkish Culture & Tourism Office
(www.gototurkey.com)
Unesco World Heritage Sites (whc.unesco.org)
United States Tourist Offices
(www.usatourist.com)

UP, UP AND AWAY

Smith **Big Air** (44 (0)845 838 0250; www.flybig.eu).
Private planes, helicopters, yachts and charter
services in worldwide locations.
Lothian Helicopters (44 (0)1875 320032;
www.lothianhelicopters.co.uk). Pleasure flights and
helicopter tours in Scotland and the UK.
Napa Valley Biplane Company (1 707 647 3758;
http://napabiplane.com). Chocks away for a vineyard
tour in a restored vintage aircraft – leather flying
helmets and goggles provided.
Smith **US Helicopters** (www.flyush.com) operates
speedy scheduled helicopter transfers from
Manhattan to JFK and Newark airports, as well
as chopper charters to Northeastern locations,
including the Hamptons and Martha's Vineyard.
Vastano Mongolfiere (39 0574 720752;
www.vastanomongolfiere.com). Float above Florence
and other Tuscan cities in a Vastano hot-air balloon.
Virgin Balloon Flights (44 (0)870 420 7300;
www.virginballoonflights.co.uk) operates from more
than 100 sites across the UK.

MAPS, MOTORING AND MORE

Smith **Classic Car Club** (www.classiccarclub.com)
hands its members the keys to a fleet of classic and
sports cars, whether you want a Maserati in Manhattan,
a Cobra in Copenhagen or an E-Type in Edinburgh.
Smith **Hertz** (1 800 654 3001; www.hertz.com) offers a
widespread car-rental network in the US and Europe.
Smith **Airport Parking Reservations** (1 800 727 5464;
www.airportparkingreservations.com). Compare
prices and book low-cost airport parking online.
ViaMichelin (www.viamichelin). Excellent maps,
online route-planning for American, European and
international destinations, plus GPS navigation
software and devices.
Weather.com provides breaking weather news,
driving tips and vacation planning, including packing
lists based on predicted weather at your destination.

BAGS, BIKINIS AND BEDROOM ESSENTIALS

Smith **First Luggage** (1 800 224 5741; www.first
luggage.com). Skip check-in queues and enjoy
hassle-free journeys: get all your baggage handled
by this door-to-door collection and delivery service.
Smith **Flight 001** (1 877 354 4481; www.flight001.com).
To-die-for travel accessories and luggage, plus retro
aviation-inspired homewares.
Smith **Heidi Klein** (1 877 694 3434; www.heidiklein.
com). Sleek designer swimwear and summertime
essentials for Mr, Mrs and mini Smiths.
Smith **Myla** (1 212 327 2676; www.myla.com) has a
seductive collection of slinky lingerie, bedtime
playthings and discreet designer toys.

BOUTIQUE HOTELS AND LUXURY TRAVEL

Mr & Mrs Smith (1 800 464 2040; www.mrandmrs
smith.com). Book hand-picked hotels around the world
– no booking fees, and best room rates guaranteed.
Smith & Friends (www.smithandfriends.com) lists
holiday rentals, private villas and country cottages.
Smith Ski (www.mrandmrssmith.com/ski) lets you
find and book super-stylish ski chalets in Europe.

Smith Mr & Mrs Smith members have access to fantastic
offers and discounts from a huge range of companies
and services, including those indicated above by the Smith icon.
Activate your free membership now (see page 4) and check out
the full range of benefits available at www.mrandmrssmith.com.

(who are Mr & Mrs Smith?)

Our reviewers are a panel of people we admire and respect, all of whom have impeccable taste, of course, and can be trusted to report back to us on Mr & Mrs Smith hotels with total honesty. The only thing we ask of them is that they visit each hotel anonymously with a partner and, on their return, give us the kind of insider lowdown you'd expect from a close friend.

REVIEWERS WHO'S WHO

Nellie Blundell JOURNALIST AND COPYWRITER
Dividing her time between London and Sydney, with many a stopover in between, Nellie has become a connoisseur of hotel beds. The memorable ones get a mention in her stories for Aussie broadsheet *The Australian*. In London, she writes a regular column for *Time Out*'s food pages and moonlights as a copywriter with branding and design agencies across the city.

Susie Boyt NOVELIST
Susie is the author of four critically acclaimed novels, including *Only Human*, which *The Guardian* called 'a spontaneous act of humane understanding'. Her latest book, *My Judy Garland Life, is* a collision of show tunes, hero-worship, biography and self-help. She also writes a weekly fashion and shopping column for the *Financial Times Weekend*. Susie lives in London with her family, and has never visited anywhere she likes half as much.

Ilse Crawford INTERIOR DESIGNER
As creative director of Studioilse, interior designer Ilse has created Soho House New York, the Electric Cinema and the influential Babington House. Other notches in her belt include the launch of *Elle Decoration* in 1989, and a vice-presidency with Donna Karan Home (where she helped launch homewares lines for the famous fashion brand and its diffusion line DKNY). Ilse is also head of department at the renowned Design Academy Eindhoven. Her latest book, *Home is Where the Heart Is*, explores ways in which design can help meet our basic, emotional needs.

Tiffanie Darke MAGAZINE EDITOR
Editing the *Sunday Times Style* magazine means Tiffanie is at the coalface of luxury stylish living five days a week, 52 weeks a year. Fortunately, at weekends, she is brought down to earth by the less charming domestic details of family living. Unless, of course, she can escape for a dirty weekend – a luxury she appreciates now more than ever. Tiffanie is well qualified to recognise the potential of a hotel room: she has written extensively about matters of the bedroom, both for national newspapers and in two published novels, including the very entertaining *Marrow*, a tale of food and sex in the kitchens of London's celebrity restaurants.

Dominic Holland COMEDIAN
An award-winning stand-up comedian, Dominic writes a regular column in *The Guardian* and has published two novels, *Only in America* and *The Ripple Effect*. His acclaimed BBC Radio 4 series *The Small World of Dominic Holland* is being developed into a television series that Dominic hopes will hit our screens sometime during his lifetime. He is married with four children.

Mark Joy MARKETING MD
Having spent the past 25 years working upwards of 50 hours a week in marketing, Mark and his wife like to use their vacations to unashamedly kick back and relax. Caribbean-holiday junkies, they have spent more than 15 years searching for the perfect small hotel in the region – somewhere that combines a great location with wonderful food and super-comfy beds.

Anne Kornblut POLITICAL REPORTER
A jaded traveller in her day job as a political reporter for *The Washington Post* (and previously, *The New York Times*), Anne can usually be found in less-than-cutting-edge hotels in places such as Iowa and New Hampshire when she is not at home in Washington, DC. A graduate of Columbia University in New York, she covered the early years of the George W Bush administration, and in so doing had the dubious pleasure of travelling to four of the six continents with the president (not exactly her ideal Mr Smith).

Amanda Lamb TV PRESENTER
At the age of 20, Amanda was discovered by Storm model agency and has advertised everything from knickers to pension schemes. After giving up modelling, but not the travel bug, she became the UK's presenter of Channel 4 property programme *A Place in the Sun*, and has spent the past eight years journeying as far afield as Fiji and New Zealand, bedding down in both beautiful and downright grotty hotels. She has recently met and fallen head over heels in love with her very own Mr Smith, and is looking forward to working her way through every hotel in this book with him.

Jonathan Lukes BRAND CONSULTANT

Erstwhile lawyer, editor and animator, Jonathan spent several years running TV stations for Time Warner, before launching his own brand consultancy, Rocket Psyence. Specialising in travel, media and the drinks industry, his favourite assignments let him research all three simultaneously. When not enjoying the trappings of hotel lobbies and airport lounges, he lives in London and San Francisco.

Howard Marks BON VIVEUR

Howard's experience of overnight accommodation is fairly singular, stemming from several years spent in five-star hotels throughout southeast Asia as an international fugitive; then nine years in European and United States jails. 'Mr Nice' has written several books about his experiences and, over the past decade, has penned travel articles for *The Observer*, *The Times*, *Time Out* and *The Daily Telegraph*.

Neil McLennan LIFESTYLE JOURNALIST

For more than 20 years, Neil has passed off having a good time as hard work at titles such as *Time Out*, *ES* magazine, *Elle*, *Grazia* and *Marie Claire*. He is currently deputy editor of chic homes magazine *Livingetc*. When not supervising food shoots, nosing around homes of the rich and famous, and dining at fine tables, Neil can be found travelling to boutique hotels all over the world, where he gens up on thread counts, premium-brand vodkas and indigenous spa treatments while accruing a fine collection of travel-sized grooming products.

Nick Moran ACTOR

Born in London, actor Nick is best known for his film roles (most notably in *Lock, Stock and Two Smoking Barrels*). His career has resulted in something of a world tour. 'I've got 14 visas from nine countries and more air miles than Alan Whicker,' he says. As a result, he's no stranger to hotel stays. He has written for *The Guardian*, *The Times* and the *Evening Standard*; is the author of the award-winning West End play *Telstar*; and was the narrator of Mr & Mrs Smith's Discovery Channel television programme *The Smiths: Hotels for 2*.

Jim McNulty YACHTSMAN

Whether staying in the *Lost In Translation*-featured Park Hyatt hotel in Tokyo as tour manager for Fatboy Slim, or working as part of a crew decamping to a converted prison in Serbia, Jim's twin passions of music and sailing have given him the chance to see the world. Now a partner in a successful yacht-charter business (as featured in our online Smith & Friends collection; www.smithandfriends.com), and a first-time father, he's enjoying travelling incognito with his baby daughter Delilah and his own Mrs Smith, Sorcha, an interiors stylist.

Alex Proud GALLERY OWNER

After incarnations as an antiques dealer, an oriental art-gallery owner and an internet pioneer, Alex opened Proud Central in 1998 and, in April 2008, reopened the legendary Proud Camden at the magnificent grade II-listed Horse Hospital in North London's Stables Market. Further launches are planned in Brighton, New York, Paris and Tokyo. His Mrs Smith is *Sunday Times Style* columnist, TV presenter and author Danielle Proud.

Serena Rees LINGERIE DESIGNER

Since luxury undies merchant Agent Provocateur first threw open its sexily-scented doors back in 1994, co-founder Serena has been the driving force behind its meteoric rise to the world's number-one fashion lingerie brand. Her passion, relentless hard work and uncompromising attention to beauty and detail makes Serena the perfect stylish-hotel spy when it comes to meeting Mr & Mrs Smith's exacting standards.

Tamara Salman CREATIVE DIRECTOR

After travelling the world throughout her childhood, Tamara's initial career inclination was to become an architect. Following a move to the UK, she turned her attention from architecture to fashion and studied textiles at the Winchester School of Art. Her early career was spent working in some of the most prestigious fashion houses in Paris and Milan, including the design studios of Romeo Gigli and Prada. Since her appointment as creative director of Liberty of London, she has revived and reworked the famous department store's iconic archive of prints into innovative new collections, including handbags and accessories, men and women's ready-to-wear, scarves, swimwear and jewellery.

Bee Shaffer FASHION COLUMNIST

Jet-setting daughter of legendary US *Vogue* editor Anna Wintour, Bee (aka Katherine) divides her time between her history degree at New York's Columbia University and penning pieces for the fashion press. Despite her youth (she's just turned 21), Bee has worked as a style columnist for *The Daily Telegraph* and a contributor to *Teen Vogue*, and has visited some of the furthest-flung corners of the globe. Her list of top trips includes searching for tigers in India's Ranthambore National Park, trekking through Libya's Leptis Magna ruins, and a week riding Vespas around Mykonos, but she assures us that her trip to Rome for Mr & Mrs Smith is up there with the best of them.

Christopher Tennant CULTURAL COMMENTATOR

Born and raised in the leafy suburbs of Boston, Christopher currently lives beyond his means in New York City. He knows a little something about high-end hospitality. In fact, he wrote the book on it. *The Official Filthy Rich Handbook*, his tongue-in-cheek, cradle-to-grave guide to fitting in with the international overclass, took him to boutique hotels far and wide. In a previous life, he worked as an editor and writer at titles including *New York* magazine, *Talk*, the *New York Post*'s 'Page Six' column, and *Radar*, the pop-culture magazine and website he co-founded in 2003.

Nigel Tisdall TRAVEL JOURNALIST

Nigel's globetrotting career began one wet Monday morning in 1985 when he went to London's Liverpool Street station and caught a train to Hong Kong. Since then, he's been roaming all over the world, writing principally for *The Daily Telegraph* and its weekend companion *The Sunday Telegraph*. Currently travel editor of *Marie Claire*, he's constantly checking into hotels. The best? 'A tent in Antarctica – until it blew away.' The worst? 'A candlelit lodge in the Peruvian Amazon, where I just happened to spot a cockroach on my toothbrush...'

Simone Topolski TRAVEL JOURNALIST

After a brief incarnation as a furniture and jewellery designer, Simone decided to swap workshops and toolboxes for boutique hotels and matching luggage, and entered the world of travel journalism. After several years of struggle, someone finally decided to pay her for it and she's since explored the globe on behalf of *The Daily Telegraph*, *Condé Nast Traveller* and *Time Out*. When not scribing for her supper, she can usually be found snoozing in a hammock in the Mexican rainforest or making fire with her bare hands somewhere in Sussex.

Matt Turner MAGAZINE EDITOR

Following an eight-year stint editing nightclub-industry trade magazine *Night*, Matt swapped dancefloors for duvets, with an international relaunch of hotel design magazine *Sleeper* in 2002. In addition to his full-time role overseeing development of the *Sleeper* brand, he has also written and commented on hotels for various magazines and broadcasters including *Wallpaper**, *The Observer*, *The Guardian*, the BBC and *FX* magazine.

Dita Von Teese BURLESQUE ARTIST

The indisputable queen of burlesque, Dita has transcended the scene in which she made her name to adorn the covers of fashion magazines on both sides of the Atlantic. Best known for her provocative shows in which she performs an old-fashioned striptease that culminates with her submerging herself in a giant martini glass, Dita has graced stages all over the world, gaining plaudits for her Forties-inspired look and for evoking a sense of retro glamour that's adored by both men and women. Briefly married to goth-rock icon Marilyn Manson, she now concentrates her energies on fronting MAC's Viva Glam campaign, and on checking out hotels in her home town of Los Angeles for Mr & Mrs Smith.

MR & MRS SMITH TEAM

Managing director **James Lohan** is one half of the couple behind Mr & Mrs Smith. James' first company, Atomic, created the infamous Come Dancing parties and club promotions. (One of his London parties was voted 'number-one place to be in the world' by *FHM*.) He built on this success with Atomic Events, producing events for clients such as Finlandia vodka and Wonderbra. He then went on to co-found the White House bar, restaurant and members' club in London. Since Mr & Mrs Smith's first book, James has visited almost 1,000 hotels. As a first-time dad, he's now also a keen advocate of our child-friendly hotel collection, Smith & Kids.

Online and marketing director **Tamara Heber-Percy**, co-founder of Mr & Mrs Smith, graduated from Oxford University with a degree in languages, then left the UK for a year in Brazil, where she launched a new energy drink. Since then, she has worked as a marketing consultant for international brands such as Ericsson and Honda. Her last role in that field was in business development for Europe, the Middle East and Africa at one of the UK's top marketing agencies. She left the corporate world in 2002 to head up her own company, the County Register – an exclusive introductions agency – and to launch Mr & Mrs Smith.

Publishing director **Andrew Grahame** launched the UK's first corporate-fashion magazine in 1990. After moving into fashion shows, exhibitions and conferences, he transferred his talents from clothing to finance, launching Small Company Investor. He started a promotions company in 1993 with clients such as Sony and Virgin and, after a spell as a restaurant/bar owner in Chelsea, turned his hand to tourism in 1997, creating the award-winning London Pass and New York Pass, which give visitors access to the cities' attractions. Andrew co-produced our television series *The Smiths' Hotels for 2* for the Discovery Channel.

Financial director **Edward Orr** has worked in investment banking and managed companies in their early stages for more than a decade. As a result, he has had to stay in many hotels, spanning five continents – and, generally, he doesn't like them. This makes him qualified not only to look after the finances of Mr & Mrs Smith, but also to have penned the odd review – and he can confirm that Mr & Mrs Smith hotels really are special enough to be a treat, even for the most jaded corporate traveller.

Editor-in-chief **Juliet Kinsman** helped develop Mr & Mrs Smith from a twinkle in James' and Tamara's eyes back in 2002 into the fully fledged being it is today, and now regularly shares her travel secrets in publications from *The Guardian* to *Grazia*, and on TV, including in our show for the Discovery Channel, *The Smiths' Hotels for 2*. Born in Canada with childhood stints in Africa and America and spells based in New York, Greece and India, her latest challenge has been continuing her globetrotting with a little one in tow. Having recently had a baby, she's still on the go, but is nervous her already well-travelled daughter's first sentence will be 'Can we get room service please?'.

EDITORIAL

Editor **Rufus Purdy** began his working life dressed as a giant banana (complete with yellow tights), handing flyers to tourists outside Tube stations. He then graduated to the heights of junior sub-editor at *Harper's Bazaar*, where he honed his skills dragging celebrities' barely literate copy into the realms of acceptability. A spell at *Condé Nast Traveller* pigeon-holed him for life, and he has since claimed free holidays as travel editor at *Psychologies*, or on jaunts for *The Observer*, *Elle* and *The New York Post*. Aside from travel, his other passions include an unswerving devotion to Sheffield Wednesday football club.

Deputy editor **Lucy Fennings** cut her travel teeth early; as daughter of a hotel PR, she visited far-flung flophouses from French châteaux to Ethiopian tukuls. After a year in Dubai, working on *Emirates Woman* magazine and enjoying the kind of dives that require a wetsuit, Lucy went to Glasgow University to study art, literature and whisky. Later, as a Legalease production editor, she learnt how to be creative with copy about tax, before exploring Asia. When Mr & Mrs Smith found her, Lucy was deputy chief sub-editor at *Harper's Bazaar*, keeping her finger on fashion's pulse and sharpening her editorial knife on hapless hotel PR copy.

Before Mr & Mrs Smith, online editor **Anthony Leyton** was at *The Independent*, writing about universities for the Push Guides. As you can imagine, it was a tough task persuading him to exchange league tables for luxury holiday retreats. He has penned pieces for publications both top-drawer (*The Telegraph*) and top-shelf (*Fiesta*), and he has had a love of travel ever since he found bullet holes in the walls of a hotel room in New Orleans. He also has too many pets. But that's another tale altogether.

DESIGN, PHOTOGRAPHY AND PRODUCTION

Creator of the Mr & Mrs Smith brand and designer of the book, Bloom is one of the UK's freshest design agencies. It is responsible for creating brand designs for some of the world's leading consumer-brand companies. Bloom's house style is bold, iconic and distinctive.

Renowned for a creative yet meticulous approach to his work, photographer Adrian Houston has shot famous personalities and unusual landscapes, as well as major ad campaigns. He has photographed the Dalai Lama, Sir Ranulph Fiennes, Luciano Pavarotti and Jim Carrey, and his images have appeared in *Vogue*, *GQ* and *The Sunday Times*. Adrian has commercial clients across the globe, and has created his best work in some of the world's most unexplored locations; the Discovery Channel featured him in its Discovery People series.

Head of operations Laura Mizon spent her younger years living in Spain and, after graduating from Manchester University, returned to her childhood home to spend four years at an independent record label in Madrid, promoting the emerging Spanish hip-hop movement. When she joined Mr & Mrs Smith as a freelancer in 2004, it soon became clear that Laura was to play a key role. She is now responsible for building relationships with like-minded brands.

Production executive Jasmine Darby graduated from Manchester with a degree in History of Art in July 2006 and accepted her role at Mr & Mrs Smith soon after, more than happy to swap the fear of studenty electric-shock nylon sheets for the hope of close contact with Frette bed linen.

HOTEL COLLECTIONS

Having grown up in the south of Spain, head of hotel collections Katy McCann moved to Madrid to become editor of *In Madrid*, the largest English-language publication in the city. She was tracked down by Mr & Mrs Smith to help develop and expand our hotel collections, which fits in perfectly with her love of travelling, her multilingual skills and her dream of opening up her own hotel some day.

Head of hotel relations Peggy Picano-Nacci was born in Indonesia but grew up in France. The past 15 years have seen her earn an unrivalled understanding of what makes a great boutique hotel tick. A former sales manager at the Dorchester and an alumnus of the Small Luxury Hotels of the World team, where she was responsible for the French, Spanish and Portuguese member hotels, she has made good use of her Spanish, English and French language skills.

Hotel collections manager Mary Garvin's first travel memory is driving from her native Brooklyn to Florida, packed in tight for 22 hours among a month's worth of luggage, her parents and five siblings; imagine her delight when she first flew first class. After graduating from McGill University in Montreal, Mary moved to London, from where she now spends her time sniffing out stylish stays across the globe.

PR AND MARKETING

Head of PR and marketing Aline Keuroghlian has worked in travel for more than 10 years. Stints at Armani and London's quirky Sir John Soane's Museum helped cultivate a love of stylish things. After university came several years of guiding professionals across Italy for niche tour operator ATG Oxford, which made use of her maternal heritage. Meanwhile she is putting both her sense and sensibility to good use by working with some of the most beautiful hotels in the world, as featured in the Mr & Mrs Smith collections.

Having been born to Finnish and Dutch parents, PR and marketing executive Sabine Zetteler was always destined to work in an international setting. She comes to Mr & Mrs Smith after stints with London-based fashion house Belle & Bunty and the BBC.

MEMBERSHIP

Membership manager Amber Spencer-Holmes may be a Londoner, but she's got cosmopolitan credentials, having lived in Sydney and Paris before reading French and English at King's College London. Before joining Mr & Mrs Smith, Amber made waves in the music industry running a number of well-respected record labels. She is married to Mr & Mrs Smith TuneSmith columnist, DJ Rob Wood.

When marketing and membership executive Daisy Byrne isn't efficiently looking after Mr & Mrs Smith members, she can normally be found running, cycling, riding and generally being all outdoorsy somewhere in the Great British countryside. When she's not at Smith HQ, Daisy also runs an up-and-coming business empire from her bedroom: communications consultancy FutureWorks.

[where in the world]

THE GLOBAL MR & MRS SMITH HOTEL COLLECTION

EUROPE

Austria Vienna, Zell am See
Belgium Antwerp, Brussels
Cyprus Limassol
Czech Republic Prague, Tábor
Denmark Copenhagen
Estonia Tallinn
France Beaujolais, Bordeaux, Burgundy, Cannes,
Côte d'Azur, Dordogne, Languedoc-Roussillon,
Lyon, Montpellier, Paris, Provence, Tarn, Vaucluse
Germany Berlin, Hamburg, Munich
Greece Athens, Aegean Islands, Ionian Islands,
Mykonos, Santorini
Iceland Reykjavík
Ireland County Carlow, County Meath, Dublin
Italy Aeolian Islands, Capri, Florence, Milan,
Piedmont, Puglia, Rome, Sardinia, Sorrento,
South Tyrol, Tuscany, Venice
Monaco Monte Carlo
Netherlands Amsterdam, Monnickendam
Portugal Cascais, Douro Valley, Lisbon
Spain Andalucía, Barcelona, Córdoba,
Costa de la Luz, Extremadura, Granada, Ibiza,
Madrid, Mallorca, Marbella, Ronda, Seville, Valencia
Sweden Stockholm
Turkey Istanbul
United Kingdom Bath, Belfast, Berkshire, Brighton,
Bristol, Cornwall, The Cotswolds, Devon, Dorset,
Durham, Edinburgh, Glasgow, Gloucestershire,
Hampshire, Harrogate, Lake District, Liverpool, London,
Manchester, Norfolk, Oxfordshire, Peak District,
Somerset, Suffolk, Sussex, Wales, Wester Ross, Wiltshire

THE REST OF THE WORLD

Australia Byron Bay, Great Barrier Reef,
Hunter Valley, Melbourne, Sydney
Belize Ambergris Caye, Pine Ridge Forest, Placencia
Bhutan Bumthang, Gangtey, Paro, Punakha, Thimphu
Brazil Bahía, Rio de Janeiro, São Paulo
Canada Montreal
Caribbean Antigua and Barbuda, Bahamas,
Barbados, Grenada, Mustique, St Barths,
Turks and Caicos
China Beijing, Guilin, Hong Kong, Nanjing, Shanghai
Guatemala Flores
India Kerala
Indonesia Bali, Jakarta, Java, Moyo
Indian Ocean Mauritius, Seychelles
Malaysia Kuala Lumpur, Langkawi
Mexico Campeche, Colima, Jalisco, Mayan Riviera,
Mexico City, Puebla, Yucatan Peninsula, Zihuatanejo
Morocco Atlas Mountains, Essaouira,
Marrakech, Ouarzazate
Oman Musandam Peninsula, Muscat
South Africa Cape Town, Cape Winelands,
Garden Route, Hermanus, Johannesburg,
Kruger National Park, Madikwe, Sabi Sands
Thailand Bangkok, Chiang Mai, Hua Hin,
Khao Lak, Koh Lanta, Koh Phi Phi, Koh Samui,
Krabi, Phuket
United Arab Emirates Dubai
United States Big Sur, Las Vegas, Los Angeles,
Miami, Napa Valley, New York, Palm Springs, San
Diego, San Francisco, Sonoma
Zambia Lower Zambezi

These are some of the worldwide hotel destinations that our website and travel team can take you to.
For more information, or to book, visit us online at www.mrandmrssmith.com, or call 1 800 464 2040.

Smith

Welcome to the world of Mr & Mrs Smith, where you'll find everything you need to plan your escape. With our boutique-hotel bibles, which steer you around the most special stays and give you the lowdown on your destination, you can design and enhance your perfect break in one hit. We've even launched an online wedding-list service, so that your friends can contribute to the ultimate gift: a stylish holiday. So visit www.mrandmrssmith.com/shop and get packing: your vacation starts here...

HOW TO PLAN YOUR GREAT ESCAPE

Five books (including this one), more than 400 gorgeous hotels, endless ideas for your precious escape...
Whether you're looking for a romantic retreat, a cosy inn or a luxurious hideaway, the Mr & Mrs Smith hotel
guides will signpost you to the most inspirational hotels around the world. Each book contains entertaining
reviews, insider destination information and first-class, first-hand restaurant, café and bar recommendations.
Inside the cover, you'll find your very own exclusive membership card, entitling you to gifts, upgrades and
discounts galore. Go to www.mrandmrssmith.com/shop to order the indispensable guides that ensure you
get the hotel address right first time.

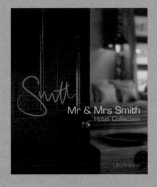 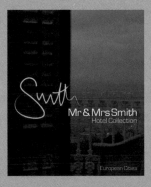 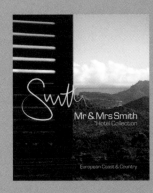 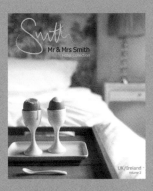

GET A ROOM!

Gift vouchers suddenly got sexy: treat someone to a weekend at one of our fantastic hotels with a Mr & Mrs
Smith Get a Room! voucher, stylishly presented in a black envelope, and you can be certain they'll get
something they really want. See details and order online at www.mrandmrssmith.com/hotel-gift-voucher.

(applause)

thank you

Adrian Houston for his inspiring interiors shots and lush landscape photography, his assistant Tom Mattey and Hasselblad cameras; Bloom, for its brand genius and design savvy, and for making this book fit to grace the most stylish of coffee tables – with special thanks to Ben White, Dan Cornell, Craig Barnes, Lindsay Reynolds, Louise Brown, Tim Reynolds and Beeker Northam; Peter Osborne, Feena Brooks and Sam Millar at Osborne & Little; Mark, John, Clive and Keith at E-Media Colour; Graham at Replika Press PVT Ltd for printing the book; Alamy, Corbis and Getty Images for supplementing our destination-guide photography; all our stockists; Lynton for his web wizardry; Ed Bussey, Peter Clements and Ian Taylor; Marin and the team at Travel Intelligence; all our reviewers for sharing their tales; the brilliant Mr & Mrs Smith travel team. And last, but by no means least, huge thanks to everyone else who has helped make *The Global Shortlist* a reality: Paul Clements, Sophie Dening, Neil McLennan, Peter Myers, Andrew Spooner and Jim Whyte for their wonderful way with words; Aun Koh for his tireless research; Kate Daughton, Teun Hilte, Ben Palmer and Lee Weingast for revealing their destination secrets; Amy Corcell for kicking our limey colloquialisms into touch; Melissa Whitworth for her invaluable help Stateside; Stewart J Wild, our eagle-eyed proofreader; Craig Markham and the team at the Haymarket Hotel, London; and, of course, all those 'other halves' who accompanied reviewers, or provided support and encouragement.

Smith

Mr & Mrs Smith

index